The $\mathcal{F}$INE $\mathcal{A}$RT
of $\mathcal{F}$UNDRAISING

The $\mathcal{F}$INE $\mathcal{A}$RT of $\mathcal{F}$UNDRAISING

SECRETS FOR SUCCESSFUL VOLUNTEERS

Carolyn Farb

Foreword by Robin Leach

For further information, contact the publisher at:

books

Emmis Books
1700 Madison Road
Cincinnati, OH 45206

www.emmisbooks.com

Library of Congress Cataloging-in-Publication Data

Farb, Carolyn.
The fine art of fundraising : secrets for successful volunteers /
Carolyn Farb.-- 1st ed.
    p. cm.
ISBN 1-57860-180-0
1. Fund raising. I. Title: Secrets for successful volunteers. II. Title.
  HV41.2.F37 2004
  658.15'224--dc22

2004016289

Interior designed by Mary Barnes Clark
Edited by Jessica Yerega
Cover designed by Mary Barnes Clark and Andrea Kupper
Cover photo by Rick Goncher, Terrell, Texas

My book is dedicated to the memory of my beloved son, Jake Kenyon Shulman.

January 9, 1970 - September 25, 2004

ON CHILDREN...

You may give them your love but not your thoughts.
For they have their own thoughts.
You may house their bodies but not their souls.
For their souls dwell in the house of tomorrow,
Which you cannot visit, not even in your dreams.
You may strive to be like them, but seek not to make them like you.
For life goes not backward nor tarries with yesterday.

—KAHLIL GIBRAN, *The Prophet*

Acknowledgments

My gratitude goes to the many generous benefactors who have donated the funds for research, children's causes, women's issues, education, the arts, and space science technology. Individuals, foundations, and corporations believing in a better quality of life for mankind have joined together, creating the philanthropic circle. My thanks to the many in-kind donors—printers, retailers, musicians, restaurants, and florists—who support innumerable causes. To the celebrities and artists who give of their talent, creativity, and time; to name a few: Jean-Daniel Lorieux, Don Henley, Tommy Tune, Ann-Margret, Marvin Hamlisch, Clint Eastwood, Larry Hagman, Carl Lewis, Mary Lou Retton, Hakeem Olajuwon, Carol Channing, Phyllis George, Dixie Friend Gay, Sharon Kopriva, Richard Wood, Kimberly Gremillion, Julie Speed, James Surls, David Adickes, and Jesús Bautista Moroles. And to the countless number of volunteers who dedicate their time, enthusiasm, and energy.

My calling began when I was a teenager wanting to do something to help others. I volunteered at Texas Children's Hospital working in the snack bar making pimento cheese sandwiches for the parents and relatives of sick children. The journey has been my passion and enriched my life for thirty years. The wings of special individuals have encouraged me through the years and helped me bring what I fondly call my "Volunteer's Handbook" to being. I'd like to recognize mentors like my beloved grandfather, Jakie Freedman; my son, Jake Shulman; Dr. David Fry, Northwood University; Dean John Bear, University of Houston; and my speech teacher, Mary Alice Krahl, who always reminded me of the power of a smile. Thanks also to Nan Booth Simpson, Patricia Scott McHargue, and Diane Stafford for their editing assistance; to my assistants, Leah Hubenak and Dawn Sanders, for the many hours they spent with me at the computer working on this book; to my friend Bob Hopkins, publisher of *Philanthropy World*, for being the first to read and bless my book; to Lance Avery Morgan of *Brilliant Magazine*; and also to Dawn Koctar; Charles Ward; Lucho Flórez; Richard Bonica; Joanna South-Shelley; Mary Horton; Linda Hofheinz; and Janice Adamson.

Special thanks also to my adorable fourteen-year-senior Shih-Tzu, Bogie, who is a great volunteer. He has been side by side with me since I began to write this book and has supported my passion to help others. Bogie is truly dedicated and doesn't mind long hours, weekends, or whatever it takes to bring an event to fruition. He can usually tell by the stacks of papers invading his space that we are getting close to the end of a project—only to begin again. He loves to hear the phone ring, likes the sound of the fax, and finds the copier fun to watch. Bogie definitely gets his fair share of fan e-mail. He's heard every speech I've ever made several times and critiques them in his own way. By his interest level, I can always tell if he's engaged. He's happiest when the house is filled with people for a pre-event, meeting, or reception. Nobody can work a crowd better than he does. He puts on the charm and manners when greeting everyone. Bogie's camera-ready and knows the drill. W. C. Fields said it best: "You don't want to take a picture with a dog or child; they'll upstage you every time." He has his favorite causes—the SPCA Telethon, Bogie's Stroll for pet awareness, and the campaign to Save Jeffrey Jerome, the hog who came to the aid of the homeless. For all of that and more, I can rely on Bogie. He's always there with an unconditional welcome and smile.

 *Contents*

 *Foreword*

In traveling the world for *Lifestyles of the Rich & Famous*, I have had the wonderful opportunity to see the finest life has to offer in some of its most beautiful settings. Many of the incredible events I have attended have been associated with very worthy charities. There is only one name when it comes to fundraising: Carolyn Farb. In fact, if you look up fundraising in Webster's, you'll find her name as the ultimate definition! She is the queen of them all; she's tireless, dedicated, glamorous, effervescent, and the word *no* just doesn't exist in her vocabulary. Dr. Farb has pioneered many successful fundraising techniques that have been copied around the world.

As you read *The Fine Art of Fundraising: Secrets for Successful Volunteers*, you will learn her insights and shortcuts to effective special events. Dr. Carolyn Farb has a soft-spoken, easy manner that belies her tenacity and determination. Some have said that if she applied her talents of discipline and dedication to corporate America instead of philanthropy, Carolyn would be CEO of a Fortune 500 corporation or in a White House cabinet post.

The phone at her home office is always ringing with many requests for her help in fundraising for myriad causes. For the past three years, she has put all the advice gleaned from her volunteer career into this book you are now reading. For Carolyn, fundraising is more a calling than a goal. Just as Dr. Carolyn Farb has started so many new charity programs that flourish today, you will have the opportunity to win the same successes in your community. In this book, you'll find everything (and I mean everything) you ever wanted to know about fundraising. She will make you feel Rich and Famous with her generosity of spirit.

Enjoy.

Robin Leach

 *Introduction*

> *"One person with passion is better than 40
> people merely interested."*
>
> —E. M. FORSTER

America has a big heart ready to take on the challenges and realities
of our world today. Close to three billion people worldwide live on
$2 a day, and more than one billion live on $1 a day. Children die
every day due to preventable causes such as hunger, disease, and lack
of water. Luckily, we have the information, knowledge, technology,
and resources to bring about a new moral energy and commitment
to make a difference.

Philanthropy has become a way of life in America. Today nonprofit organizations answer innumerable needs and are advocates for
many causes. Competition for the philanthropic dollar is intense
because the same group of donors is called upon repeatedly to support a variety of causes in the community.

What John D. Rockefeller once described as "the business of
benevolence" requires a concentrated effort involving imagination,
hard work, and keen business sense. To become a fundraiser, you
must believe in and be passionate about a cause. Understand the
mission of the group and your reason for commitment. Once you
determine this is where you want to dedicate your energy and time,
you can bring about innovative and creative problem solving solu-

tions and ideas for change. Trust your intuition when making choices. Follow your dream and create a vision to accomplish it.

Remember, volunteering is part of your life—not your whole life, so keep it in perspective. Make every project mean something. Try to be selective when choosing projects so you won't burn out. Saying "yes" when your plate is full will limit your effectiveness. The responsibility comes from the top, so make your chain of command short. Keep your committee's attention. Think lean with a limited budget, make every dollar count. Ask yourself, "How do I get others to work with me to support a worthwhile cause?" Your knowledge, combined with the efforts of people who will touch the hearts of others, will inspire support for your cause.

Reggie Bibbs was born with Neurofibromatosis (NF). He has inoperable tumors all over his body, and yet every day is positive for him because he is valued for his contributions. Despite his medical problems, Reggie's quality of life continues to improve. Although there is no cure for the disease, through research the genetic cause has been discovered, allowing scientists to learn more about how to control it. Through genetic research and philanthropy, treatment options are becoming available. For children with NF, barriers to education and treatment are being minimized.

When you sign on to chair a fundraising committee for a cause such as this one, give committee members the opportunity to be involved. Engage the mind, talent, and spirit of each volunteer. Tap into the strength of others, and they will work harder as a team. Think of yourself as a coach. Always recognize the contributions of others. Social change occurs when individuals realize their effectiveness in making things happen collectively. Everyone involved must own the outcome. Team motivation can spread to in-kind donors. Work collaboratively with others to make a difference. And, when working with others, show respect. Make them feel like equal members of the team.

Appreciate the value of volunteers, their commitment and their creativity. Learning to be a team member and developing good verbal and writing skills is key to the success of any fundraising event. When giving of your time, make it count. Deliver on your promises and keep to a timeline. Don't lose focus. Stay committed until your goal is realized.

Volunteerism asks that we reach outside ourselves. You have to be passionate about what you do, because if you take on a project for any ulterior reason, you won't achieve success. You have to be yourself and recognize your own unique characteristics and talents. You have to know what you can do and what you can't do. If you do nothing to benefit others, you do nothing to benefit yourself.

By sharing my experiences as a volunteer, I hope to ignite your passion, encourage your creative resources, and empower you to follow your own dream.

LEARNING TO GIVE

The desire to effect a change and improve the quality of life for those less fortunate lies beneath the surface in most of us. For me, community service has been my calling, and I am fulfilling my purpose when I am in the process of helping others. Volunteerism remains a cherished part of my life. Every day brings new opportunities to touch someone with an act of kindness, patience, and understanding. For more than twenty-five years, my passion has not dimmed.

My mentor, my beloved grandfather Jakie Freedman, was best known as an early pioneer in Las Vegas and a high-stakes risk-taker. In his teens, he left Russia to come to the United States to pursue the American dream. He loved Texas but eventually left to be a part of the boom out west where he built his place in the sun, the Sands Hotel in Las Vegas, Nevada.

As a young girl, I spent summer vacations working in my grandfather's executive offices, where I first learned about giving. Along with other hotel owners, my grandfather was always involved in campaigns for deserving and worthwhile causes, such as Saint Jude's Hospital. Besides his philanthropy, he was a networker supreme, which kept us in the company of movie stars, columnists, politicians, and business leaders. With Las Vegas as my special window of opportunity, I became a keen observer of people.

This is where my charitable passion and management style began. Anyone who plays a game of chance will tell you that the key to winning isn't luck or nerve. It's management—how you manage your finances, time, and expenses. Nothing encourages concentration more than having all your chips on the line. Although I wasn't allowed to gamble, I learned lessons in showmanship and charitable planning. I discovered that a successful fundraising effort requires a certain wisdom. These are the secrets I learned to successful fundraising:

1. Be passionate about the cause you champion.
2. Create a vision and a plan.
3. Pioneer new ideas.
4. Set realistic goals—and surpass them.
5. Expand your reach.
6. Make a commitment.
7. Motivate others to the cause.
8. Put together a strong team.
9. Decide on a format and follow through.
10. Follow the timeline.
11. Be proactive—initiate.
12. Practice zero budget.
13. Adopt change—take risks.
14. Stand out from the crowd.
15. Embrace challenges.
16. Emphasize the details.
17. Spread the word.
18. Share the good works.

MEETING THE CHALLENGE

In the end, knowing what motivates people to participate in worthwhile causes doesn't matter much. The *doing* is what really matters. With this book, I hope to inspire people who want to make a difference at every level. Just making the commitment to change the dynamics of a situation is personally rewarding. Your deed may be a simple act but one with powerful results. The memory of an ordinary childhood experience may spark magical ideas that become your passion and can change the world. Believe in your own can-do ability, accept challenges, stay focused, and give your best. Starting early and being well prepared is a game plan for success. The willingness to give extra effort to meet challenges creates an ethic for achieving goals. You'll realize you have the power to make changes for the betterment of others. Seek to learn at every available opportunity from inspiring role models. Fundraising is hard work, but it is very uplifting. It is how people know me. They always say, "If anybody can do it, you can."

All of us must ask of ourselves who we really are and who we want to become. My best advice is to answer your calling—connect your best talent and skills to your values and beliefs. Bring your mind in sync with your soul. Let your moral compass guide you on the path that's right for you. Dare to dream—you never know where opportunities will lead you—and don't be afraid to take risks. Always follow the language of your heart. Believe that you can make a difference, and that belief will bring about change.

 *Chapter One*

FOLLOW YOUR PHILANTHROPIC PASSION

"Service to humanity is the best work of all."
— DR. ARTHUR E. TURNER

Giving is a belief in optimism, ideals, and principles that elevates individuals and offers hope. Fundraising is the way to fund medical research, endow scholarships, support the arts, build libraries, and promote global initiatives. I believe that the desire to serve is a quality that most of us possess.

WHAT KINDS OF CAUSES NEED SUPPORT?

Nonprofit organizations and international agencies work diligently on behalf of myriad causes that concern everyone. These organizations depend on volunteers to achieve their goals. People who want to volunteer have many opportunities for involvement: fundraising, chairing special events, soliciting underwriting, serving on boards, hands-on volunteering, and/or donating funds. A good source of information about existing nonprofits in your area is a local volunteer organization. For example, my local group is called Volunteer Houston. It posts both short- and long-term volunteer opportunities on its Web site.

Volunteerism is about feeling good, and it's also a wonderful way to make new acquaintances and establish long-term friendships. It gives you a sense of belonging. Volunteers should be serious in their commitment to an organization and be enthusiastic about their assigned duties. Working together, everyone can take pride in a successful team effort.

Educational

For the past hundred years, the American Public School System has done the best job worldwide in providing universal access to education. American schools have traditionally been supported through local taxes, but in the last few years, parents have become proactive in their efforts to obtain more state funding. Moreover, Parent-Teacher Organizations (PTO) are increasingly expected to raise funds to provide essential items for equal opportunity for all students—computers for classrooms, library books, new sheet music, student tutorials, participation in local and national competitions, and training seminars for teachers, to name a few. Without the help of PTO fundraising activities, such after-school programs as art, dance, karate, and fencing would be neither available nor affordable. In less-affluent neighborhoods, PTOs face an even greater challenge, and the work they do makes a greater difference in the lives of the children they serve.

Revenue from cold drink and candy machines is a major source of funds for enrichment programs at many schools. Another source of revenue is the selling of advertising space on the football scoreboard. Such annual advertising revenue ranges from $15,000 to $20,000 a year and is usually directed to a special activities fund. The most aggressive fundraising activities take place with the Booster Clubs for various sports teams. The clubs are made up primarily of parents who may host weekly barbeque suppers or pancake breakfasts, for example. If they charge $10 per person for a meal costing $4, a significant profit can be generated over the period of a school year.

One of the major issues the education system faces is the inability of schools that have a large population of students from lower income families to raise funds for the "extras." There is federal funding for the instructional programs (buildings, books, and teachers) for these schools but little funding for enrichment programs. For example, many low-income children do not have access to the Internet at school and do not have computers in their homes. In looking at the inequity of school funding, the greatest challenge in philanthropy may be in narrowing that digital divide.

The Travis Elementary School in Houston holds an annual Spring Auction and Dinner. The event's volunteers have become very proficient at fundraising. The co-chairs send out letters with a donation form giving the readers an overview of the event. They list different ways the donor will be acknowledged and the number of households that will be reached. The purpose for the fundraiser is stated, letting prospective donors know of enrichment activities and special projects that will be funded for all Travis students. The volunteers offer to coordinate the pickup and/or the delivery of the donation. All donations are tax deductible in accordance with IRS guidelines.

Other parent organizations are using events such as book fairs to raise money and awareness. Houston's West University Elementary School raised $2,300 by auctioning the opportunity to be "Principal for a Day." With PTO fundraising, both teachers and students enjoy increased opportunity to dream and inspire.

Many school districts have created their own foundations to raise funds for district-wide projects and distribution. These foundations are 501(c)(3) accredited (see page 57) and raise money in various ways. These funds support student enrichment activities that federal and state funds do not provide, such as getting a special teacher, building a swimming pool, or supplying computer labs.

Foundations such as the Communities Foundation of Texas, based in Dallas, understand the commitment to preschool opportunities, reading incentive programs, scholarships, and interdisciplinary educational programs. The generosity and caring of these foundations have fulfilled the meaningful legacies of their major benefactors.

The Arts

There's not a symphony orchestra, regional theater, opera, or ballet company that can exist without volunteer fundraising. The answer lies in private donations from corporations and individuals. Depending on the economic and political climate, corporate and foundation endowments may shift their support from arts to social causes. Innovative approaches are needed to overcome the lack of funding by municipal and state arts budgets. Ongoing support by local business leaders is essential to generating more money for the arts.

To boost the income of a regional theater company, you can create a level of benefactors, give them an identity (Barrymore Circle, Leading Ladies and Gentlemen), and ask them to contribute a specified amount annually. As an incentive to give, these benefactors are invited to attend dress rehearsals, opening nights, lectures, and private receptions, and to enjoy other privileged opportunities.

An "arts summit" to bring together numerous organizations in your community would be helpful in assessing changing giving patterns, spurring volunteerism, and creating a positive mindset among corporate leaders. Involving a well respected, dynamic keynote speaker from the arts community will get people interested. People who might not have cared about the arts previously may now bring new ideas to the table. Reaching out and working collaboratively is a critical part of building support for the arts.

Medical

In addition to lending our support to such organizations as the American Heart Association, the American Cancer Society, and the March of Dimes, volunteering to serve a medical cause may be motivated by a personal connection with a person who has a disease or a special need. For example, when a symphony orchestra member's five-year-old child suffers from cerebral palsy and can not speak or walk, how are the parents to cope? Insurance pays for only a portion of therapies needed, and the balance falls back upon the family.

In this real-life scenario, a benefit concert was organized to help the family by creating a fund to offset staggering, long-term financial challenges. This is an example of how a group of concerned friends (orchestra leader, musicians, singers, stage hands, other arts groups for which the orchestra plays, public relations practitioners) came together to make a difference. This noble effort raised $50,000.

The follow-up care and education that a nonprofit organization can offer to children and their parents makes an enormous difference. Ongoing emotional support and nurturing is essential. Helping parents learn how to cope, putting them in touch with others whose children have the same issues, helping them get over the hurdles and through the rough spots, and giving directions on where to find supplemental funding in situations in which there is no cure are just a few areas in which assistance is invaluable.

Celebrities can help to create awareness, especially if they or family members have been affected by a disease. Michael J. Fox's personal battle with Parkinson's disease has heightened awareness, has raised money for advanced research previously not available, and has created compassion for those who have the disease. Cyclist Lance Armstrong, who refused to be counted out in his sport after he battled cancer, went on to win multiple Tour de France races. Lance was honored at The University of Texas M. D. Anderson Cancer Center "Living Legend" luncheon event in Dallas. Following an inspiring interview he did with former NBC Sports Anchor Scott Murray, Lance's cycling shirt was auctioned spontaneously for $100,000.

Actress Dina Merrill is a national board member of the Juvenile Diabetes Foundation. Dina, whose son is diabetic, was instrumental in Houston being selected as the site for the foundation's first annual tennis classic. The attendance of Dina and late actor Jack Benny's daughter, Joan, helped to bring Juvenile Diabetes to the public's attention. A parent making an appeal when a child has a chronic illness is very effective in reaching out to the community.

Unpopular Causes

Many causes are tough and, therefore, are not as appealing to donors. Some people would like certain causes to simply go away because they make people feel uncomfortable. Social ills come to light before our eyes as the nightly news focuses on daily domestic violence, disturbances, and fatalities. Even though donors may support an unpopular cause initially, they still may feel that there is a stigma attached to supporting such causes as fighting AIDS, drug and alcohol abuse, cancer, domestic abuse, mental illness, and homelessness.

Unfortunately, these causes that so often take a backseat with donors are truly deserving and in need of support. Organizations, through their programs and services, make a difference not only in the lives of the individuals with the problem, but also for their caregivers. Once an unpopular cause gains acceptance in the community, the task of fundraising becomes easier.

Shelters that help the homeless are funded through the generous support of individuals, foundations, corporations, and the volunteerism of corporate employees. For example, Houston's Star of Hope Mission relies on Rice University's partnership program, America Reads and Counts, which provides literacy and math aid for children. Baylor College of Medicine partners with the Star of Hope Mission to provide counseling services for its clients. Dr. Louise Moorehead of Baylor set up a Vision Clinic at the Star of Hope Men's Center. Some of the ways that volunteers help shelters fulfill their missions include serving meals; volunteering for kitchen chores, maintenance, and storehouse duties; teaching computer skills; tutoring adults and children; mentoring; improving literacy skills; and assisting with resumes and cover letters.

Individuals who participate with church and service organizations like Rotary, Community Partners, and the YMCA support family shelters and the homeless by responding to a basic-needs wish-list (such as clothing, business attire, gently worn shoes, dresses, gently used towels and linens, toiletries, umbrellas, tote bags, luggage, hosiery, watches, baby items, and toys). Many shelter organizations have Web sites that provide a description of services, contact information, location of emergency shelters, overviews of their programs, current needs, and giving and volunteer opportunities.

Global Issues

The volunteer support of national service organizations, alumni groups, and religious organizations has been especially effective in third-world countries where the very basics—food, clothing, shelter, health care, and education—are nonexistent. Don't be afraid to embrace global causes. Join the Peace Corps and help spread democracy. Volunteer with a Rotary Group to work with children and families in a small village in Nicaragua. Work with others to build homes for Habitat for Humanity in your community.

Some causes have more universal appeal, but it takes time to build awareness and support for causes that don't directly impact our own lives. Sadly, environmental issues often take a back seat, but recent world and domestic situations have caused many Americans to reconsider the consequences if they don't lend their support, either financially or by volunteering. Indiscriminate destruction of the world's rain forests will destroy the earth's natural laboratories and lessen our opportunities to find a cure for diseases such as cancer and AIDS. Each time a medicinal plant becomes extinct, it is as if a library of information has been burned down.

If people do not have water or food for their children, then we have to help create solutions so they can become self-sufficient. The Rain Forest Foundation is one of several organizations that focus on securing the natural resources for the long-term benefit of the indigenous peoples. In seeking ways to preserve and protect the environment and the culture of the local people, the foundation makes the world aware of how environmental degradation within a single country can result in a nonpeaceful environment for everyone.

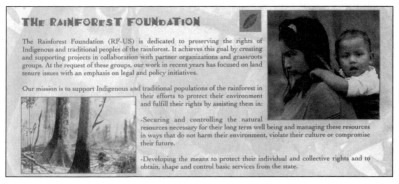

THE RAINFOREST FOUNDATION

The Rainforest Foundation (RF-US) is dedicated to preserving the rights of Indigenous and traditional peoples of the rainforest. It achieves this goal by creating and supporting projects in collaboration with partner organizations and grassroots groups. At the request of these groups, our work in recent years has focused on land tenure issues with an emphasis on legal and policy initiatives.

Our mission is to support Indigenous and traditional populations of the rainforest in their efforts to protect their environment and fulfill their rights by assisting them in:

-Securing and controlling the natural resources necessary for their long term well being and managing these resources in ways that do not harm their environment, violate their culture or compromise their future.

-Developing the means to protect their individual and collective rights and to obtain, shape and control basic services from the state.

Materials that both illustrate and state an organization's
purpose are invaluable to its success.

But it doesn't take a large organization to tackle a global issue. Actor Richard Gere's black-and-white photography exhibit represents his personal and spiritual voyage through various Tibetan communities. His portfolio has helped raise awareness of the plight of Tibetans and fund projects of the Dali Lama.

Gary Bowersox, a modern-day Indiana Jones, helped fund the war against the Soviets when he traveled to Afghanistan in 1988. He and a team of local miners uncovered more than $2 million in precious stones while traveling on horseback for a month at a time. Today, Bowersox sends profits to the Northern Alliance and continues to work with villagers, training them in mining exploration. His goal is to educate these people so they can earn income and work toward developing foreign exchange and taxes for the new government. Outside interest in mining jewels and stones in Afghanistan has created a positive turnabout situation in which the harvesting of these stones has helped fund the Northern Alliance in its struggle against the Taliban.

Animal Protection

Funds for spay/neuter programs and shelters can be raised through a fashion show format, like the one put on by retailer Donald J. Pliner, who created a line of clothing for his dog, Babydoll. A fundraiser featuring clothes for both people and their pets and modeled by high-profile individuals and their celebrity pets was well received in the community. A percentage of all clothing sold that evening, and for a limited time thereafter, went directly to the cause.

THE HUMANE SOCIETY OF NEW YORK

has ongoing support services
for animals affected by the tragedy of September 11

♦ Comprehensive veterinary care for victims of trauma
♦ Foster Care Network
♦ Relief Supply Center

Photograph by Debbie Bogard

If you need help, or would like to make a donation
in support of animal relief please contact:

Humane Society of New York
306 E. 59th St., New York, NY 10022
(212) 752-4842
www.humanesociety.org

Fliers like this one can raise public awareness
of nonprofit services in times of need.

The terrorist attack of September 11th made us even more aware of agencies such as the Humane Society of New York, which offers ongoing support services to animals affected by the tragedy through the relief supply center and foster care network. The lesson to be learned was that animal agencies everywhere need to be prepared in advance for unexpected natural disasters in their cities, such as floods and hurricanes. Another service of these agencies is to provide aid to neglected and mistreated domestic animals and to rescue abandoned exotic pets.

How to Promote a Cause You Cherish

Passion and commitment are critical to successful fundraising. If you're passionate about a cause, your commitment will flow naturally. Remember, spearheading a fundraiser means total immersion in a project. As a volunteer, it is important to motivate others with your own sense of commitment. Taking volunteers on site visits or field trips to a museum, homeless shelter, public library, hospital, hospice, or university helps volunteers gather information about the organization so they can speak with conviction about the project. In this way, both volunteers and donors learn what can be accomplished through their efforts, dedication, and financial support. The more knowledgeable you become about the organization, the people it serves, and its needs, the more successful you will be in convincing others to share your vision.

When I chaired an event called "The Quest for Excellence," benefiting the University of Houston College of Natural Sciences and Mathematics, I wanted to understand how the various schools within the college would benefit from the funds we were going to raise. A tour of these colleges—which included a session in the University's Virtual Environmental Cave and lengthy conversations with Nobel laureate Dr. Paul Chu, Dean John Bear, and other outstanding professors—proved to be motivating. I then understood the college's needs and purpose for the funds. I was able to speak in my own voice with passion and conviction as I diligently worked to raise $3.5 million for this important and worthwhile project.

For another project, a group of Intercontinental Rotarians and I traveled to Chinendega, Nicaragua, to meet with Father Marco Dessy, an Italian priest who had heroically rescued children from the city's dump. We wanted to learn first-hand how our efforts could make a difference in the lives of these children. The Rotarians have since organized seven successful fundraising campaigns to provide food, clothing, shelter, and education for these children. The children do their own part in breaking the cycle of poverty by creating art-work for Christmas cards each year and selling recordings of the Getsami Children's Choir worldwide. The choir traveled to Italy, where they were heard by the great tenor Luciano Pavorotti. He was so moved by the voices of the talented children and by their story that he donated the funds to build a music conservatory for them.

In the long run, most volunteers embrace their work as the most rewarding endeavor of their lives—the one thing that truly makes sense. Helping others never gets old; you always feel needed. Your life becomes enriched through the hope you've given others. And believe me, the people who work alongside you on the volunteer bandwagon are some of the finest folks you will ever meet—they're kind-hearted, upbeat, fun, and excited about life.

So, if a friend tells you that her life lacks direction, recommend volunteering. Working hard to improve the lives of those less fortu-nate than you will put your problems in perspective faster than any-thing else.

Think about it: You can have fun doing meaningful work.

THE CHANGING FACE OF FUNDRAISING

There was a time when the word "fundraiser" brought to mind events like Girl Scout cookie sales, raffles, bingo games, car washes, garage sales, and community bazaars. These efforts still serve their purpose nationally to the tune of millions of dollars for various causes. "Mega-fundraising" efforts have added another level and brought about changes in fundraising techniques.

Naomi Levine, director of development at New York University, says, "No organization, big or small, can exist without raising money. Years ago the needs were less, and the federal, state, and city governments gave more. But today, fundraising is absolutely essential." There are now many professional fundraisers whose responsibility is to guide donors in major gift decisions, orchestrate planned-giving approaches, and conduct full-blown capital campaigns.

Few people realize how many vital services charities provide and how much funding flows through them each year. With more than 1.4 million charities, including religious organizations in the United States, and donations from about 70 percent of the households, the estimate for charitable giving is 2.3 percent of the gross domestic product. The greatest contributions come from individuals, bequests, foundations, and corporations, in that order.

Charitable Giving in 2003, as reported by Giving USA	
Individuals	$183.73 billion
Bequests	$18.1 billion
Foundations	$26.9 billion
Corporations	$12.19 billion

Americans are the most generous people in the world. Even in a difficult economic year like 2003, charitable giving increased 2.8 percent to $240 billion or, stated another way, 2.3 percent of the U.S. gross national product. Some nonprofits in the billion-dollar category include the YMCA of USA ($2.8 billion), the Salvation Army ($2.5 billion), Boy Scouts of America ($648 million), and the American Cancer Society ($540 million).

Most of the charitable giving occurs by people in their local places of worship, with educational giving being the next largest sector. Corporations also undertake fundraising events of large magnitude by utilizing their employees and networking skills to bring other contacts and companies on board. Companies of all kinds are made up of people who embrace the philosophy of philanthropy.

The September 11th relief effort generated $2.6 billion in contributions with 61 percent coming from individuals. Corporations, foundations, and other institutional donors' contributions made up the difference, producing the greatest relief effort in history.

According to the Bureau of Labor Statistics, each year 63.8 million Americans volunteer their time for worthwhile causes and spend a median of fifty-two hours on their endeavors. The median American donates $894 in time annually to charity. For a charity to hire a full-time employee to cover the work of volunteers, the charity would have to pay the industry standard rate of $17.19 per hour for the invaluable tasks performed at no cost by volunteers. (The Bureau uses the Current Population Survey, which is a monthly poll of 60,000 US households concerning employment and related matters, to determine the number of volunteers for tomorrow. Visit www.volunteertoday.com for more information.) You may become one of those generous individuals hoping to make the world a better place.

In 1889, industrialist Andrew Carnegie wrote an essay, *The Gospel of Wealth*, suggesting that the rich have a moral obligation to give away their fortunes toward good works during their lifetimes. Carnegie donated virtually all of his wealth, which in today's dollars would amount to roughly $3 billion. Millionaires such as Carnegie and John D. Rockefeller Sr. were predecessors in philanthropy to today's generation of super-wealthy corporate executives and high-tech entrepreneurs worth billions. In 1913, John D. Rockefeller created the Rockefeller Foundation, which gave away $540 million (about $6 billion in today's dollars) during his lifetime. His son, John D. Jr., continues the tradition of giving in an equivalent amount.

"George Soros is the only [modern-day] American who rivals the great philanthropists of the 1890s—John D. Rockefeller Sr., Andrew Carnegie, and Julius Rosenwald," said Nelson Aldrich Jr., editor of *The American Benefactor*. Individuals like Mr. Soros hope their giving will prompt other foundations to support risky projects and research. "I don't have all of the answers," Soros said, "But I know what questions to ask. And after all, I can't take it with me." The Open Society Institute Board is a nonprofit foundation that supervises Mr. Soros's domestic giving.

Today, the ranks of the wealthy have never been stronger, and many are working as hard at giving away their fortunes as they did in building them. The new philanthropists want to be more personally involved and to take on global issues such as famine, world HIV/AIDS, education, peace, health care, and water conservation. In turn, this new generation of philanthropists expects recipients to be accountable and to produce results. Oracle Corporation's Lawrence J. Ellison has given $100 million to support medical research on aging. He says he believes results count more than the size of the gifts: "Until you start solving problems, until you start delivering results, what difference does it make how much you give?"

Television mogul Ted Turner was a catalyst in this new era of giving when, in 1997, he pledged an historic one-billion-dollars to the United Nations, extending a challenge to other wealthy individuals to do likewise. John R. Alms, President of Coca-Cola Enterprises, Inc., provides intensive support for at-risk kids in Los Angeles from middle school through college. He draws up a plan and volunteers time outside of his regular business hours implementing it.

Bill Gates and Jim Barksdale are major representatives in the increased giving trends by America's high-tech sector. In his campaign to improve health care for the world's poor, Bill Gates initially placed $16.5 billion into his Seattle-based foundation. Since that time Gates and wife, Melinda, have put a total $25.6 billion, some 60 percent of their current net worth, into their foundation, making it the world's largest. The Bill and Melinda Gates Foundation announced an initial $100 million commitment to support an initiative to slow the spread of HIV/AIDS in India. This foundation is dedicated to improving people's lives by sharing advances in health and learning with the global community.

Former Netscape Chief Executive and one of Silicon Valley's leading venture capitalists, Jim Barksdale, and his wife, Sally, recently donated $100 million to create the Barksdale Reading Institute to fight illiteracy. Other gifts include $5.4 million to the University of Mississippi to create the McDonnell-Barksdale Honors College and several donations to the Medical Center in Jackson for full medical scholarships for African-American students.

As philanthropy has evolved into a profession over the past thirty years, there is a need and interest for universities to offer programs that teach the many aspects of fundraising and offer a degree, as exemplified by New York University's Center for Philanthropy and Fundraising. Nonprofit organizations such as UNICEF and the M. D. Anderson Cancer Center Foundation, as well as professional fundraising firms, such as the Dini Partners or Doug Lawson & Associates, offer internships for students wanting to learn about fundraising.

A magazine devoted to philanthropy, *Philanthropy World*, celebrates the spirit of giving. The magazine spotlights people who make a difference and have a major impact on the quality of life in communities around the globe. With so much money at stake, high-level events have assumed greater significance, with talented fundraisers continually raising the bar. Furthermore, all of this takes place, according to surveys, in an environment that is increasingly competitive. More and more causes are vying for fewer and fewer dollars, which means that the key figures in fundraising must have plenty of creativity, initiative, and energy.

CHECKING OUT THE CAUSE BEFORE YOU SIGN ON

Once you make the decision to volunteer, you want to choose a well-run nonprofit organization that promotes a cause you fully endorse. Ask yourself, "Do I really believe in this cause? Could I knowledgably carry on a conversation with a potential benefactor and convince that person to lend his or her support?"

Volunteer Commitment

Three in five large charity organizations have paid volunteer coordinators on staff. Any volunteer should welcome an interview and perhaps go through a training orientation before signing on with a nonprofit. Before making a commitment, it's a good idea to reflect on your personal goals. Ask yourself the following questions:

1. How much time can I realistically give in a week, month, or year?
2. What's my availability to volunteer, in terms of days of the week and times of day?
3. What unique talents do I possess that could help this charity achieve its mission?
4. What do I hope to gain from the experience?
5. Do I want a new skill set that can carry over into the workplace?
6. Am I interested in meeting new people with similar interests?
7. Do I want a sense of fulfillment?
8. What do I want to accomplish and which charities work best to achieve those goals?

Whether the cause offers care to hungry, impoverished, and uneducated children; funds research for an insidious disease like ALS (Lou Gehrig's) or Neurofibromatosis; supports the arts; or creates educational and scholarship opportunities, ask yourself, "How effective is the organization's track record? Do they deliver?" Understand what is expected of you, how many lives will be assisted, what hope is promised, and what the recipients will take away. Is there follow-up? Are there success stories? Can you build on these points?

Learn About the Management

Study the dynamics of the nonprofit organization before making a commitment to become involved. Find out how insiders rate the group. You will be giving the organization your time and energy for many months to come, and you want to be interested enough to commit fully. Clearly, a nonprofit with a high degree of long-term nurturing is meaningful to both benefactors and clients.

Get to know the executive director and visit with two to three members of the board. Determine the role of the board president. How involved is he or she in working with the nonprofit organization? Does he or she bring leadership and guidance to the table, setting the tone for the organization? A board president who leads with integrity will inspire responsibility and accountability in the team. What are the dynamics that exist between the board members and the executive director? Can the board members go directly to the executive director with their ideas and suggestions? What's the protocol?

If you've been asked to become a board member, consider the reasons you have been asked to serve on the board. Is it to contribute, bring new benefactors to the organization, network in the community, be a goodwill ambassador, or chair an event?

Be aware of the activities of other nonprofits to make certain that the organization asking for your help is not duplicating the mission of a similar group. You also want reassurance that targeted groups will indeed be the recipients served.

The merger of not-for-profit organizations makes an even stronger statement for a mutual cause. If the missions are similar but the approaches are different, such changes can create an administrative structure more beneficial to the client or cause being served.

Combining budgets will reduce expenses and non-programmatic operations. As the demand for funding partners grows, mergers of nonprofits are a new direction in fundraising. For example, the Greater Houston Collaborative for Children and the Initiatives for Children recently merged and became the Collaborative for Children.

Look at the Organization's Mission Statement

Before you sign on with an organization, you should understand its mission statement. Essentially, a cause is a need that inspires an individual or group of people to take action to address a specific problem. The group adopts a mission—a defined task that will accomplish its goal. The mission statement adopted by a nonprofit organization states its purpose for being and what it hopes to achieve. The goal of the group should be stated clearly, along with its plan of action.

A well-run service organization should be able to define its mission in fewer than four sentences. For example, "The Shepherd Society supports the field of music at Rice University and in Houston," or, "The mission of the Susan G. Komen Breast Cancer Foundation is to eradicate breast cancer as a life-threatening disease by advancing research, education, screening, and treatment." Another inspiring mission statement is the Lance Armstrong Foundation's: "Enhancing the quality of life for those living with, through, and beyond cancer."

A simple, direct mission statement gives donors a clear picture of what is being accomplished with their charitable dollars. "Quid Pro Quid"—Something for Something—is the motto of Houston's Chinquapin School for economically disadvantaged youths, and this motto is practiced daily. Students there give time and effort to the school in return for the opportunity to receive quality education in a caring, family-oriented environment.

"Most of what I really need to know about how to live and what to do and how to be I learned in kindergarten... when you go out into the world, watch out for traffic, hold hands, and stick together."

—Robert Fulghum,
All I Really Need to Know I Learned in Kindergarten:
Uncommon Thoughts on Common Things

Mission Statement

The Mission of the Houston Public Library is to offer a broadly defined program of informational, educational, recreational and cultural enrichment opportunities for Houstonians of all ages and educational, cultural, and economic background.

Born to Read, La Nueva Casa de Amigos Health Clinic

An organization should clearly state its mission.

Key Issues to Address in a Mission Statement

- Who are we?
- What is our purpose?
- Who does the organization benefit?
- What is our plan of action?
- How will we accomplish our goal?
- How will the success of fundraising efforts be measured?

 *Chapter Two*

CHAIRING A FUNDRAISING EVENT

*"The wind and waves are always on the
side of the ablest navigators."*

—EDWARD GIBBON

The success of any fundraising campaign depends on how committed the chairperson is to the mission of the organization and how well he can articulate its purpose to others. It is the charge of the chair to create the concept, theme, and goal. The chairperson should be a prominent or high-profile individual from the business, arts, or social community. His acceptance makes a powerful statement about the importance of the campaign and serves to promote the cause and the mission of the organization to others.

The chair should be willing to dedicate her time, work hard, and perform any number of duties, from creating benefactor letters to making follow-up calls, from compiling mailing lists to working with different committee chairs to create a successful event. As the chair, you must be prepared to lead by example and to help potential and current donors fully grasp the organization's needs.

The chair always welcomes benefactors and in-kind donors at all events. He offers remarks pertinent to the organization's mission, acknowledges donors, and shares his own vision. It is important for the donors and the volunteers to bond with the chair, and upon hearing her words, they are often inspired to make an even greater commitment. When I am serving as a chairperson, my remarks are usually limited, and I try to include a poignant and relative quote that reaffirms what I am saying.

Each chair has his own management style, but it's the personal appeal that counts. Letters to the chair can be put aside for a later time, but a direct call generally requires a more timely response. An effective leader will attract others of comparable position or resources who possess special skills and will involve them in the event. The most dedicated, hardworking person cannot succeed in organizing an event if she cannot enlist others to lend their time, effort, money, and name to the project. The general chairperson with a good track record will be able to secure volunteers' involvement; furthermore, such a person will play an essential role in attracting major benefactors. The general chair should be an individual to whom people will want to say "yes." Personal contact by the event chairperson is essential for identifying and bringing on board a group of benefactors and donors. By representing an organization in a positive way, the chairperson can increase awareness and create a bond of trust with prospective benefactors that will ultimately result in their commitment to your organization. As a chair, you should make certain your organization is not duplicating the efforts of other groups, thus diluting your own organization's impact.

In deciding whether to accept a chairmanship or to politely refuse, always trust your instincts. If an organization is trying to pressure you into chairing an event about which you don't feel strongly, or if you feel that it is not the right time (economically, politically, or socially) to hold such an event, or if you are concerned about the public's support for such an event, then step back and reevaluate this undertaking. To be effective, you have to be 100 percent committed to whatever cause you support. If you decide not to undertake a project, don't beat yourself up. It doesn't mean that you do not care about what happens to the cause.

When you are following in the footsteps of a highly successful previous chairperson, don't reproach the previous year's donors, whining, "Well, you did such and such for last year's chairman." This approach will permanently turn-off donors. Response from donors varies from year to year. Never insult formerly involved donors by telling them how disappointed you are that they are contributing less or not meeting your expectations in their level of giving. You want to be sure to invite previous donors to be involved in the upcoming special event; however, be considerate of personal situations.

If you have been asked to chair an event, you can count on the organization to offer assistance. Directories and access to other needed information will be provided. For example, you may need the previous donor mailing list to review. Ask the organization to provide you with those names, and input the ones you are adding along with those submitted by your committee members. Make sure the list is in a format with which you are comfortable. There should always be one contact person with whom you work directly at the nonprofit, as well an alternate contact in case vacation leave or illness occurs.

When you are selected chairperson, it becomes your task—and your committee's—to cultivate a fresh group of benefactors to broaden the organization's donor base. There are donors who support the organization's effort on an annual basis simply because they believe in the cause. Others come onboard because of loyalty or friendship with a specific chairman. Some stay involved because their previous experience was a positive one. As the new chair, you must move forward, making your own contacts.

PROJECT A POSITIVE OUTCOME

Once you have accepted a fundraising challenge, there are many calls to be made and letters to be written. Each and every worthwhile project has its own potential benefactor/in-kind donor base. No one enjoys making calls asking for contributions or following up on initial requests. Develop a personal mantra that works for you to make the "ask" process easier.

A mantra provides a protective shield. Say to yourself something like, "I'm not doing this for myself. I believe in this cause. There are people in need. To make a difference, I need this person's commitment." This will give you the confidence and courage to make dreams come true for others. It's an especially helpful way to boost your courage when you have a really big favor or request to ask of someone. After a brief dialogue with myself that includes repeating my mantra, I feel confident and reach for the phone.

Before making a fundraising call, talk with others at the charitable organization you represent, making sure that you know the facts as well as the answers to key questions you may be asked. Some donors may ask about your personal involvement. How committed are the board members? Do they support the foundation monetarily? Do you look for contributors to volunteer as well as to give dollars? Be prepared to answer all of their questions. If you don't know the answer, tell them you'll get back to them with the information they requested. To quote Oprah Winfrey, "Luck is a matter of preparation meeting opportunity."

DO YOUR HOMEWORK

It is also helpful to have as much foreknowledge as possible about the individual, corporation, or foundation you are contacting. The nonprofit organization should have a list of donors and their giving history. Try to direct your correspondence to someone at a corporate office who you know or may have met socially, preferably someone in a senior-level position or a department head who sits on a committee that grants funding requests. There may be a board member of your charitable organization who has contacts within the corporation. Exchanging business cards when you attend events of any kind is a good way to build donor prospects and will help you personalize a future letter or call. It is helpful after attending a reception or a meeting to make a note on the back of the individual's business card, jotting down when and where you met them. This information will refresh your memory when you are making a fundraising request of any kind.

I served as chairperson for the first ever telethon for the Houston Society for the Prevention and Cruelty of Animals (SPCA). Since this was its first annual telethon, we realized in order to be successful we needed at least half of our projected financial goal committed before we ever went on the air. The opportunity to host a telethon came with a short time frame. Many of the major corporations had already prepared their philanthropy budgets for the year, so this created quite a fundraising challenge. We utilized the previous donor base of the society and, at the same time, worked diligently to enlist new individual and corporate sponsors.

Because of our limited time frame to secure corporate sponsorship, we relied heavily on the popular appeal of the cause of protecting animals. I had to focus on goals to bring quick results. The evening before the telethon, I went to a dinner, which former President George Bush attended, and I asked him if I might speak with the former First Lady about the SPCA's telethon. The next day I telephoned Mrs. Bush's office describing the event to her assistant and sending over some information about the organization. "Please tell Mrs. Bush that my reason for calling is to see if First Dog Millie might phone in a pledge during the telethon to Bogie, my dog, who is serving as the telethon's official mascot." Mrs. Bush and Millie were so well loved that her call added a warm and friendly touch to the public awareness of the Houston SPCA. Can you imagine the excitement of the volunteers working the phone bank as well as the viewing audience when Barbara Bush called in Millie's pledge? Even if you are unable to approach someone with a national platform, you could create a similar buzz in your own town by enlisting a local celebrity of sorts to appear on a locally televised fundraiser.

When an organization is represented by an inexperienced chairperson, a staff member needs to make certain that potential problems don't become apparent to the guests. The person chairing the event should have had enough previous experience to be organized, beginning with the simplest of details. An organized chairperson should always make clear such specifics as guest arrival times and dress code. Try to make sure everything flows according to schedule. Use discretion when seating guests. Thank benefactors, in-kind donors, wait staff, and volunteers. When people arrive at an event, they expect to see the chairperson and committee members in place, welcoming and assisting with any details relevant to the event. If anything happens out of order—say the flowers arrive after guests have been seated—that can show a lack of organization and preplanning.

WORKING WITH EXISTING PLAYERS

High-visibility methods of fundraising have spilled over into key operating segments of some nonprofit organizations, and sometimes no clear boundaries exist between an organization's professional staff and its chairperson for the fundraising event. It is very important that the volunteer chairperson feels comfortable working with the development staff. As the chair, you need to understand the staff's responsibilities so that everyone works well together as a team.

The Executive Director

The executive director interacts with the president of the nonprofit's board on matters pertaining to budget, strategic planning, and fundraising. He then takes this information before the board or appropriate committee head on the board. An executive director must have strong leadership skills and be prepared to go out into the community to research, identify, and cultivate new donors, as well as to assist the event chair when she begins working on the fundraising project. Most important, he needs to work well with the organization's board, staff, and volunteers. In a small- to average-size nonprofit organization, the executive director wears many hats and assumes development duties in addition to other tasks.

The Director of Development

The director of development initiates government grant applications and funding proposals and seeks top-level benefactors to lend support to fundraising events. It may be her responsibility to identify top-level business leaders or volunteers from the community to chair annual fundraising events.

The Board of Directors

Board members are selected for a variety of reasons, including their fundraising abilities, leadership skills and team player qualities, willingness to participate, and a strong interest in the cause. Nothing is impossible if the board membership believes in the vision for the fundraising event and is prepared to make the required commitment to raise or give money. The board chairman and board members should expect to attend more than a few fundraising breakfasts and luncheons to open donor doors and enlist donors. Encouraging the participation of board members to give or solicit will make the difference in overall revenue development success.

The board membership is generally comprised of talented individuals in fields relating to the organization in addition to CEOs, bankers, attorneys, accountants, community or civic leaders, and other strong volunteers. Prestigious board members should lend their names to the letterhead and help generate increased awareness for the organization. All members should serve as goodwill ambassadors for an organization, bring fresh ideas to the table, and work to acquire funds. Under the direction of the board president, they are a great resource for new contacts and will work with the executive director on matters pertaining to fundraising and strategic planning. This ensures that their appeals to donors won't overlap with those of the organization's development team.

If a special event is part of the overall fundraising plan, members of the board need to attend and become actively involved. It is up to them to introduce new friends to the organization to help broaden the donor base. The board needs to be open to change for the overall good of the organization. An attitude of "this is what we have done in the past" can keep even the most successful nonprofit organization from moving forward. It's easier not to make change, but as we all know, that's not how progress comes about.

Try to be receptive to fresh ideas and philosophies. For example, technology provides unlimited opportunities in fundraising and is cost efficient. If you've planned an auction, listing silent and live auction items on a Web site gives added recognition and appreciation to in-kind donors.

Advisory Board

Consider enlisting board members-at-large. They are individuals who do not fit any certain profile, but who would be great additions. They bring resources to the organization through their contacts and previous experience in working with other nonprofits in the community. They may be able to serve as a catalyst for a specific project and convince others to become involved. Each board member brings his own unique talents to the board. Make sure you don't inadvertently exclude those who can be effective but may not fit any niche.

FURTHERING THE ORGANIZATION'S STRATEGIC PLAN

When you are appointed chair of the board of a nonprofit group, you should host an orientation session for new board members at which you review the past year's activities, highlight programs, acknowledge the positives, and set new goals of the organization. Divide the board members into working committees. Try to give new members a choice of committee. Schedule an annual retreat to generate enthusiasm and review the organization's strategic plan. A retreat gives members the opportunity to bond as a team, as well as give their input for long-range planning. An outside facilitator may be retained to manage the process.

The strategic plan should be born from the organization's mission. The plan takes time to properly develop, as you establish specific objectives and coordinate efforts. Suggest that a designated number of board members and the executive director plan to meet at an offsite location for a weekend or for a series of creative think tank meetings to create the plan. An unbiased outside consultant might prove helpful and guide your group through the process. It is important to understand the difference between planning work and planning strategy. Once the strategic plan has been decided, the work plan should coincide with it, taking the agreed upon objectives and implementing them.

Sometimes the simplest plan can be the most complex, and working out the path to accomplish the organization's desired objectives can be a long-term job. The plan needs to be fully understood and endorsed by all involved to work in harmony, just as the music of a symphony orchestra blends together.

A proper strategic plan enabled The Girl Scout Council in Wilton, Connecticut, to create a three-year funding development strategy that revitalized its annual giving. Annual giving increased from $42,000 in 1994 to more than $200,000 in 1997, and membership also increased. Given this success, a comprehensive strategic plan was needed because the increased membership created a burden on staff, volunteers, and available money. The council (as do many other nonprofits) faced several socioeconomic challenges—the changing role of women, social programs based on that change, and a more diverse membership.

The Chinquapin School in Houston dedicated its 2002 Annual Report to its past and present board members. The school acknowledged the visionary leadership of its board members and their importance to the fabric of the school's principles. Former board member William F. Kuehn quotes General George S. Patton, "Accept the challenges, so that you may feel the exhilaration of victory," when he talks about the challenges of birthing an endowment, getting it funded and functional, and securing the future for Chinquapin.

Seize the Moment

Some larger organizations have board memberships of more than a hundred people. If you are chairing an upcoming event and have good news to share, take advantage of an opportune moment to attend the board meeting. Ask to be put on the agenda. Have fact sheets, response forms, and invitations to events available so the board of the nonprofit can be among the first to support an effort to benefit the organization.

You can never start planning too far in advance, as many corporations have their charitable budgets in place at least a year in advance. At the board meeting, the chairman or a committee member can demonstrate how the promotions on the Web site and registration for events will work. A report from the chair will keep them up to date on the progress of the events. They will appreciate your willingness to share information. Give board members the opportunity to be informed, to participate, and to enlist the support of others.

AGENDA
JOINT ANNUAL MEETING
AND MEETING OF THE BOARD OF TRUSTEES
HOUSTON GRAND OPERA ASSOCIATION, INC.
Thursday, June 7, 2001* 4:30 P.M.
THE BALLROOM * RIVER OAKS COUNTRY CLUB * 1600 RIVER OAKS BOULEVARD

	Trustees' Coffee	4:00 PM
I.	CALL TO ORDER/APPROVAL OF MARCH 8, 2001 MINUTES................	Archie Dunham
II.	REPORT OF THE GENERAL DIRECTOR............................	David Gockley
III.	HGO ENDOWMENT.....................................	William Moore
	Endowment Campaign Feasibility.................................	Bruce Flessner
IV.	PROGRAM HIGHLIGHTS	
	A. Development Council.................................	Harry Pinson
	B. Special Events..	Pat Breen
	Opera Ball...	Carolyn Farb
	C. Finance & Administration Report and Approval of FY'02 Budget°°	Robert Hunter
	D. Marketing & PR..	Gracie Cavnar
	E. Public Policy..	Richard Mayor
	F. Education & Outreach..................................	Brenda Harvey-Traylor
	G. Houston Grand Opera Studio..................................	Fabian Worthing
	H. Trustees Committee.................................	William Guggolz
V.	HOUSTON GRAND OPERA GUILD................................	Patte Comstock
VI.	DISTINGUISHED SERVICE AWARD – TEXACO...............	Jim Hackett
VII.	BYLAW AMENDMENT/RESOLUTION*...........................	Walter Stuart
VIII.	2001-2002 BOARD OF TRUSTEES ELECTION* 2001-2002 HGO GUILD OFFICERS & TRUSTEES ELECTION*...	William Guggolz
IX.	ELECTION OF OFFICERS, EXECUTIVE COMMITTEE, MEMBERS-AT-LARGE & BOARD VICE PRESIDENTS OF BOARD OF TRUSTEES, ENDOWMENT TRUSTEES, LIFE TRUSTEE°°...	William Guggolz
X.	RECOGNITION OF 2001-2002 BOARD OF TRUSTEES.......	Archie Dunham
XI.	OTHER BUSINESS..	Archie Dunham
XII.	ADJOURNMENT...	Archie Dunham

Be prepared to present your ideas at a board meeting
to garner your organization's full support.

Board Meeting Tips

- Schedule major board meetings a year in advance in consideration of members' schedules.
- Limit number of meetings.
- Stress the importance of attendance.
- Provide brief highlights of matters up for discussion. Have a staff member clip pertinent newspaper or magazine articles to include with reminder memo.
- Keep your board strong and engaged. When people rotate off the board, express appreciation for the time they have served and welcome new members.
- Be an enthusiastic participant.
- Be open to changes that will benefit the organization. Saying "that's what we have always done in the past" can hold a group back.
- Bring in several advisors or speakers who have a sincere interest in your organization but don't have the time for board membership. They can energize a board that needs a fresh perspective.

 *Chapter Three*

MAKING SURE YOU'LL MAKE MONEY

"High expectations are the key to everything."
—SAM WALTON

There should always be a bond of trust between the organization and the donor. When a donor makes a contribution or a volunteer asks for funds on behalf of a nonprofit organization, both are entitled to know that the monies they are giving or asking for benefit the specific cause and not other needs of the group. When a request you have initiated is granted or an in-kind donation is received, following up with a thank-you goes a long way in pleasing donors.

An organization's accurate financial data upholds the standards of that organization and maintains its public image. You need to ask yourself, "What would an investigative reporter say about how we've spent the money we've raised?" The net results tell the story. Keep your expenses low with tight reigns on your cash flow when raising funds. Watch the bottom line!

COMMITTING TO A ZERO-BASED BUDGET
I use the term "zero budget" philosophy, meaning you don't have to spend money to raise money. There are certain fixed expenses that are unavoidable and sometimes impossible to have underwritten.

Some examples of these fixed expenses are food and beverage at a hotel or venue ballroom, entertainment, floral and linen, decorations, printing, valet parking, and other line items. Try to generate as much in-kind support as possible to offset expenses so you can deliver the sought-after bottom line.

When structuring a budget, try to keep your event expenses contained to less than 25 percent (10 to 15 percent is preferable) of the projected revenue, not including in-kind donations. Remember, it's always easier to spend money than it is to raise it.

It is very advantageous to the zero-budget philosophy if all pre-parties (or the actual fundraising event, if it is small in size) can be held in either a restaurant willing to donate its services or in a private home. People who have moved into fabulous new residences or those who enjoy entertaining on a large scale often are willing to open their homes to deserving organizations. This will reduce your expenses, increase the excitement for the upcoming event, and boost the bottom line. The key point is to entertain your benefactors with a special evening of good fare and fine wines.

The ideal profile of a host would be a restaurateur/entrepreneur who could have several of his restaurants offer food stations, waiters, and entertainment. You can also have a pre-event with a clever theme (such as Hawaiian), serving only cocktails and hors d'oeuvres. At these gatherings, guests are not limited to one dinner partner and have an opportunity to mingle and network. There is a trend to make these events less formal—no tie, still casually elegant.

I recently chaired a tea and book signing for actress Carol Channing on the publication of her book, *Just Lucky, I Guess: A Memoir of Sorts*. Northwood University has chapters of its National Women's Board and Friends in both Dallas and Houston. To benefit the college, we were able to host the events a day apart in the two cities. Carol Channing was a delight and an inspiration. Everyone marveled at this energetic eighty-two years young superstar and author.

Since it was the inaugural tea at the InterContinental Houston

Hotel, the management generously underwrote the expense of the event. The hotel was happy to partner with our group and felt the awareness the event created would be beneficial to the facility in the future.

Every detail of your event should complement your overall message or theme.

For the Carol Channing Tea, the decorations complemented the theme of the role she's best known for, *Gentlemen Prefer Blondes*. We did the room glamorously red with sparkles and red roses adorning the tables. The linens and the chair covers were red, as well. I previously had worked on a gala with two local businesses called Lexis Florist and Distinctive Details, so they generously donated the centerpieces, linens, and chair covers for this event. The proceeds created numerous scholarships for students on the Northwood University campus.

Potential Special Event Income and Expense Budget

Income and Revenue
- Underwriting and major gifts
- Table sales and individual tickets
- Contributions
- Auction items
- Centerpiece sales
- In-kind donations
- Raffle items
- Program ad sales
- Retail percentage sales

Expenses
- Food and beverage costs
- Orchestra and entertainment
- Awards
- Venue charges—rental, electrical, VIP room charge
- Decorations
- Photographer
- Office supplies
- Printing—invitations, programs, catalog
- Meeting room space
- Equipment rental—tables, chairs, linens, computers
- Lights, sound, and audio-visual
- Moving and storage
- Travel expenses
- Limousine rentals
- Security
- Valet parking

MANAGING THE CAMPAIGN

Use a software program to accurately track all phases of the campaign process. Select a program with the ability to categorize benefactors, corporate partners, potential in-kind donors, revenue, and expenses. Take the time to enter helpful information about each person, so that he is approached in the proper manner. For example, some do not want to attend events and prefer to make direct contributions. Others want to be recognized in a specific way for their contributions, perhaps listing both their name and their company. And there are those who wish to remain anonymous. If individuals have indicated an interest in volunteering for any aspect of your event, keep them informed of such opportunities. Make them aware of current projects and others that are in the planning stages.

Once your underwriting letters have been sent and early commitments have been made by benefactors, the nonprofit organization will begin to receive affirmative responses in the form of checks and credit cards. Checks aren't keepsakes. The organization's finance director's job is to receive the checks, make a copy of them for the nonprofit's records, and deposit them. Give all checks to the treasurer; don't hold onto them! If there is a special situation with the way the organization's treasury is set up, be sure to follow all necessary procedures. For example, if you are raising funds for a college branch that is part of a central campus in another state, the checks may need to be sent by a carrier that tracks packages, like FedEx, to the main registrar to be immediately deposited.

If a check is given directly to a volunteer, she should immediately make a copy and give it to the responsible person at the organization to be deposited. I said this earlier, but I can't stress this enough: Copies of checks or credit card receipts always should be kept on record at the nonprofit office. This serves as a check and balance on monies and credit card charges received. And don't forget to acknowledge receipt of the contribution with an appreciative thank-you-letter form that the donor can also use for tax purposes.

Make it clear to your donors to whom they should make their check payable: "Victory/American Cancer Society," "Friends of the Nelson Mandela Children's Fund, Inc." On your response form, give them the option of paying in the current year or by a specified deadline in the following year. If your donor is a corporate employee, see if the company will consider a matching donation.

Tracking Funds

Recent questionable behavior and ethical lapses in the corporate sector have made the public and the media more concerned about the philanthropic and nonprofit sectors. This may be related to the rapid growth or the number of nonprofits that now represent 7 to 10 percent of the economy.

Conscientious donors want to know exactly where the net proceeds will go. Benefactors prefer that their charitable contributions not be spent on administrative costs. Whenever possible, let them

Your organization's annual report should be available to donors.

choose the specific programs they wish to support—research, preventative medicine, scholarships, or endowments. A brief description of the various programs could be included and mailed with the benefactor package.

Invite potential donors to your office to learn firsthand about your organization. You should always have your organization's balance sheet up to date and readily available to donors. Requesting this information demonstrates an informed effort on the donor's part to know the inner workings of your organization. The balance sheet should reflect revenues and expenditures for both the current period and the fiscal year to date. A spending plan or budget will assure donors that your nonprofit is being well managed.

Minding the Store

The late Stanley Marcus, chairman emeritus of Neiman Marcus, created a retail enterprise known throughout the world as a epitome of quality. The title of his book, *Minding the Store*, emphasizes an important aspect of both business and fundraising. I interpret "minding the store" to mean that both individuals and organizations need to have hands-on involvement in whatever the commitment. You can always save a situation, but once it has gotten out of control, the damage is done. In other words, as a volunteer you should always have a watchful and helpful eye looking out for the best interest of the organization.

For example, the chairperson needs to mind the store if a committee head goes overboard on decorations or any other unnecessary expenditures. Prospective benefactors will definitely be turned off if they hear that funds are being spent in a frivolous manner.

By the same token, don't allow in-kind donors to demand too much from the organization in exchange for their donation. The nonprofit organization shouldn't make promises it can't realistically keep in order to lure donors. For instance, charities are not in the consignment business for jewelry, furs, carpets, cars, or real estate.

Never deviate from your purpose, and always remember the cause is the priority. It is best for a donation to be given outright without any strings.

If someone offers to donate a piece of jewelry, the organization is not responsible for the expense incurred to create the piece of jewelry. The organization may host a reception at which the jeweler presents his collection. In this way, you can thank the donor and honor his generosity. However, the charity is not responsible for the lack of success of any high-end retailer who participates in the event. The charitable organization is merely presenting the opportunity to the donor, and the donation is given in good faith and becomes the property of the charity.

Tax Exemptions

The proof is in your nonprofit status. You *must* list your organization's status with the Internal Revenue Service as a nonprofit organization. You may add a sentence about the purpose, such as: "Provides loving care to persons living with HIV/AIDS." Donations are tax deductible to the extent allowed by law.

An organization must meet requirements set forth in the Internal Revenue Code. It then becomes tax-exempt by applying for recognition of exemption from the IRS. To apply for recognition of exempt status by the IRS as described in section 501(c)(3) of the code, an organization must use Package 1023, Application for Recognition of Exemption. The application must be complete and accompanied by the appropriate user fee. The organization should request an employer ID number even if the organization does not have any employees. Except for churches and their integrated auxiliaries, the public charities whose annual gross receipts are less than $5,000 will not be treated as described in section 501(c)(3) unless they notify the IRS they are applying for recognition. If they do not notify the IRS within fifteen months of their creation, they will be classified as Private Foundations. For more details, visit www.irs.gov.

You should have your IRS designation and other information available to donors. When you are planning a special event at a hotel, convention center, or similar venue, don't forget to provide your tax exemption information to the hotel banquet manager or on-site caterer. Nonprofit organizations are generally exempt from sales tax but not from gratuities or service charges. Check with your state taxing authority about your organization's specific exemption rules. Consider every opportunity to reduce any related expenses.

Maintaining Credibility

In the case of nonprofits, you must delineate the true value of the organization. When you're trying to communicate this important information to the public, you can count on one fact: People almost always buy into the goals of a charitable organization that ensures that at least 85 percent of funds raised go directly to the cause. Posting this achievement will insure a good rating on any charity watchdog list.

Honesty and integrity count. You can't make exaggerated promises. A product whose claims are super-sized beyond belief will never be a lasting success. (On the flip side, many products and services are better than their reputations suggest, which means that the public has not been alerted to the quality of these products/services.)

Watchdog groups like the American Institute of Philanthropy bring to the public any concerns about how donations are being used. For example, with the Red Cross Disaster Relief Fund, the question arose regarding the establishment of the Liberty Fund after 9/11 and whether it was honoring donor intent. The commingling of 9/11 monies with other Red Cross Disaster Relief funds gave the impression that the Red Cross was using the crisis as an opportunity to raise money for more general purposes.

In a damage-control statement about the misuse of the Liberty Fund, the Red Cross stated that donations of $500,000-plus would go directly to the victims of the terrorist attacks. Lawsuits by the

New York Attorney General were pending, but the Red Cross's announcement provided a level of satisfaction for the families and an improved image for the agency. This underscores that the public should remain the ever-constant watchdog.

There is donor demand for accountability, as well as for evaluation of the effectiveness of the charity and how it spends its funds. The IRS doesn't do a lot of monitoring of nonprofits, and even if financial information is available, due diligence can be difficult. Only recently has the IRS questioned charities regarding their fundraising activities.

Nonprofits should strive to be accountable for their own spending—not only how much they spend but what aspect of their mission each dollar is contributing to. For example, if you receive a direct mail solicitation to raise money for a cancer group, and at the same time, the letter tells you ten ways to avoid having cancer yourself, the pitch is in part educational and the nonprofit probably considered that mailing an educational expense rather than a fundraising expense. For information on the soundness of charitable organizations and their ratings, go to www.charitynavigator.org, which provides a database of more than three thousand charity ratings.

Cost-Efficient Tips for Nonprofit Organizations' Events

- Get wines donated and work with the banquet manager on a reasonable corkage fee.
- If the event is a dinner, serving fish or chicken instead of beef can reduce cost per person.
- Save on a luncheon menu by offering only two courses. Try a grilled chicken salad or cold poached salmon entrée as a main course with a great dessert (key lime pie, apple crisp, pecan ball). You can make this happen in the range of $20 to $30 per person including tax and service charge, depending on the venue. This works well when there's a program and short time frame and will help guests get out in a timely manner and back to their carpools or offices.
- Dinner should consist of three courses, especially when there is an entertainment program, and you can provide this meal in a range of $40 to $65 per person. If you add a fourth course, it adds another $7 to $10 to the cost.
- If providing meals for the volunteers, keep the menu simple and cost effective—a deli buffet works.
- Make arrangements with the venue manager to have as much time as possible for setting up in advance. This will avoid labor/overtime costs from production and decorating crews.
- If the venue has its own audio-visual department, use those services, as their bids will typically come in lower.
- To avoid additional expenses, be flexible with the event decorator regarding setup.
- Try to get valet parking donated. You can offer to provide corporate custom logos on the valet parking tickets. In this way, you're giving sponsors something in return. A car wash or party vendor would be a likely prospective underwriter for the valet parking. They will be advertising to a targeted audience for a fraction of the cost.

 *Chapter Four*

BUILDING SUPPORT FOR
YOUR ORGANIZATION

*"Determine that the thing can and shall be done,
and then we shall find the way."*
—ABRAHAM LINCOLN

People need social services today more than ever. With families scattered across the country, there are no longer the support systems that once existed. Economic circumstances have changed over the past thirty years. Health care costs have skyrocketed. With both parents working in most households, the volunteer pool has diminished. People are living longer. Technology is advancing rapidly. There is greater concern for the underprivileged, creating a larger need for philanthropy in our society. We are challenged to create resources to fund the organizations that address the changing times in which we are living.

FINDING SOURCES OF ANNUAL SUPPORT
Every organization should consider developing a special group of benefactors to boost annual support. This group of benefactors will provide a dependable source of revenue and create a circle of philanthropists for the organization.

An organization can provide incentives for benefactors to become involved. For example, members of the Houston Ballet Ambassadors are offered such opportunities as enjoying an annual lecture/luncheon, hosting visiting performers in their homes, and attending private receptions.

Your organization might plan a special day and show benefactor appreciation by hosting a series of Sunday brunches in private homes. Depending on the number of participants and the levels of membership decided upon, these benefactors could provide a dependable amount of added annual revenue to the organization. For example, three hundred members at $2,500 per year would bring in $750,000, less any expenses for catering, printing, valet, and other miscellaneous items. (Not all members of these groups attend every event, and the organization should base its budget accordingly.)

Once people have become long-term supporters, they will often evolve into future event chairs, guild officers, and board members. Include a questionnaire/response form in the organization's newsletter or event program encouraging your benefactors to inquire about the various ways they can become involved—guild membership, advisory board membership, season subscription, and/or charitable gift annuities.

Let your major benefactors express in their own words why they are making a major contribution to your organization. You can print their letters in your newsletter. For example, a message from philanthropists John and Rebecca Moores was printed in the University of Houston Moores School of Music newsletter sharing their reasons for underwriting the new building for the school. After touring the old buildings of the school, they saw the need and decided to donate the funds for the new facilities to meet the needs of a growing student body and distinguished faculty. Sharing a personal message will inform your readership of just who the benefactors are and why they are making such meaningful and substantial gifts. This can be very empowering to others who are considering becoming involved.

Invite new donor prospects to a reception or performance as the guest of a board member or the organization's executive director. Keep your mailing list fresh. Don't rely on the same list for every mailing. Instead, continue to build and cultivate new donor prospects. Long-time benefactors won't appreciate being solicited for every fund drive, special event, and campaign the organization sponsors.

Benefactors are sometimes inspired on their own to help others. Aside from being motivated by a specific fundraising plan or publicity campaign, a donor might see a human-interest story or heart-warming photo published with a caption that will motivate him or her to give. The late Joan Kroc, widow of McDonald's Corporation founder Ray A. Kroc, was moved by the work of the Salvation Army during the Depression. This later led to the establishment of the Ray and Joan Kroc Corps Community Centers, which are being built across the country.

Respecting Your Benefactors

There are many reasons why people give of their time and money. Try to understand what motivates the potential benefactor to give and tailor your appeal to his or her sensibilities. They may be idealistic and genuinely concerned for those who are less fortunate. For some people, giving reflects their hope of bringing order and comfort into the lives of others. Giving can be motivated by a sense of duty. Many people derive their own sense of well-being from helping others. Be sensitive to the causes people choose to support and be appreciative of their giving.

When it comes to working with donors, know when to ebb and flow. Donors come with different wishes, and you must learn to honor them. Some donors are low key, while others require higher maintenance. There are those who want a presentation and to be taken lunch. While some say, "Don't call," others prefer a phone call. Go slowly and try to follow each donor's lead. Don't be overly aggressive, or you may send the donor in a different direction.

People take their time when considering a major gift. Be patient.

It's a process I like to define as the basics of fundraising: Listen to your potential benefactors, get them involved with the organization, keep them informed, develop a relationship over time, and practice patience.

Give donors the opportunity to contribute as their finances allow and let them know that all gifts are appreciated. Remember not to "over ask" and always remember your "last ask." Gently approach the donors to see if they might consider a move to the next level of giving. Keep in mind that competition is intense for philanthropic dollars. And very importantly, remember to say thank you.

Building the Prospect Pool

Work with your board of directors to create a wish list of individuals, corporations, and foundations to expand your benefactor base. Bond your potential supporters with the needs of the group. You can cultivate these prospects by sending them information on your organization, evaluating their interests, and including them on invitation lists to special events. An arts organization might invite potential benefactors to a special performance so they can experience firsthand the organization's cultural impact and value within the community.

When you are trying to raise funds for a nonprofit organization, you need to create awareness. Have the executive director or a well-spoken board member highlight educational and community outreach programs that are a vital part of the curriculum of the organization. An opera company might send the latest CD or video of past opera performances to prospective benefactors, invite them to attend a small recital by opera studio artists, or introduce them to cast members at a post-performance party. Enumerate the positives about your organization with your prospective donors.

A picture is worth a thousand words. Stephen Roddy, director of the Houston Children's Chorus, has mastered the art of captivating the hearts of his potential benefactors. He puts together a small photo album filled with pictures of the children's chorus at work and uses poignant photo captions to describe their performances. He includes a personal note with the album and sends them out to his past and prospective donors. How is that for a sincere, refreshing appeal that anyone would find hard to resist? The chorus performs annually for more than 750,000 people in Houston and is always a sellout. Whether the choir sings with Celine Dion or before visiting dignitaries, participates in teaching music to inner-city children or represents our country at the Vatican in Rome, these young ambassadors spread goodwill.

Images of your donors' dollars at work can add
impact to your fundraising appeals.

KNOWLEDGE IS POWER

To better serve their organizations and address the competition for funding, the development staff and key volunteers (board chair, board members, and upcoming chairpersons) of nonprofits should stay abreast of the latest in philanthropy news. They should stay in touch with elected officials, be aware of local, civic, and social issues, and volunteer with other nonprofits to observe how their boards interact. When you are appointed as a chairperson or other key volunteer, being well informed will strengthen your organization. Appoint a board member or another key volunteer to serve as a resource librarian—clipping newspaper articles relative to potential donors and filing articles for easy access. Check out the business section of local newspapers and business journals, not only in your city, but also statewide. There are new companies relocating into your region daily, and the executives and their spouses will be looking for ways to become active in their new community.

A "Bids and Proposals" column in the classified section will list local grant proposals. The social columns cover special events and generally acknowledge major benefactors who make such events possible. Individuals, companies, and foundations that support charitable events by attending fundraising activities may be potential benefactors for your cause.

Look over other event programs to see if there are names that have been overlooked on your mailing list. This is another way to build your donor list. When you attend events, take note of individuals in attendance who might have an interest in your organization. If your organization hosts a free lecture, movie, or concert, have a guest book available for people to register and perhaps offer a contribution. In this way, you may bring additional donors into your organization. The personal contacts of board and committee members can serve as another resource for new prospects.

Be Open to Offers of Generosity

Don't overlook a gift horse. This may sound cliché, but it would have served as a good reminder in one instance among my fundraising colleagues in Houston. A former member of a symphony orchestra left the group to start a catering business. His ongoing love of music and a desire to stay involved prompted him to offer his catering services and partially underwrite the cost, discounting his services. To his dismay, no one took him up on his proposal. So, he offered his services to other arts groups, who readily embraced his generosity. When people make an offer to give back in-kind rather than in cash, organization leadership should pay attention.

BUILDING A MAILING LIST

A good mailing list is invaluable. The best mailing list consists of your own contacts as well as those of your friends, board members, and volunteers of the organization. Your mailing list is never complete—it needs to be regularly updated and broadened. For each event, review lists to determine which donors to include for that specific event. Your decision should be based on the donor's personal preference, interests, and record of giving.

Mailing lists are available for a price, and some are free. The Neiman Marcus catalog list indicates an average income and lifestyle, and for that you pay a fee. Horchow provides in its catalog mailing list a consumer profile, which includes income, age, marital status, education, spending, and family dwelling style. Others are available by Zip Code.

You can ask committee members, friends, or associates who are working on the special event to provide lists of names that would not ordinarily be available. This could include a directory listing of memberships from a country club, Junior League, alumni association, dance club, or church membership, to name a few. It doesn't mean that having the list will ensure instant success. Going through such a directory will help you discover additional contacts that have been overlooked. Determining how to get the best results for your organization is almost like analyzing a puzzle; there are many pieces that you must put into place to help create the whole.

WHAT'S IN IT FOR YOUR ORGANIZATION'S SUPPORTERS?

Nonprofits are becoming more creative as they compete for the charitable dollar. They remind benefactors that anyone, not only the wealthy, can make a generous gift and, at the same time, receive immediate or long-term benefits. Some of these benefits might include guaranteed fixed payments (partially tax-free, immediate income tax charitable deduction), reduction of capital gains tax if appreciated securities are part of the contribution, and removal of the contributed assets from taxable estates.

Because each benefactor's needs will be different, it is important that the charitable organization suggest that the would-be donor consult with his or her financial and legal advisors to explore the opportunities that will best fit his/her desire to support a worthy cause.

Charitable Gift Annuity:

☐ I/we would like to know more about the benefits of a Charitable Gift Annuity.

Name _____

Address _____

City/State/Zip _____

Telephone _____

☐ I/we have already included Houston Grand Opera in my/our will(s) or other long-range estate plan.

☐ I/we wish to be recognized as a member of the Laureate Society. Preferred program listing: _____

_____

☐ I/we wish to remain anonymous.

☐ I/we would consider including Houston Grand Opera in my/our will(s) or other long-range estate plan.

HoustonGrandOpera
Laureate Society

Keeping the Flame of Opera Burning Brightly

"I expect to pass through life but once. If, therefore, there can be any kindness I can show, or any good things I can do to any fellow human being, let me do it now, and not defer it or neglect it, as I shall not pass this way again."

William Penn

A simple, standard gift form might look like this one.

Gift annuities especially have popular appeal with senior Americans interested in philanthropy. Nonprofit organizations often use the soft economy and the volatility of the financial markets as a way to reach this specifically targeted audience. Gift annuities can compare favorably with conservative investments.

How Does the IRS View Charitable Shares?

Your benefactors won't need to involve a broker when donating stock if they have the stock certificates in hand. All they'll need to do is fill out the back portion of the form and make it payable to the nonprofit organization. Then the recipient can take the stock certificates to a broker to sell. If the benefactor's shares are held in a brokerage account, the broker can assist with the transfer.

Benefactors can avoid a capital gains tax, get a current tax deduction, and support their favorite cause by supporting a Benefactor-Advised Fund. A gift must be irrevocable to qualify for a tax deduction, and made to an I.R.S. qualified recipient. Setting up a Benefactor-Advised Fund is a simplified, lost-cost procedure compared to creating a private foundation. The benefactor leaves more money for philanthropy. Once tax-free assets growth is funded then future income and gains are not taxable. Benefactors receive immediate tax deductions while supporting their charitable beneficiary. See the National Charitable Gift Fund Trust at www.managed-giving.org.

WHAT IF POTENTIAL BENEFACTORS AREN'T RESPONDING?

Encourage research. Do surveys to find out how your donors feel about things, and don't wait until there is a crisis. Have museum visitors and conference attendees fill out questionnaires, or hire consultants to get more relevant feedback from donors.

Have the questions cover all areas, and tailor rating scales so that respondents can give both positive and negative ratings. Be prepared to enter the data received from the questionnaires so that the information can be assessed.

You can hire a research firm for assistance with data entry and tabulation. Interview several fundraising consultants before making a choice. Shop around to compare fees for a professional plan. If you choose to go with a professional, the benefits may outweigh the expense.

Experts can guide you through the project if you provide a clear objective for the information you want. Choosing the right questions and wording these correctly are two important aspects of survey-taking. If your intent is to attract a specific donor type, tailor questions to that donor profile.

 *Chapter Five*

COURTING CORPORATIONS AND FOUNDATIONS

*"Example is not the main thing in influencing
others, it is the only thing."*
—ALBERT SCHWEITZER

Causes that appeal to a broad audience have greater opportunities to partner with corporations, retailers, and other local businesses in the community. This is known as cause-related marketing. Companies work with nonprofits to demonstrate their community concern and involvement. When the cause is compatible with a corporation's culture, cause-related marketing offers added strength, revenue, and visibility for both partners.

CAUSE-RELATED MARKETING

Partner with a corporation by enlisting the support of a CEO who is actively involved in the community. For example, you might ask the CEO, president, or managing partner of a local bank, retail center, investment firm, or energy company to serve on your nonprofit's board in a leadership role or to spearhead a capital campaign. Ultimately, the benefit of his or her knowledge, as well as of the company's image being tied to your organization, will open doors and provide greater access for a nonprofit to explore new donor possibilities.

Once a CEO makes a commitment to your organization to serve as the head of your board of directors or to chair a specific capital campaign, you can count on his or her performance. These individuals are used to being in the public eye, hitting their mark, and achieving their goals.

Make it easy for corporate leaders to commit to your nonprofit organization. Remember, most of these high-powered individuals already have busy, committed lives and will not accept the responsibility unless they feel they can deliver. Try to discover a common interest the CEO might have with your organization before you and the nonprofit executive director seek his or her support. If a corporate leader relates to your cause, and it falls within the corporate guidelines, he or she will make his/her resources available. For example, the Dave Thomas Foundation for Adoption lends its support to help children in need of adoption. It was established by the Wendy's founder, the late Dave Thomas, who was raised in a Catholic orphanage.

A medium to large corporation can undertake events of significance and network to bring other individuals and companies to a cause. It is not uncommon for corporate leaders to sit on two or three nonprofit boards or to serve as chairman of the board of directors of a nonprofit organization. They apply the same business ethics and practices that have created successes for their own companies. Their active participation is invaluable. It allows nonprofit organizations to prioritize and begin strategic plans for future growth.

Lead individual or corporate sponsors encourage others to embrace a cause by stepping forward. When the first major sponsor makes a commitment, this gives wings to your project. It is very important that your lead sponsors receive proper recognition.

A nonprofit's partner involvement will continue to develop if the company is satisfied with the relationship. The company can participate in a variety of events that reinforce the partnership, such as store openings, guest appearances, walk-a-thons and marathons, galas, literary evenings, and dinner and theater events.

In the fight against breast cancer, major retailers such as Saks Fifth Avenue, Estée Lauder, and jewelry designer David Yurman support breast cancer awareness and funding for research, and, at the same time, directly target their consumer markets. Nearly everyone knows someone who has had breast cancer, so there are many companies that want to become involved in these partnerships and embrace this cause.

Evelyn Lauder, the daughter-in-law of Estée Lauder, is both a passionate advocate for breast cancer research and a talented photographer. On several occasions, arrangements have been made for an exhibition of her photography at an art gallery, with the proceeds from the sales going to The Breast Cancer Research Foundation. Her visit is often partnered with a retailer, such as Neiman Marcus, to include other in-store events such as a luncheon and reception in her honor. This example of cause-related marketing can take place at venues across the country and can be duplicated by other worthwhile causes.

In 1995, the number-one foot care company in North American teamed up with the March of Dimes for the 25th Anniversary of Walk America. As a Silver Anniversary National Sponsor at $222,500, Dr. Scholl's Foot Care Products generated awareness and support nationwide for the charity. Dr. Scholl's individual brand and trademark messages were tied to a respected cause-related event that raised interest and educated consumers about its products and the March of Dimes. As former Rice University president Malcolm Gillis said, "What could be a better fit than a foot care company sponsoring Walk America?"

American Express's commitment to the restoration of the Statue of Liberty project was viewed positively by its clients, because it underscored the values of the company with the patriotic spirit of America and its people. Consumers are more apt to embrace a company that supports a cause about which they care. Given a choice, consumers will tend to select one brand or retailer over another because of the company's association with a particular cause. Partnering is a way for companies and nonprofits to work side-by-side and to mutually benefit.

Joint ventures between an organization and a corporation can result in a large donation to the cause. For example, the Ultimate Drive raises awareness for both the nonprofit Susan B. Komen Breast Cancer Foundation and BMW North America. This partnership works well because it creates awareness for both groups, builds the volunteer base for the Komen Foundation, and validates BMW's belief that once you drive a BMW, you'll want the car. There are no out-of-pocket expenses for the consumer. For every test mile driven by volunteers, one dollar is contributed to the Komen Foundation. This event happens simultaneously all over America. In Houston, dealerships have united to offer drivers the option of going from one dealership to the next—or even to a dealership in a nearby city—all in the name of a good cause.

Each year a breakfast is held recognizing the participating dealerships as well as deserving honorees. Such guests of honor might be cancer survivors or prominent professionals in the medical field. The Ultmate Drive also has involved groups like the Girl Scouts and the Houston Museum of Fine Arts to keep the event from becoming stale. For example, one year the Girl Scouts contributed to the event by making one thousand paper cranes following a Japanese proverb: "If you fold a thousand paper cranes, your wish will come true." This project fulfilled the wish to survive made by a teacher who had cancer, and provided a way for philanthropy to be experienced by the young. The cranes were displayed at the various dealerships, where people could take them in exchange for a donation of their choice. With the funds raised, the foundation can continue research to find a cure for cancer, provide mammography for indigent women, and reduce the time for women waiting to learn their diagnosis.

Sometimes the key to a successful fundraiser is to join forces with another nonprofit organization that shares your goal. Combined efforts of groups like the Kiwanis and the Rotarians can address international causes or crises such as the Skip a Meal Program and the Intercontinental Program to Eradicate Polio in Our Lifetime. For some endeavors, your organization may be able to get an international consulting firm to work pro bono as a partner. For the Juvenile Diabetes Foundation, individuals, government (U.S. National Institutes of Health), and foundations (the Welcome Foundations in the United Kingdom, the United States, Canada, and Australia) were leveraged and maximized to research funding opportunities. If a partner gives two dollars and your organization gives three dollars (or vice versa), research efforts can be doubled, resulting in greater impact for your dollar.

FEMAP is an El Paso, Texas, foundation based in Ciudad, Juarez, that is dedicated to improving the quality of life among Mexicans living in poverty. "We started the foundation eight years ago to help people on the other side of the border, but they have turned around and helped us," says Adair Margo, founder of the FEMAP Foundation.

Guadalupe de la Vega of Juarez founded FEMAP's Hospital de la Familia near the national bridge linking the El Paso and Ciudad to provide health care and support to the underserved women of Mexico. She was inspired to work to improve these conditions when she read about a depressed mother of nine children who tried to commit suicide because she could not provide for her family. This desperate need for education on family planning and maternal and child healthcare touched Lupe de la Vega profoundly, and through FEMAP, she is able to prevent such tragedies from occurring.

First Lady Laura Bush first began supporting the organization when her husband was Texas governor. Most of the hospital's patients are from Mexico, but a number of U.S. residents also cross the border to receive care. When Adair Margo, Guadalupe de la Vega, and I were inducted into *Philanthropy Magazine*'s Hall of

Fame in El Paso, Texas, in 1997, we visited the hospital, and I was inspired by this amazing partnership that provides services to large numbers of patients.

Another strong partnership exists between Teach for America Los Angeles and the UCLA Center on Aging. The two groups partner to connect retired teachers in mentoring roles with outstanding recent college graduates. When the young teachers become Teach for America Corps members, they commit to teaching two years in a low-income or urban community. The mentors from the UCLA Center on Aging then pair up to share their wealth of practical experience and professional support with the corps. Small groups of two to three corps members meet periodically with a mentor for classroom visits, workshops, social visits, and one-on-one consultations. Not only do both organizations benefit from this partnership, but all contributions to this endeavor directly impact the lives of underserved children by providing them with talented, dedicated teachers and role models. Donations are used to cover the cost of recruitment, as well as the selection and training of Teach for America Corps members.

The concept of partnership employed by these organizations would work well with other centers on aging and nonprofit organizations around the country.

Another example of a profitable partnership occurs annually during the holidays, when Macy's sets up annual Giving Trees at their stores filled with the wishes of hundreds of children in underprivileged communities throughout the country. When a shopper purchases a gift for a needy child, Macy's staff members then wrap and deliver it. Stores may choose to make additional gifts for children in the names of loyal customers.

Local Partners
Approach local retailers to offer a percentage of individual sales to nonprofits when hosting in-store events. This saves the nonprofit

group the expense of renting a venue. Consider asking new retailers moving into the community to host a benefactor party celebrating their official opening. The format could include dinner and dessert buffets, full bars, live music and dancing, and private shopping all evening with a percentage of the sales going to benefit your cause. For example, the gala opening of Nordstrom's in Houston offered different sponsorship levels to benefit the Project S.A.F.E.T.Y. at M. D. Anderson Cancer Center, which educates children about over-exposure to the sun and promotes preventative behavior that will reduce the development of skin cancer. The sponsorship levels ranged from $500 to $10,000, with individual tickets at $150. The top benefactor level at $10,000 included a VIP cocktail reception, priority seating for a full runway fashion show with entertainment, and a commemorative gift for the host couple, plus other perks. The tax-deductible amount of the highest level of contribution was $9,140.

There are many other ways to raise money by involving business-es. Take something as simple as enrolling your local grocer. Once your organization has been assigned a number with a grocery store, a small percentage of the item's dollar value for every purchase made by your supporters will benefit the organization. Schools in Texas have used this method for raising funds to great effect. It's a win-win, because caring about the basic needs of others enhances the retailer's perception in the community.

The Randalls and Tom Thumb grocery store chains offer their cus-tomers a way to direct donation dollars to their favorite charity through the Good Neighbor Program. Through the program, non-profit organizations sign up to be assigned an exclusive account num-ber, and members and supporters of the organization can link their grocery cards to that number. Then a small percentage of those cus-tomers' purchases goes to their designated charity. Through the Good Neighbor Program, Randalls and Tom Thumb have donated more than $20 million to more than 7,500 participating organizations.

Do some research in your own area to find similar opportunities with conscientious retailers who support local organizations where their customers live and work.

Proprietary Products

T-shirts, mugs, and bumper stickers are ways to create awareness and raise money for your cause. A T-shirt usually costs five dollars to produce and should be sold at a price that equals twice the cost. You can apply the same pricing formula to mugs, bookmarks, and other merchandise.

Bo's Place was named in memory of Laurence Bosworth "Bo" Neuhaus, who died of cancer at the age of twelve. His parents established Bo's Place, a grief center that recognizes that children and adults experience grief differently. Bo had always wished for a black lab but was unable to have one; instead, he had a small stuffed dog named Raisin. To raise awareness and funds for Bo's Place, a black lab stuffed animal called Raisin was marketed. It sells for $16 in supermarkets, bank branch offices, pharmacies, and local department stores. One hundred percent of all the proceeds from the sales benefit the children of Bo's Place.

Retail or thrift shops operated by nonprofits do very well if they are attractive and have a good location. The Society for the Prevention of Cruelty to Animals in Houston generally makes in excess of $35,000 a year through its retail operation. The products sold at such outlets should relate to what the organization does or who it serves. For example, the SPCA sells pet supplies. You might contact a consultant to help design the layout of the store, decorate it, merchandise products, and offer product recommendations. Classes can be conducted for volunteers on sales in a workshop scenario.

Reach for the Stars

Celebrity participation enhances attendance at your events—and boosts your net. Including high-profile individuals often encourages corporate sponsors to be involved and can take your event to another level. Try to contact a celebrity who is appearing in your city for a concert tour, charitable event, or book signing. You can watch the news, listen to radio and television promotions, and try to get a packet of information and a request delivered to these individuals while they are in your city. It is best if someone at the venue where they are performing or hotel where they are staying can personally deliver the package. You can leave contact information with a concierge or manager. Or, you can attend their presentation or performance and try to hand them a packet yourself. I employed this technique when Don Henley was doing a book signing in Galveston, and as a result he agreed to donate a performance to the "Marvin's Million Dollar Dream" event benefiting the M. D. Anderson Cancer Center. My secret was that I had done my homework before I approached Don Henley; his mother-in-law had just recovered from cancer. All performers have causes that touch them, and—just like you—they would be far more likely to donate time to those causes than to others. You can learn about what causes might interest celebrities by visiting their Web sites. (And those same sites may give guidance as to how contact them through their management company or agent, as well.)

Once you get to know most celebrities, you'll find they are just people. Offer transportation and hotel accommodations and all of the other reasons to say "Yes." After a celebrity agrees to participate, try to maximize (in accordance with her availability) the impact of your guest of honor. To coincide with your special event, ask the celebrity to teach a master class at the local high school for the performing and visual arts, to be a guest speaker, or to lead a panel discussion at a fundraising luncheon. Some stars will be happy to meet donors; others flatly refuse.

When working with celebrities, you may have to be flexible to accommodate their busy schedules. For example, there was a film schedule conflict when actor Robert De Niro was to receive the Jacqueline Kennedy Onassis Medal to be presented by Caroline Kennedy and the late John Kennedy. The original date on the benefactor letter had to be changed to accommodate the honoree's schedule. This is a rare occasion, but in such cases, you should notify your benefactors as soon as possible. Explain the reason for the change, and express your hope that their involvement won't be affected.

If your keynote speaker happens to be a politician, there is always the possibility that an important government session or an unexpected emergency might arise. Be prepared by putting an asterisk by the speaker's name in the program, indicating pending schedule, so invited guests will not be disappointed.

Consider the downside as well as the pluses of working with celebrities. You must be willing to grant their needs, no questions asked. When I worked with Carol Channing, the request was simple. She just wanted bottled water and fresh fruit. Singer Don Henley asked for a stationary bike and other workout equipment to use before performing. Another star might want her stool set at a certain height on stage or her clock set ahead forty-five minutes. Always be prepared to accommodate your prestigious guests, whatever their demands.

Value Past, Present, and Future Donors

Seeing promises fulfilled and the continuing presence of those initially involved in developing programs keeps corporate benefactors interested. For example, the family members of the Challenger tragedy stay actively involved with the Challenger Learning Centers. Bonding the public to the education-and-space legacy of the fallen heroes, Kathie Scobee-Krause and June Scobee Rodgers—daughter and wife, respectively, of the late Commander Chuck Scobee—represent the families as articulate spokespersons.

Tips for Reaching Potential Corporate Supporters

- Getting past the gatekeeper, meaning the CEO's secretary or administrative assistant, is the first hurdle to overcome in contacting those in high-level positions. Involve the administrative assistant or secretary who potentially stands between you and success. Interest that individual in the project, talk about the cause and acknowledge any assistance in helping you make the contact. An invitation to a pre-event to learn more about the organization is always appreciated.
- Getting someone to return a call reminds me of fishing. You have to make certain your bait will peak the fish's interest enough so that he will nibble and bite. Your call has to have phone appeal. The lure is all that stands between you and the donor.
- Don't leave the call open-ended. Good closers include: "I need to speak and/or meet with you at your earliest convenience with exciting news to share." "We need to catch up so I can update you on the progress the research you funded has made possible." "There's an article in a journal where your generosity has been acknowledged as being the catalyst for the entire project." "You've had faith in my projects in the past, and I hope I can count on your generosity once again in a matter of equal importance."
- Remember, you can always cast your line again if the first school of fish does not bite. There are challenges in getting callbacks just as there are challenges in any sporting activity. This gives you an adrenaline rush and adds to the excitement of the task at hand. Just ask yourself, "How do I get them to call back?" Perhaps you can say, "Perhaps, I can bring lunch to your office from this new gourmet restaurant that raises take-out to a new height." Or, "We have tickets to the theater. I'd love you to see the great job our artistic director is doing."

continued

Tips for Reaching Potential Corporate Supporters (continued)

- Peak the interest of your benefactors. Share some of the special activities that are a part of the giving opportunity. Most donors have experienced typical perks. Try to create a special opportunity that she couldn't otherwise arrange. One of the special benefactor opportunities on the Philip Johnson Endowed Chair project at the University of Houston College of Architecture was a visit to the Glass House designed by architect Philip Johnson, which is now part of The National Trust. On another occasion, benefactors were invited to a private reception and dinner at Bayou Bend, the former home of philanthropist and patron of the arts Miss Ima Hogg that is now part of the Museum of Fine Arts Houston. If you are working to benefit the symphony, perhaps you could let a benefactor be the maestro for the evening, conducting the orchestra. Be creative and make your benefactor's generosity a joyous occasion.

- Because of the many requests corporations receive for funding from worthwhile and deserving organizations, companies have established corporate contributions committees to review and determine the outcome of each request. CEOs, managing partners, or other individuals at the top should have the opportunity to intervene regarding support for a particular cause if there are extenuating circumstances. The company's top executive should have knowledge of your organization's request should it become necessary to override a decision made by the corporate contributions committee.

- Corporation and foundation guidelines may not permit a group to support your special event. Don't despair; ask to see a copy of their guidelines so that you may tailor a request for funding or services to meet their specifications. It is certainly worth the paper and ink.

Be Open to New Donor Fields

There's an untapped and unlimited audience waiting to hear from your organization. The next wave of growth may be small business owners and tomorrow's entrepreneurs. Look into this segment of the giving community. In addition to my suggestions in Chapter 2 for approaching new donors, there are lists that can be purchased that will target the audience you want to reach. They will conduct mailing list research for your marketing campaign and provide you with a "niche" list for review with complete details on those you want to pursue. For example: There are more than 287,000 growing businesses out there eager to learn about your organization and how they might become involved. To target the more than two million executives and business owners and make your organization one of their destination stops, you can build your donor lists by signing-on or e-mailing one of the many mailing list brokers. They will give you a quote on your project that could be monthly, annual, or a rental fee. They can also base their fee on the number of leads they supply. This will give you an edge on your competition.

Keep abreast of the trends in giving. The World Wide Web has been among the most significant new aspects in fundraising in the past decade, both in terms of the dollars raised and the number of nonprofit organizations using Web sites for fundraising. Year-to-year, growth of Internet users continues at more than 50 percent. If you haven't already, you should continue taking your organization's fundraising efforts to a new, online level. According to one online survey, online fundraising reached nearly $2 billion in 2003.

GOING FOR GRANTS

What do the Alzheimer Family Center, Catholic Charities, Habitat for Humanity, YWCA, and Goodwill Industries have in common? They all benefit from the knowledge of the *Directories of Social Services Grants, Health Grants, Operating Grants, Building and*

Equipment Grants, which targets at least six hundred state-by-state foundations for grant and funding requests. Each profile lists address, phone number, and areas of interest supported. Geographic restrictions, range of grants, and lists of organizations funded are included in the foundation profile when available.

The *Directory of Computer and High Technology Grants* is a great tool for both the small and large nonprofit organizations. It informs you about ways to obtain basic high-tech equipment that your organization may benefit from: copy machines, fax, modems, sophisticated telephone systems, and high-tech typewriters. If you apply for—and receive—a high-tech grant, funds your organization previously budgeted for this equipment can then be directed to other areas that benefit the program.

Five Easy Rules When Applying for Grants

- Give funders the requested information in the exact order and format as outlined in their guidelines
- Success breeds success. Don't give the funder the impression that this may be the last donation your organization receives.
- Always ask the foundation for a specific amount of money. Make certain the budget has figures as close to the penny as possible and make sure that the grant you've received pays for the item or project. If there is any excess grant money, ask them how you should return the unused portion to their office.
- Be specific and straightforward. Your CEO or executive director should personally sign each and every proposal. Should there be a discrepancy and the foundation seeks recourse against the organization, the executive director's signature will serve as a binding contract assuming final responsibility for the organization.
- No typos!

This directory will also guide you to the right sources for software, computer, and high-tech equipment grants. Find the funders that work with your specific type of organization. You'll save time and energy by knowing about and securing grants that support underwriting salaries, rent, office supplies, and general overhead expenses.

Nonprofits shouldn't try to "mail merge" a generic proposal to funders. Write them individually and request guidelines. They will send you a copy of their guidelines, or they will send you a letter saying that any format is fine.

ENDOWMENTS AND TRUSTS

Endowed giving is based on the concept that gifts will be invested and only a portion of the earnings will be used to carry out the intention of the donor's gift. The amount of earnings to be spent is determined by an endowment spending plan. Endowment giving is a permanent naming opportunity and can be established to reflect the name of the donor(s) or someone they wish to honor. The agreement is usually approved between the donor and the recipient, e.g. a university, scholarship, or awards program. The YMCA Endowment Fund provides the YMCA with guaranteed growth. A gift may be given to support a specific branch or service area, provide program scholarships, or perpetuate an annual gift.

M. D. Anderson Cancer Center in Houston has created a Research Trust with a $100 million philanthropic goal. This endowment is to serve as a permanent source of money for up to twenty-four researchers in areas that will best enhance the goals of their worldwide research effort to find a cure for cancer. The trust will enable them to establish laboratories and see their research programs through to maturity.

Endowment giving offers unique opportunities for individuals to support the arts with challenge grants. The Houston Grand Opera

High School Voice Studio, generously funded by The Bauer Foundation, is a program designed to help high school seniors to continue their vocal music studies into college. Various monetary awards given through the endowment help selected first-year college students with their expenses.

The Minute Maid Company and Houston Grand Opera cosponsor a contest requiring entrants to describe their experiences at the opera in the form of a drawing or essay. As part of the Houston Grand Opera's education and outreach programs, the Student Performance Series bring school children into the theater, expanding the arts curriculum with the magic of opera.

WAYS TO ACKNOWLEDGE YOUR "ANGELS"

Recognition and awards for benefactors reflect good business as well as good manners. Letters of thanks have been standard practice for a long time. Always remember to thank them both verbally and with a written note for their generosity. It is important for donors to know that their contributions, no matter how large or small, make a difference. Cherish your donors, and never take them for granted.

It also is most important to set up a system whereby donors periodically receive reports on the results of their giving. Benefactors and partners should not hear from an organization only in requests for funds. When corporations contribute money or time, they appreciate being acknowledged for their philanthropy. Keep them informed through e-mail, newsletters, or phone updates. Find out how they prefer to be updated on recent accomplishments, achievements, and major donor contributions. Maintain contact throughout the year. Take a supporter to lunch; offer to provide transportation to an event; arrange for complimentary valet parking; include them as your guest at an event. Send an autographed book from a well-known author who has been an honoree at an event. Thoughtful mementos will always remind givers that they are appreciated. At a gala event, presenting the chair with a bouquet of flowers is a lovely way to acknowledge his hard work in making the evening a success. And if your donor receives special recognition in the community, send a congratulatory letter or make a phone call.

Remembering the anniversaries of their original good deeds, as well as the completion of a building, the endowment of a professorship, or an addition to a library, is another way to recognize the generosity of benefactors. Try keeping track of all of your donors and any anniversaries you'd like to remember by creating a database in a computer spreadsheet program. You might begin by entering the donor's name and basic contact information. A record of the donor's initial involvement with the organization as well as the amount of her first contribution should be listed. This is important not only so you can recognize important milestones in her giving, but so that you don't make a request when you have just received a donation. It will also help you determine when it would be appropriate to approach that donor about elevating his level of giving. Any history or information such as birthdates, anniversaries, or special interests also should be added to the information. All of the above will bond the relationship between donors and your organization.

There are many ways to acknowledge and show appreciation to outstanding individuals. Reward their good works by naming something in their honor, such as a street, a day, or a scholarship; presenting a special honorary badge from the police department; or, when possible, sending a signed celebrity photograph or a photo from a fundraising effort in which they were involved. (I was deeply touched by an inscribed photograph given to me by the Challenger family members.) Have your governor name an individual as an Ambassador of Goodwill or have a resolution adopted by the legislature. Present an American flag or state flag that has flown over the capital to a noteworthy individual.

Politics aside, there's nothing like a proclamation from a high-ranking local or state official to honor your benefactors' efforts, make them feel proud, and, at the same time, focus positive attention on the charitable organization. When honoring a dignitary or someone who has made significant contributions, a proclamation from the mayor, governor, or president will have special meaning. You should place a call to city hall and speak to the person in charge of proclamations. They will advise you on the procedure to follow for your request, which will need to be submitted in writing.

Write or call the scheduling office to see if the mayor or another city official might be able to attend and present the proclamation. The proclamation will be more personal if you include biographical information on the honoree. State in your request the reason the individual or corporation is being honored. Try to arrange to have the proclamation framed and, if possible, ask a frame shop to donate the labor and/or materials.

A proclamation is an effective way to recognize an honoree at an event.

When planning festivities such as a ribbon cutting or the opening of a new building, ask your major benefactors to take the first steps through the doors or to cut the ribbon. If there is a program, include them in the opening remarks. At the Museum of Medical Science in Houston, major benefactors were the first to experience hands-on science activities in this new state-of-the art facility. Other considerate gestures include advanced invitations to view traveling art or medical exhibitions and permanent recognition on a donor wall in the building. This special attention and recognition of their giving will keep them involved and enthusiastic about their support.

Invite donors to groundbreaking ceremonies; offer a personal hard-hat tour when a building is under construction and some permanent exhibits are already in place. Have a quick fact sheet available describing your nonprofit and a floor plan showing the new building's design. Ask the architect to make remarks about the design and functionality of the building. Give the benefactor the opportunity to become involved at the beginning.

If a dedication is planned for a new building, try to make special

A ribbon-cutting ceremony officially dedicates a space and recognizes donors.

arrangements for those attending, especially if there is a construction problem. Have representatives ready to greet guests at the entrance to the parking lot. You can even reserve a special parking lot near the dedication ceremony and arrange for buses to shuttle guests back and forth to the project. Have a map that pinpoints the location of the new building and a schedule of the various activities. Be considerate of the time factor—some people might want to be there only for the reception, a special exhibit, or the unveiling of the donor wall.

Individuals, corporations, and foundations make gifts not only directly to organizations, but also to establish endowments supporting the educational, religious, social welfare, scientific, or medical achievements of certain prestigious individuals. Seeking out individuals worthy of such an honor in your own organization is another way to expand upon your organization's fundraising and to attract new donors and cultivate existing ones.

Ways to Recognize Major Gift Sponsors

- Designated research project or sponsorship of a research fellow in their name
- Fund a senior research award
- Title sponsor of a patient education seminar
- Send-a-child to camp

The creation and awarding of a prize is not dissimilar from endowing a chair for medical research, naming a building on a college campus, or recognizing an individual with an endowed lectureship. It creates a win-win situation for the donor and the recipient. An artist or sculptor might be commissioned to create a limited edition artwork to commemorate the prize. It may ultimately become the nucleus in the underwriting campaign of an annual special event to raise funds for the organization's programs and operations. The award inscription could read, "to honor an individual(s) who has contributed to the enrichment of the community in the spirit of the founder." In many cases, the award is given in an individual's honor, making that person the first recipient. The presenting of the award then becomes an annual occurrence.

Prizes are meaningful and encouraging to outstanding recipients and to those whom they mentor. Nominations for honorees should be considered by a board committee within a designated time frame, with the deliberation and voting kept secret. All prizes should be awarded irrespective of nationality, race, creed, or ideology, creating a permanent legacy for the giver.

The William E. Simon Foundation awarded its 2004 Prize in Philanthropic Leadership to David Robinson, former N.B.A. all-star with the San Antonio Spurs. He is one of the founders of a new private school, the Carver Academy. His interest in a founding a school was sparked when he was mentoring a teenager who was two grades behind where he should have been. "I realized how hard it was to help someone catch up who was so far behind," he said. "I thought that if we started with children when they were young, we could make a difference." The $9 million David Robinson donated to make the academy possible is thought to be the largest single charitable gift by a professional athlete.

Donor Etiquette Tips

- Develop an ongoing relationship with donors. This builds lasting relationships that will benefit your group far more than one or two gifts donated reluctantly.
- Don't go overboard in your first solicitation.
- Be straightforward when soliciting donations and grants from individuals, corporations, and foundations.
- If you use superlatives (the oldest, the largest, the biggest), make sure you're correct and that your group is the "est" you describe. Don't be half-right. Donors and foundations are very savvy, and they may know more about your competition than you do.
- Don't judge a donor only by appearance or reputation. One executive director I know made an error when he valued image above everything else by choosing to woo an individual from the corporate world over two ordinary long-time supporters. The upshot of the incident was the corporate giant was indicted for fraud, and the two ignored donors made their contributions elsewhere.
- Do your homework and know something about the person you are approaching. One foundation trustee received a proposal from an environmental group whose activities included protesting a local chemical company. The problem was the trustee had controlling interest in the chemical corporation, where he had worked for thirty years until his retirement. Protesting the place where he spent his life was not endearing.
- Use common sense with making a donor pitch. Each prospect is unique. If a prospect is conservative, mention that your program will increase self-sufficiency, decrease dependency on governmental subsidies, and allow clients to become more independent.
- Be serious about your ask and sincere in your thanks.
- Try to find a committee member or friend to initiate the contact

continued

Donor Etiquette Tips (continued)

with the donor. Be prepared with information you need. A corporate benefactor will want to know the ways his or her company will be acknowledged.

- Don't promise what you can't deliver. You can always develop interesting ways to recognize donors after the initial meeting, depending on the size of the gift or pledge. Expect to go to several meetings when you are proposing a large gift.

- Stay in touch. Be donor friendly. Send donors recent articles about your organization. Try to be as personable as possible. Congratulate them when they are recognized in the community. Celebrate the birth of children or grandchildren. Remember, if you only contact donors when you need support, they will feel as though they are being used.

- Listen to your donors and prospects. They will tell you everything you need to know. On occasion, executive directors may be so focused on their pet project that they may forget to listen to the donors—and they may lose the grant as a result. Find out what your donor wants to support.

- Give credit. If a donor is noteworthy, nominate that individual or corporation for an award. (Grant writer Janice Adamson says that when she nominated Albert Herzstein for the Columbus Foundation's Philanthropist of the Year, and he won over Walter Annenberg, she would never forget the priceless look on his face when he said, "Jonas Salk picked me?")

- Help people who help you. If a volunteer turns out for all your events, attend one that he or she stages. Buy a table for the event spearheaded by that terrific friend of yours who always buys tables from you.

- When people are thanked from the podium, make sure the emcee

continued

Donor Etiquette Tips (continued)

knows exactly how to pronounce your donors' names. Nothing is as rude as an acknowledgment by someone who hasn't bothered to learn your name. The same rule holds true for spelling donors' names in print.

- Make your events people-friendly, and donors will warm up to your organization.
- When contacting a donor, remember the name of her executive assistant who schedules appointments and may be involved in determining which charitable organization the donor chooses to support. Use common sense and practice good manners when soliciting donations.
- Be judicious in putting out fires. If your donors are upset and feel that they have be slighted, meet with them and find a solution for the problem. In this way they will feel validated.
- Keep your ethics intact. Don't give business to a vendor who says, "If you buy my system, rent my product, etc., I'll make a donation to your agency." The truth is, if someone sincerely wants to donate to your cause, you won't have to make a deal.
- Leave your business card out of the holiday greeting card envelope.
- Show in-kind donors how grateful you are.

 *Chapter Six*

CHOOSING THE RIGHT EVENT

*"Anything that the human mind can conceive
can be produced ultimately."*
—DAVID SARNOFF

The fine art of fundraising begins with an event, the purpose of which is to demonstrate the organization's mission. All events should reflect the "heart" of the organization. Never miss an opportunity to introduce the people who make the event happen (your key constituents) in your fundraising efforts.

Once you have agreed to chair a fundraising event for a charitable organization, you need to come up with a concept for the event. If it is not an annual event, consider the audience to whom you are appealing and a creatives concept to capture its interest. Gather your board members, nonprofit executive director and/or development officer, friends, and interested volunteers for a brainstorming session.

Let the creative energy flow. Evaluate the skill level among the team and the number of available volunteers. How much time is everyone willing to donate to the project? Define the target audience and level of support. Is there underwriting money available? Describe the purpose for the event. What is your net goal? Discuss a timeline for accomplishing the plan. Select a target date for the event.

The following events appeal to a wide range of people and have proven very successful as fundraising projects.

FAMILY ACTIVITIES

The most common family fundraising activities raise money for student organizations or schools. Parents are great volunteers who want to support their children's fundraising efforts. If you are involved with planning such an event, encourage parent participation through incentives such as a weekend getaway or a dinner at a local restaurant. Be sensitive to busy schedules and stretched pocketbooks by confining your fundraising activities to a few high-impact projects. Parents will double their efforts if they know they will be called upon only once or twice a year. Involved parents feel a stronger connection with their child's school.

Fundraisers the whole family can enjoy, however, go far beyond educational events. Fundraisers geared toward young children might include carnivals, caroling concerts, kite flying, cat or dog shows, magic shows, and rubber ducky races. Tried-and-true suggestions for teen fundraisers include car washes, lawn mowing, window cleaning, and treasure hunts.

School Book Fair

Parents are essential to the success of a school book fair. This event is usually held to raise funds for purchasing new library books. An education- or youth-oriented book company can provide an inventory of its books for the school and the volunteer committee to consider. Selections are made from each genre, and the number of books needed is determined. The fair generally runs about two or three days; the size of the book fair determines the percentage of the school's profits.

In an effort to be more efficient, schools are now holding book fairs at bookstores. For example, children are bussed to a Barnes and Noble and are allowed to use special book discount cards for purchases. The school negotiates a percentage of gross proceeds, depending upon the number of books sold. Certain registers at the bookstores are designated during the fair, and additional personnel are on hand to accommodate the crowd. Parents can charge books using their discount cards to make the event even more successful. The school does not receive cash, but earns credit with the bookstore. A successful book fair can greatly reduce or eliminate the cost of new books for the library.

Visit from a Distinguished Alumnus

Often, distinguished alumni are more than happy to lend a hand in their hometown for a good cause. In one such event, Tommy Tune brought his singing, dancing, and big band show, featuring the Manhattan Rhythm Kings, to honor his former teacher and mentor Ruth Denny as she turned ninety. This event launched the renovation campaign for the Lamar High School auditorium that was to be named in her honor. The event was organized by the Lamar High School Parent Teacher Organization, and invitations to attend a rehearsal and an evening performance were made available to alumni. The invitations were sent to 25,000 alumni with only 1,300 seats available, so early reservations were essential. Ticket prices for teachers and students for the matinee performance ranged from $25 to $50. For the evening performance, ticket prices ranged from $200 to $500. Top ticket-level sponsors were invited to parties afterward at nearby residences.

In another successful alumni fundraiser, Amazon.com founder and CEO Jeff Bezos and other distinguished alumni helped River Oaks Elementary School celebrate its seventy-fifth anniversary. The school didn't have to do much asking to prove that it was worth honoring; River Oaks serves more than six hundred students from culturally and economically diverse backgrounds.

BENEFITING THE LAMAR HIGH SCHOOL AUDITORIUM RENOVATION

★ "Reach For The Stars" ★
STARRING

Tommy Tune

WITH HIS ALL SINGING-ALL DANCING
BIG BAND SHOW FEATURING
THE MANHATTAN RHYTHM KINGS

**Tommy Tune Returns
to Lamar High School
for One Night Only!!!
25,000 Alumni   Only 1,300 Seats**

Reserve your seat now!!!

Thursday, February 12, 2004

Performance 7:00 p.m.
Rehearsal 2:00 p.m.

Lamar High School Auditorium
3325 Westheimer

Starring Tommy Tune, a 9 time Tony Award winner
A once in a lifetime performance on his home stage

To honor Ruth Denney as she turns 90
To kick off the campaign for the auditorium renovation

Dress attire: Broadway Casual
Hardhats and work boots optional

Performance Tickets 7:00 p.m.
$500 – Premium Floor
$500 – Premium Balcony
$200 – Rear Floor or Rear Balcony

Rehearsal Tickets 2:00 p.m.
$50 – Community
$25 – Student or Teacher

Contact Fran Callahan, Cynthia Urquhart and Jan Young
Lamar High School

ONE NIGHT ONLY

Events featuring distinguished alumni are effective in raising money for schools.

Patriotic Barbeque

If your fundraising goal is to honor veterans, try hosting an Armed Forces Day barbeque that the whole family can attend. The funds can benefit a National Veteran's Museum and can show your support for today's military personnel and veterans. You might want to try holding the event at a park on a weekend afternoon or evening at a cost per meal of ten dollars per adult and five dollars per child. Flyers distributed in your community, along with radio and television public service announcements, can spread the word about your event and help boost attendance.

Multi-family Garage Sale

A well-planned neighborhood garage sale can successfully raise money for any number of local causes. For example, this is a good way to raise money for your local school's cultural enrichment programs, field trips, sports equipment, or computer equipment. If you were planning a large-scale garage sale to honor such a school-related cause, you might begin in the fall by asking high school students to send out letters asking for items to be donated to a garage sale to be held in the spring. Locate a central storage space or several family garages that will serve as mini-warehouses. When the time for the event comes, invite the volunteer high school students' parents and friends to have the first opportunity to purchase at a pre-opening sale that usually lasts about two hours. Everything after the pre-sale event is open to the public. Any remaining items from the sales should be donated to a worthy organization.

Popcorn Sales

The Boy Scouts have proved how successful popcorn sales can be as fundraisers. They market their popcorn in much the same way as the Girl Scouts sell cookies. They pre-sell and take orders in advance by going door-to-door. Orders are taken, popcorn is delivered, and funds are collected, with the scouts netting 50 percent of their sales.

Savvy scouts are now using e-mail to reach their potential and existing customers.

Fundraising Guidelines for Children's Activities

- Establish a time frame for the fundraising campaign. It may be from two weeks to three months.
- Clearly define the reason for your fundraiser, i.e. equipment for sports team, French class trip to foreign country, scholarships, building expansion, additions to library.
- Believe in the power of word-of-mouth. Network through your community; inform the public by flyers, e-mails, or posters about your bake sales, church bazaars, car washes, bingo lunches, cause plate sales, holiday cards, or school auctions.
- Sign up volunteers to organize the fundraiser. For example, if there are bulk products to receive and distribute, you need volunteers to set the event in motion.
- Learn about ways your charity can be part of a product sale fundraising campaign. Product sales involve purchase and resale of popular consumer products by a nonprofit group, such as candy, gift-wrapping paper, candles, and holiday décor.
- A sales representative from the products company will be the liaison between the charity volunteers and the product supplier. The company offers advice and support and supplies products. The sales representative helps energize and maximize sales, yielding greater results for the nonprofit group.
- Clip, shop, and charge programs are effective ways to earn extra dollars for a school program. Initiate a school campaign for which students clip box tops from their favorite General Mills food products to yield ten cents a box top.

Telethons

A telethon has energy that brings the community together in support of causes. Those who are critical of telethons say that they are not cost effective and are too labor intensive. Your organization has to weigh the pros and cons of the concept to determine its viability. If an auction is involved, volunteers need to collect, assemble, store, display, and arrange for delivery of the donated items.

The late comedian Milton Berle did the first telethon to benefit New York's Damon Runyon Memorial Cancer Center Fund in 1949. Uncle Miltie had celebrities and chorus girls on the phone lines, and it was a huge success. Jerry Lewis has been doing the Muscular Dystrophy Association Telethon since 1966. He's been known to stay awake throughout a seventy-seven-hour telethon despite personal health problems. How's that for dedication? This telethon has raised more than $900 million, with the 2001 telethon alone bringing in $54.6 million.

To boost their visibility, even politicians such as Hubert Humphrey and the late former President Richard Nixon tried their hand at this unique way to raise funds. Sometimes the reverse of what one wants to achieve can happen, as when the late former President Reagan garnished all of the call-in support during a Democratic telethon that took place Memorial Day weekend 1983. Only 20 percent of the calls yielded pledges for the Democrats.

Well-known charitable organizations including the United Way, the United Negro College Fund, and the Children's Miracle Network (which supports a group of children's hospitals) still host telethons that combine show business and philanthropy. The public becomes mesmerized by its own generous response, the emotionally driven music, the sense of urgency to respond, and the excitement of the tote board updates.

Channel 8 KUHT Public Television was the first public television station in America to host an annual telethon. Before the telethon concept was discontinued, monies raised had increased from

$122,000 in 1971 to $1 million gross in 1990. There were twenty auctions in all. The Super Sports Night benefiting KUHT Public Television in 1973 raised $252,264 and, for the first time, involved athletes pledging support to a deserving nonprofit organization. The auction items included autographed basketballs, tennis rackets, and golf clubs, complete with high-profile celebrities doing the auctioneering (golfer Doug Sanders, Olympian Carl Lewis, and former Secretary of Commerce Robert Mosbacher).

FASHION SHOWS

Fashion shows can stand alone as a popular fundraiser, or can be the icing on the cake for another fundraising event that targets a largely female audience—a garden party, brunch, luncheon, or tea, for instance. Ask a local producer to coordinate the show. She will suggest a fabulous theme and compliment the fashions with appropriate music. You don't want to put the audience to sleep, so limit your production to no more than forty-five-minutes. Have well-known people in the community or people who are connected to the charitable organization participate as models. If the audience sees the clothing on regular people, they will appreciate the show more and be more apt to shop.

If the fashion show is presented before the food is served, have your first course pre-set. This will take the edge off your audience's appetite. An offering of cheese and nuts before the first course works well, and you will have their undivided attention.

SPORTS AND LEISURE EVENTS

Sports and leisure events that organizations have used to raise funds include air shows, archery competitions, hot air balloon races, car rallies, clay pigeon shoots, cycling races, fishing tournaments, a day at the horse or dog races, charity polo matches, and regattas. Indoor activities that might work for your organization include badminton, bowling, ping-pong, poker or pool tournaments, and dart competitions.

Clay Pigeon Shoots

A sporting clay invitational has become a popular annual event for some nonprofit organizations. Unique auction items relating to the fine sport of the English game fair can be offered. A precocktail reception the night before could relate to an exhibit and lecture on custom gun making at one of the auction houses or a museum venue. This type of event will appeal to sophisticated donors who can cross over from a black tie gala to a sporting clay invitational. Teams can be organized at different levels of sponsorship.

Croquet and Jazz Brunch

Locate a croquet champion in your area. Organize a group of people who are enthusiastic about the game. Give your supporters an option of playing or enjoying the jazz and cuisine. Ask the participants to select their time to play and offer the option of croquet teams of up to two persons per mallet. Pray for good weather. If possible have a rain date. This is a delightful way to introduce a new cause and possibly a new fundraising concept to your community.

Golf or Tennis Tournament

Enlist a committee that includes people who are familiar with the activity. If the event involves golf, invite local celebrities to fill out the foursome. Choose a facility that is centrally located and guest friendly. Get a retailer involved to underwrite the awards to be presented and another to offer to fill the goody bags. Consider introducing creative and affordable auction items based on the sports theme—include dinner with a celebrity, sports memorabilia, an opportunity to play with a celebrity, or private lessons with a professional.

Soliciting registration for a fundraising athletic tournament
can be as simple as a trifold brochure.

Walks and Runs

Walks and runs are popular ways to raise money for a cause—and
the further in advance you plan them, the more money you're likely
to raise. Pick a beautiful park for a walk; choose downtown streets
for a jog. After you set the date, here are a few pointers to get you
started: Create a logo and brochure; make banners for the event; get
goodie bags together for participants; have event T-shirts made;
secure permits (alcohol, sound, security, park rental, traffic, street
closings); provide water, tents, food, and beverages; set up a registration day before the event; and consider having entertainment on
hand, such as clowns, fire eaters, jugglers, tarot readers, or face
painters.

BAZAARS

Bazaars are a good way to involve a large volunteer group. The following vehicles might fit your needs perfectly: antiques sales, art fairs, craft fairs, holiday markets, plant sales, or toy fairs. Generally, a nonprofit hosts such an event by bringing in vendors and providing a place for them to display and sell their wares. The organization makes its profit from leasing the space and/or taking a percentage of the vendors' sales. Bazaars often have other components such as preview parties or food booths for added revenue. Many churches and private schools raise money with annual bazaars that feature home-cooked frozen entrées and baked goods, handmade holiday decorations, or rooted cuttings and bulbs from members' gardens.

PROGRAMS, LECTURES, AND TOURS

Hosting a dinner with a prominent guest speaker is an excellent format to appeal to a broad audience in the mood for a more sedate evening. Authors are popular guest speakers, for instance; the exposure for their books such events offer is a major incentive for authors to participate. At an event featuring an author, arrange for a book signing during the reception prior to or after your event. Be aware the some of the most popular authors have speaking fees; however, if the author is receiving an honor or award from your organization, he may waive his speaking fee.

For instance, when I was chairing a series of events to raise money for the M. D. Anderson Cancer Center, Fran Drescher's book *Cancer Schmancer* was the perfect match for a book signing benefit. Fran agreed to be a guest at an event because she had recovered successfully from uterine cancer and wanted to give her support to research in this field.

In another high-profile example, former President George Bush and editor Jim McGrath had their book signing benefit the Houston READ Commission. Literacy is a cause close to both George and

Barbara Bush. The event was held at George Bush's favorite barbeque haunt, Otto's, and tickets were $35, including food and a
copy of *Heartbeat: George Bush In His Own Words.*

BARBARA TAYLOR BRADFORD
Author, Journalist, Screenwriter
NORTHWOOD UNIVERSITY
Distinguished Woman 2001

Best-selling novelist Barbara Taylor Bradford, beloved by millions of readers around the world, is published in 89 countries and 39 languages. She is the author of seventeen novels, all of them international best sellers. Her eighteenth novel, *Three Weeks in Paris*, was published by Doubleday in February 2002. She also has written ten non-fiction books, seven of which are on interior design.

Barbara Taylor Bradford began writing as a child, sold her first short story at the age of ten, and went to work as a reporter on the *Yorkshire Evening Post* when she was sixteen. Graduating to London's Fleet Street at the age of twenty, she was a journalist for a number of years but never lost sight of her desire to write fiction. It was her first novel, *A Woman Of Substance*, now a classic, which launched her literary career. Long acclaimed as the foremost chronicler of women's lives today, her books have sold over sixty-three million copies worldwide. Ten have been made into TV mini-series or Movies of the Week by her husband movie producer Robert Bradford, whom she married in 1963.

In 1990, Mrs. Bradford was awarded an honorary Doctor of Letters from the University of Leeds, her hometown. The university houses her literary archive in its famed Brotherton Library. She also holds honorary doctorates from the University of Bradford in Yorkshire and Connecticut's Teikyo Post University.

Mrs. Bradford is a member of the James Madison Council of the Library of Congress and is on the Council of the Authors Guild of America and the Authors Guild Foundation. She has received numerous honors and awards over the years, including the Matrix Award in Books from the New York Women in Communications in 1985, induction into the Matrix Hall of Fame in 1998, the Special Jury Prize for Body of Literature from the Deauville Festival of American Film in 1994 and Birmingham-Southern College's "Gala 12" Women of the Year Award in 1995. She has received awards from a variety of not-for-profit organizations, including the Albert Einstein College of Medicine, the City of Hope, the Police Athletic League and Girls Inc. of America. Her most recent honor, the Northwood Distinguished Woman citation, was presented at award ceremonies in Phoenix, November 2001.

"*Lunch with Barbara Taylor Bradford*"

11:30 a.m. *Reception*

12:00 noon *Welcome & Introduction*
of Distinguished Guests
Tom Koch
ABC Channel 13 KTRK-TV Anchor

Luncheon

Dr. William Oliver
Provost, Texas Area
Northwood University

Carolyn Farb, Chair
Northwood Distinguished Woman 1996

Barbara Taylor Bradford
Author, Journalist, Screenwriter
Northwood Distinguished Woman 2001

Booksigning to follow luncheon

A biography in an event program is an effective way to spotlight an honoree.

Tours of historic and architecturally significant homes and buildings, or of fine private and public gardens, make good fundraising
events because they are often of interest to a broad range of people.
If you are planning an outdoor tour, keep in mind that a rain plan
never hurts. An alternative to touring a public facility is to offer a
tour of a private home featuring rooms designed by professional
interior designers. Such an event can provide both exposure for the
designers and funding for the nonprofit. For added revenue, invite
past benefactors to a preview party, or include a tearoom in a show
house fundraising event.

AUCTIONS AND RAFFLES

Auctions and raffles are often part of another, larger event. Chapters 12 and 13 will outline the details of planning an auction, but here is an example of a popular idea: The Instant Wine Cellar. Who wouldn't love to acquire a superb wine collection in the name of a charity? You can add another layer to your special event by asking event supporters to become involved in putting together the wine cellar. They can donate a bottle of wine, port, or champagne from their personal cellar or sponsor a bottle of wine from a vendor who has agreed to coordinate the wine cellar project. Establish a contact person at a retail store. He or she can reserve your selection over the phone as well as offer recommendations to complement other selections. The designated coordinator will make certain the cellar has an appropriate selection of wines. Donors of wine or champagne will be recognized on signage near the wine cellar display.

Another popular auction item along the same line is a dinner for serious collectors at a private commercial cellar where wines are stored. Ask the owner of this specialty shop to sponsor a dinner for a designated number of guests with exquisite wines to complement each course. Invite a sommelier to talk about the exceptional wines being served. This auction offering would tempt any food and wine connoisseur.

GALAS AND OTHER EVENING ENTERTAINMENT

A special event provides opportunities to reiterate the organization's basic goals and philosophy to its own constituency that isn't always as knowledgeable as you would like to think. In the context of a special event that is attracting interest and attention, the message is often received with greater clarity. If you are looking to plan a large annual event on a somewhat informal scale, give these party ideas some thought: a cabaret, casino night, karaoke event, murder mystery night, musical revue, wine and cheese tasting, or a themed fundraising event to celebrate Halloween, New Year's, or Valentine's Day. But if your campaign has a net desired goal in excess of $500,000 in mind, a large gala event can work magic.

Galas differ from other fundraising events in that they are large scale, combine layers of activities, require more volunteers and, hopefully, raise both funds and awareness for the nonprofit organization. It is important to enlist a strong chairperson who will look upon an event of this magnitude as a labor of love combined with personal vision, commitment, and dedication. He needs to be willing to commit a year of his life and gather a strong team of vice chairs and committee volunteers who will perform in the truest sense of volunteerism.

I knew we had the potential to make a difference when I took on the journey to chair "A Night at the Alhambra" gala for the Houston Grand Opera. My personal goal was to raise $1,400,000 and to focus on the opera's community outreach programs. From benefactor packages and pre-event parties to dining selections and auction items, myriad details demanded attention. A case study of the many steps necessary to plan this event is outlined in detail in the appendix. A year of hard work by dedicated volunteers and generous community support culminated in an exquisite and exciting evening for the guests and a well-deserved and appreciated gift for the Houston Grand Opera.

When I chaired Marvin's Million Dollar Dream benefiting M. D. Anderson Cancer Center, having guest concert performers like Don Henley and Lyle Lovett donate their talent made dreams come true. We aimed high and set a fundraising goal of $1 million. This was the first time that the table sponsorship in Houston was elevated to $75,000 dollars. There were lots of angelic contributors. I was inspired by Daniel H. Burnham's words, "Make no little plans. They have not magic to stir men's blood. Make big plans, aim high in hope and work." When I contacted Don and Lyle, they said yes.

The intricate details of planning a major annual gala will be outlined in later chapters.

 *Chapter Seven*

ASSEMBLING YOUR TEAM

*"Of all the things I've done, the most vital is coordinating
the talents of those who work for us and point
them toward a certain goal."*
—WALT DISNEY

As chairpersons, in some cases you'll be assembling your team after
the format of the event and a tentative date have been chosen by the
organization you are benefiting. In other instances, the organization
will expect you to assemble a team, choose the event format, find a
venue, and make all the arrangements. Either way, the right committee members make fundraising efforts easy.

FINDING THE RIGHT VOLUNTEERS TO CHAIR VARIOUS COMMITTEES

When you put together a committee for an event, make sure each
member has something to contribute. Members with high profiles
can open doors to new donors. Others can help increase community
awareness of the organization. Other committee members may be
worker bees who wish to do the work and remain in the background. Try to choose committee members who can be actively
involved in one capacity or another, whether that means organizing
silent auction items, working on an invitation committee, assisting a
photographer at an event, writing press releases, working with the

media, or simply volunteering when needed. Giving each team member a vital role to play empowers him in a common goal.

When you are assigned a project to chair or coordinate, enlist the help of in-kind donors and volunteers who have worked together on other projects. Meet with your group of supporters to fill them in on the new endeavor and see if they want to participate. If so, they will form the nucleus for the project. Then, branch out to other possible committee members. For example, if you are planning a gala, you would try to include dependable people who are involved in lighting and sound, table decor, centerpiece and floral design, invitations and printing, or computer and electronic communications. Often, these in-kind donors will partner or work at a discounted rate with non-profits if they believe in the cause. Their payoff is the joy of helping a charity and the possibility that other job opportunities might develop for them as a result of their association with your non-profit—a key point that I emphasize in my zero-budget philosophy.

A host of specialized committees will help any nonprofit or event chair stay organized and keep a hand in cultivating of all different aspects of the fundraising endeavor. The following are descriptions of specialized committees that you may find it beneficial to form (or join, when you're not serving as chairperson) for your organization as a whole or for a major event that your organization is planning. (Note: One category that might seem to be missing is a treasury committee. However, a charitable organization will usually have its own director of finances handle all financial aspects of the fundraising event, so you will not need to form a committee to handle these matters. It is important for all of your committees to work with the director of finances, however, to be sure that all financial decisions made are informed ones.)

Honorary Committee

You may want to extend your resources by forming an honorary committee. Members of such a committee would serve as goodwill ambassadors for the organization and offer the names of philan-

The Crescent Gala

The Honorable William P. Clements, Jr.
and Mrs. Clements
Chairmen

Mr. and Mrs. Cloyd D. Young
Mr. and Mrs. Lawrence R. Herkimer
Co-Chairmen

Mrs. Carolyn Farb
Commemorative Program Chairman

Honorary Committee
Miss Marian Anderson
Mrs. Helen F. Boehm
Mr. James Cagney
Mr. Aaron Copeland
Miss Katherine Dunham
Miss Lillian Gish
Mr. Larry Hagman
Miss Helen Hayes
Mrs. Wallace F. Holladay
Mr. Danny Kaye
Mr. Gene Kelly
Mr. Jack Lenor Larson
Mr. Gian Carlo Menotti
Mr. Wolfgang Puck
Mr. Rudolf Serkin
Mr. James Stewart
Mr. Claude Taittinger
Mr. Mark Thatcher
Mr. Virgil Thomson

Mrs. C. Richard Ronchetti
Contribution Ticket Chairman

Mrs. Ben R. Weber, Jr.
Reservations Chairman

Mrs. Linda H. McElroy
President, Dallas Chapter of the Friends of the Kennedy Center

Mrs. Theodore H. Strauss
National Chairman, Friends of the Kennedy Center

Mrs. Martin S. Buehler
TACA Liaison with the Performing Arts

All contributors should be recognized in your
organization's invitation and event programs.

thropic individuals, corporations, and foundations to approach. Begin by sending a letter to prominent citizens asking them to lend their good names and support by serving on the honorary committee. Their participation lends importance and prestige to the event, and they can talk about the plans for the special event and encourage others to join them. The presence of high profile and distinguished names will attract and encourage other participants.

Underwriting Committee

The underwriting committee is responsible for approaching corporations, foundations, and benefactors for the purpose of selling tables at an event and/or securing underwriting. It's helpful to have committee members who have the ability to reach many sectors in the community for securing financial and corporate support. The underwriting needs to be done well in advance of the invitations being

Dream Underwriters

Diamond Dream Makers
$75,000

Anonymous
Janey and Dolph Briscoe
Compaq Computer Corporation
Continental Airlines,
the official airline of "Marvin's Million Dollar Dream"
Enron

Golden Galaxies
$50,000

Mr. Charles Butt
Exxon
Gallery Furniture
Houston Chronicle and Mr. and Mrs. Richard J. V. Johnson
Hyatt Regency Houston
Linda and Ken Lay Family in honor of Dr. Charles A. LeMaistre
Julie and "My Beloved" Ben Rogers, Regina Rogers
Mrs. Wesley West

Silver Stargazers
$25,000

Ammirati Puris Lintas
The Houston BMW Group:
Advantage BMW, Charlie Thomas' Intercontinental BMW, Momentum BMW
KTRK-TV, Channel 13
MTV Networks
in memory of Joni Abbott
Dr. and Mrs. John P. McGovern
Charlie Thomas Ford, Charlie Thomas Chrysler Plymouth,
Charlie Thomas Chevrolet, Charlie Thomas' Intercontinental
Motors, Charlie Thomas' Intercontinental BMW

Be sure to recognize donors and their levels of
sponsorship properly in all printed materials.

mailed. Before a gala, benefactors will be recognized at pre-events encouraging those who are still considering being involved to sign on. One of the perks for benefactors and in-kind donors who make early commitments is being listed in the invitation and recognized in any advance print media. Enlisting early benefactors gives an indication of how successful the event will be.

Invitation Committee

An invitation chairman will work with the general chairman on the design of an inclusive print campaign which may include a save-the-date card, event stationery with a logo, an invitation, an auction catalog, a program, and, possibly, Web site design. Should the chair choose to select a professional to create the design theme, he then should work closely with that individual to approve the design concept and to assure completion of all the print material according to the timeline.

RAINFOREST GALA 2002 *"I believe in God, only I spell it nature."*-- Frank Lloyd Wright

Maximize the impact of your invitation by using
an eye-catching design related to your theme.

The chairperson will determine schedules for the printing deadlines and organize a group of volunteers and committee members to hand address, stamp, seal, and mail the invitations six to eight weeks prior to the event. The chair should carefully select people with legible penmanship, supervise the committee that is addressing the envelopes, and make certain that everything is presented well. It is also the chair's task to find a comfortable space and provide snacks for the volunteers.

The invitation chair determines the number of invitations, response cards, programs, auction catalogs, campaign correspondence, and respective envelopes to be printed. It is responsible for obtaining invitation lists from board members, past and present honorees, and benefit committee members. Invitation lists need to be updated regularly. Returned invitations should be corrected and resent.

Decorations Committee

When a theme is selected for a gala or large event, this committee chair is responsible for all decorations from conception to installation. She needs to determine materials needed for event décor and then solicit and coordinate in-kind donations for these materials. The committee chair also will handle such tasks as working with hotel personnel to schedule event installation according to the timetable, asking the banquet manager the size of the tables to be used, and making sure the linen company provides the proper size table linen. (If there is a dais or head table, be sure the draping adequately covers it so that you don't see the feet of those seated.) The decorations chair should enlist volunteers and coordinate the schedule in preparation and execution of design installation. Depending on the budget, the decorations chair may even consider hiring a special event consultant.

This committee also would be responsible for obtaining table favors and other items that will be given to guests. If you chair, serve on, or assist a decorations committee, you should always make

certain that the favors are properly packaged for presentation—
sometimes a ribbon and sheet of wrapping paper makes all the difference in the world. The committee and volunteers are responsible
for getting the favors to the venue on time and placing these and
other gifts according to the level of sponsorship. For example, if
your event has gold-, silver-, and bronze-level sponsors, they would
receive appropriately different benefactor gifts.

You want your décor to stand out and be memorable, but you
don't want to be remembered as the decorations chair who went
overboard with expenditures. It's a challenge to create a special environment without spending money—but it's possible if you use your
imagination and enlist the help of generous in-kind donors. With a
school benefit, involve the students and the art department in a project to create the decorations. Members of a parents' group might be
willing to help. This would give them an opportunity to get to know
one another.

Some of the decoration expenses can be offset through the sale of
centerpieces, as well as through the generosity of in-kind donors
who may underwrite flowers, props, or linens. The decorations chair

The elaborate décor of "A Night at the Alhambra" enhanced the theme of the evening.

needs to establish an installation timeline for the lighting, sound, staging, table and chair set up, table decorations, floral, favors, and programs. The teardown and return of rentals and props is another assignment of this chair.

Reservations Committee

The reservations chair is responsible for receiving all reservations either at home or the organization's office and must be reachable during the daytime hours should changes occur or additional information need to be clarified. He opens the responses, records the credit card information, and gives the checks to the organization's director of finances. He may also receive reservations via fax or responses via e-mail. This committee's task is to keep an accurate database for reservations received and payment status. The reservations chair provides benefactor names and addresses for invitations to be sent for all pre-events. The chairman keeps the underwriting committee and other committee members apprised of reservations received.

The reservation chair should list attendees by individual and company name, as well as in alphabetical order, and prepare the final list for the registration desk. It is very important that this list is accurate. The quickest way to offend a donor is to misspell her name. This chair works with the hotel for proper registration table set up and organizes volunteers to guide guests to their assigned tables.

The reservations chair assists the chairman in the placement of tables and in assigning individual reservations to tables. For some events, the reservations chair prepares place cards for major benefactor tables and works with the decorations committee chair on the placement of the cards at the event. It is not advisable to change place cards when a benefactor host has arranged for a particular seating plan. The host may have good reasons for seating certain people next to each other. If there are no place cards at the table, it is good manners for guests to wait until the table host is seated before taking their places at the table. This is a good time for guests to introduce themselves, because once the program begins, there will not be an opportunity.

It is the responsibility of this chair and the food and beverage chair to double-check that the assigned numbers on the tables match the way the tables are numbered on the floor plan.

Entertainment Committee

The entertainment committee is responsible for interviewing, selecting, and scheduling any talent for receptions as well as main events. The reception music at an auction, for example, could be a pianist, string ensemble, or harpist, and its purpose is to provide a backdrop for the guests to preview the auction items. The committee should listen to tapes or view live entertainment and interview several groups before making a final decision. Discover a "new act" and ask if they will consider donating their talent for the exposure and future job opportunities. When talent is donated for an event, it is important to highlight the group of performers in any press releases and print material. Another entertainment option would be to engage a talented group of students to perform during the reception.

If your event includes dancing, a combo or dance orchestra needs to be engaged. You might try finding such a group of performers in your community. Well-recognized orchestras also have been known to travel great distances to play at major galas. It adds interest to your event especially if they have never played in your city or are returning by popular demand. If the talent is not donated, then you must negotiate and sign a contract. Be sure to include such important details as their method of transportation, accommodations, arrival time, performance time during the event (two sets, one set, all evening, when a break will take place and for how long), attire, or any other special requirements (salaries, sound and lighting, size of the stage, etc.).

Food and Beverage Committee

The food and beverage committee is responsible for selecting and approving the menu and wines for the event, as well as the valet parking arrangements. His committee should schedule a tasting three to six weeks prior to the event with the venue banquet manager. It is the chairperson's responsibility to supervise the food and drink, review

> DREAM RECEPTION
> Hyatt Regency Grand Lobby
> Underwritten by the Hyatt Regency Houston
> Hosted by Arthur C. Zehnder, Associate Director of Catering
> Created by Lance N. Stumpf, Executive Chef
>
> Petit Spanikopita
> Crisp Phyllo Stuffed with Spinach and Feta Cheese
>
> Peking Duck Beggars Purses with Asian Vegetables
> Ginger-Soy Sauce
>
> Smoked Salmon Roulade
> on Rosemary Toast Round with a Sprig of Dill
>
> Grilled Miniature Chicken Quesadillas
>
> DREAM DINNER
> Imperial Ballroom
>
> Chilled Crab Moussiline with Field Greens
> in a bed of White French Vinaigrette
>
> Petit Filet Mignon with a Rosemary Demi Glaze
> paired with a Marinated Grilled Norwegian Salmon
> Tarragon - Citrus Sauce
>
> Pommes Dauphinoise
> Tomato Provencal with Wilted Spinach and Parmesan
>
> Sourdough, Honey Whole Wheat and Herbed Silverdollar Rolls
>
> Triad of Candied Orange Valencia accompanied by
> Miniature Pistachio Cannoli and Hand Dipped Chocolate
> Truffles with Fresh Raspberries
>
> Colombian Coffee, Decaffeinated Coffee
> and Tea Selections
>
> *There is no demand too great, no idea too far-fetched,
> no problem too challenging, for the creativity and dedication of
> Art Zehnder and the talented staff of the Hyatt Regency Houston.*

Here's to eternity. May we all spend it in as good company as this night finds us.

Highlight your carefully selected menu by featuring it in your program.

any china, crystal, and flatware that will be used, and fine tune the napkin fold, as well as decide whether to have ice or lemon slices in the water glasses and sugar bowls and salt and pepper shakers on the table. All of these details need to be considered. The food and beverage chair presents the final luncheon or dinner menu to the printer to be included in the program. It is a nice gesture to acknowledge the chef for creating the wonderful menu. A good way to enhance the event is to have the names of the different courses relate to the theme or honoree. See about getting the wine and champagne donated, and negotiate the corkage fee. And always respect people's dietary needs as indicated on the response card.

This committee addresses any costuming for the wait staff. For example, when the attire is listed as "White Dinner Jacket," the wait staff should wear contrasting colors so guests can tell the servers from the other guests. Ascertain from the banquet manager the number of staff that will be provided for your event. Determine the layout of the floor plan. You need to have an accurate count of how many guests are attending and how many are at each table. By doing so, you won't have to pay for empty spaces. Verify that the table numbers correspond to the ones on the plan, and set aside a couple of extra tables for unexpected guests.

Commemorative Program Committee

The chair is responsible for the design, copy, and printing of the program to be given out at any major event. The program is coordinated with the print design and should be an inspiring vision and a keepsake for your guests

A commemorative program can also raise additional revenue in the form of advertising sales. The committee is responsible for selling the ad space for the program, getting the company's or individual's artwork submitted by the printer's deadline, and securing payment for the ads. A list of prospective advertisers should be divided among members of the committee with a plan of action set forth by the committee chair. If a program from a past event is available, use it as a helpful selling tool for soliciting ads for the current program.

Auction Committee

If you're planning an auction as your major annual event, the auction chair is responsible for organizing a committee of auction volunteers in cooperation with the event chairperson. These volunteers will review the donor list from previous years and work together to create additional donors. They should prepare and mail donor letters, response forms, and return envelopes. The auction committee gathers the information on how the auction items should be listed, coordinates any images and logos in-kind donors want to use, and works closely with the printer to meet listing and printing deadlines. This committee is also responsible for securing storage space and contacting a moving company to assist with pick-up and delivery of auction items to storage and to the event. (See Chapters 12 and 13 for more details on the process of putting together an auction.)

A live auction is easier to assemble and less labor intensive than a silent auction. Select three to five items. You have the potential to raise more funds in twenty minutes during a live auction than you can with the entire silent auction. But to hold a successful live auction, you have to wisely choose items such as valuable artwork, a luxurious trip, an automobile, designer jewelry, or an upscale shopping spree to put up for bidding.

Publicity/Media Committee

The publicity/media chair works with the event chair to determine and identify proper avenues for maximum event publicity. The chair or in-house media staff writes and forwards press releases to proper news organizations and arranges radio and television interviews. He determines photo needs, contacts a photographer, and schedules photo shoots. Also, this chair obtains event updates from other committee members for continuing event press releases throughout the campaign.

For Immediate Release

Media Contact:
Name
Title
Phone/fax number
Email address

"AN EVENING WITH PHYLLIS GEORGE"
Benefits Northwood University
April 22, 2003

On a memorable night, with two of Houston's stellar philanthropists at the helm and the memory of yet another sparking a warm nostalgia, Phyllis George, Miss America of 1971, author, pioneering sportscaster and star in her own right, returned home to Texas for a very special cause and a very special welcome.

Fundraiser extraordinaire Carolyn Farb and her cochair Carolyn Bookout, both respected stalwarts on Houston's charitable scene, worked together to bring both long-time friends and new supporters to rally for Dallas/Ft. Worth based Northwood University and its annual Spring Gala at Houston's River Oaks Country Club.

Billed as a "romantic spring evening", it was all of that and more. The opening silent auction of precious items, included a Doris Panos Seed Pearl Necklace, a round of golf and lunch at Whispering Pines Golf Club, and an Ultimate Weekend Escape at the Houstonian Hotel, Club, & Spa. Proceeds will provide a "smart classroom" for distance learning and intercampus connectivity and will be named for Houston's late Eleanor Searle Whitney McCollum. The striking black and white ballroom décor by Distinctive Details with all white floral centerpieces by Lexis Florist created the perfect backdrop for the music of the David Caceres jazz ensemble. But the fun had serious purpose as well.

continued

Jeff Early, president of Northern Trust, spoke eloquently of the role of Eleanor McCollum, who had influenced many in the room with her myriad involvements. The printed program for the evening also included warm remembrances of Mrs. McCollum's vocal talents and long career as both an entertainer and philanthropist, penned by Farb.

Northwood president Dr. David Fry brought enthusiastic applause from the audience when he made the surprise announcement that on May 22nd at ceremonies in Arlington, TX, Carolyn Farb will become "Dr. Farb" as she receives an honorary degree from the nationally-based management university. Farb, Bookout, and McCollum each had previously received the Northwood Distinguished Women's Award.

The spirit of the night was exemplified by Phyllis George (also a Northwood "DW" as of the 2002 annual ceremonies). Speaking from her latest book, *Never Say Never: Ten Lessons To Turn "You Can't" into "I Can,"* this "beauty with brainpower" transfixed her audience with common sense, motivational ideas which spoke eloquently to the questions many of us face in life. Ms. George, author, television star, former gubernatorial first lady, and the mother of two, is also a devoted daughter struggling with her mother's early Alzheimer's. A woman with a mission, her time is spent today balancing professional responsibilities with personal ones, and helping others to do the same. That she manages with such grace and beauty was the real inspiration to the audience, who (in the vernacular) just plain loved her!

Attending was a veritable "who's who" in the business and civic community. Among the guests were Northwood Distinguished Women Rose Cullen and Billye Halbouty, Carolyn and John Bookout, Sidney Faust, Cora Sue and Harry Mach, June and Virgil Waggoner, Allison and Geary Broadnax, and Don Vannerson to name a few. Dr. William Oliver, Provost of Northwood's Texas campus and his newly named successor Dr. Kevin Fegan greeted the crowd and promised to continue the private-enterprise-based university's special mission to train young business leaders into the future.

Press releases like this one are key promotional tools
both prior to and following your event.

Choosing an Event Planner

If the budget allows for an event planner, use the following tips for making this position a key part of the plan:

- Make sure the event planner you select shares the vision of your event chair. They need to work together harmoniously to make the event a success.
- Ask for references from nonprofits with which prospective event planners have worked.
- Consider the person who referred an events planner. (Do you know the individual making the referral, and how much does she know about what you need in an events planner?)
- Ask the planner his thoughts on event budgets. He should know that it's de rigueur to get at least three bids from caterers; rental companies that provide crystal, china, flatware, table chairs, staging, and outside tents; and entertainment booking agencies.
- Check out her work ethic; you want an event coordinator who earns her fee and doesn't just take the easy way out (such as buying a mailing list and using a mail house to send invitations).
- Discuss fees with the planner to make sure you're both on the same page.
- After you have chosen an events planner, be sure that all checks and credit-card charges go to a designated person at the nonprofit office and not to the planner's office.
- Follow up. You have to make sure that your special events coordinator assumes his responsibilities and meets critical timelines.

Additional Volunteer Assistance

Carefully assess the number of event volunteers needed and be specific about the tasks they will be performing. For example, volunteers are needed to perform such tasks as stuffing and placing gift bags with favors on the tables. You also might ask them to set out table tent cards, set up signage, or arrange the auction item display for the silent auction. Or they might assist with special chair décor, such as arranging a pashmina on a chair that is being offered for sale or tying a sash or beads on a chair back. Always provide snacks, a break room, and validated parking for your event volunteers.

Volunteers make it all happen. For example, they can staff gift boutiques, answer telethon phones, and provide hospitality. They mentor volunteering students, decorate galas, position centerpieces, tie chair backs, and fill gift bags. They address envelopes, seal invitations, take reservations, handle logistics, return loaned props, and even provide pet supervision when dogs or cats are included in fashion shows. Volunteers also accommodate any guests of honor— transporting them, making sure their needs are met and delivering hospitality baskets.

Some of the most active volunteers in the fundraising community are guild members. A guild is adjunct to a nonprofit organization made up of dedicated and stalwart supporters. Guild members provide financial support through memberships and programs designed to educate and generate interest in their cause. Membership is based on willingness and ability to support and participate in the activities of the guild. There is an annual guild meeting to elect officers, transact other business as may come before the meeting, inform members of the current activities of the guild, and present programs relating to the nonprofit. Guilds afford many volunteer opportunities for each member, and members are recognized annually with awards for their qualities of commitment, dedication, generosity of spirit, and sensitivities to co-workers.

Regardless of the nature of your organization or of where your volunteers come from, give your volunteers choices so that they can discover what works for them and for their schedules and personalities. Volunteers who like interacting with the public might enjoy working in an organization's boutique. People who like sales may enjoy selling subscriptions during intermissions at events. If someone wants to meet performing artists and visiting dignitaries, she may find a place on a hospitality or hosting committee to be ideal. Others may want to venture into community schools with various educational programs. For every enthusiastic volunteer, there is a perfect opportunity. Volunteers make the fundraisers flow smoothly. You want to keep them happily involved and attend to their needs.

SETTING UP COMMITTEE COMMUNICATION

Create a Timeline

Details make or break any event. Many important details relate to last-minute tasks that will be performed by the event chairman and key volunteers the day before or the day of the special event. You should prepare a timeline, which I call a "manifesto." All volunteers and organization and venue staff should receive a copy of the manifesto explaining everyone's specific duties and responsibilities.

Even with expert planning, something can and probably will go wrong. Volunteers must be prepared to pick up the slack if something unforeseen occurs. The event installation needs to perform as a finely tuned orchestra. The manifesto should include a timeline with a listing of each of the committees' members and any vendors involved, complete with each person's daytime phone number, cell phone and pager number, and e-mail address. In my fundraising experiences, for example, the success of one event was endangered when the event's coordinator became ill and did not leave a timeline for other volunteers, who were forced to take charge. This caused a great deal of anxiety for everyone on the day of the event.

Schedule Weekly Meetings

Staying involved with the team's progress will keep the event on schedule and resolve any potential problems. Meet on a regular basis with your key people—committee chairs and/or members, the organization's staff, volunteers, and vendors. Do whatever it takes to enhance communication with others on your team.

When scheduling a meeting, remember that committee members may not be familiar with the location of the nonprofit organization, so give good directions or fax a map that will be helpful to those people who are traveling from different parts of the city. If the location of the meeting is somewhat off the beaten track, offer landmarks with which they might be familiar. Let them know where to park their cars and that there will be security provided should the meeting take place after business hours. Also give everyone involved your contact information for after hours—voice, fax, and e-mail address—plus the phone numbers of other key committee members. Try to accommodate the majority of the volunteers' schedules.

Send those who miss the meeting minutes recorded by the secretary. In some cases, you can conference call members who are unable to come to the meeting. The Internet also comes in handy for organizing virtual volunteers. You can use the nonprofit's Web site for volunteer orientation, coordination, and committee signup. A cyberspace meeting place helps individuals who want to volunteer, but who have limited time for in-person meetings.

Build Team Spirit

By following the Golden Rule (do unto others as you would have them to do unto you), you can build a highly motivated and enthusiastic team. Making people feel appreciated usually leads to a successful and imaginative event.

Get everyone involved in carrying out the theme. This provides continuity during the time leading up to the event. Convey your vision to the design/decorating team and then focus on the budget. Keep the detailing and the big picture in the proper proportion.

Remind participants that your group needs to think creatively and engage in-kind donors they know to offset expenses. Let them know that you are doing the fundraiser based on a "zero budget," and have everyone keep in mind that it's always easier to spend money than to raise it.

Establish a Chain of Command

The chair needs to make clear that any problem that arises must be brought to her attention. Never count on anyone other than yourself if you are a project chairman. No one else will be as passionate nor envision a project any better than its creator. For a pre-event designed to promote "An Evening at the Alhambra," I contacted the director of a Flamenco dance company who agreed to perform, in keeping with our theme. He had very specific requirements as to the type and size of the dance floor. After analyzing the layout of a well-known restaurant's space, we successfully converted it into a stage for the Flamenco troop. No matter what obstacles might stand in your path—even if those obstacles are literal—it is ultimately up to you to get the job done.

Stay in Touch

E-mail is today's way of communicating, insuring reduced cost, fast delivery, and quick response. It's a good way to impart exciting news from your organization to your supporters and volunteers and to build organization awareness. The chairperson needs to determine if the individuals can receive Web-enabled e-mails such as newsletters with photos.

"Be prepared" should be the committee's motto. Make it clear to the nonprofit organization's executive director that the person who answers the phone at the office should know the following about the event: the who (speaker, honoree, orchestra), what, why, where (venue), when, and how much (individual ticket prices and sponsorship levels). If the contact person doesn't have all the facts, he will need to take the name and number of a person calling for information and refer the caller to the proper individual. Have a fact sheet about the event available to fax, mail, or e-mail to anyone who requests information.

If the nonprofit has a Web site, make sure information is available on that site, as well. In order to avoid losing a prospective donor, the contact at the office also should be prepared to take credit card information. It is a good idea to print a form with the credit card information to be faxed or e-mailed back to the donor for her signature and then returned to the organization. This also provides the donor with a record and receipt.

Team Members

- Chairperson
- Executive Director
- Director of Development
- Board of Directors
- Advisory Board
- Volunteer Committees:
      Honorary
      Underwriting
      Invitation
      Decorations
      Reservations
      Entertainment
      Food and Beverage
      Program
      Auction
      PR/Media

 *Chapter Eight*

EARLY PLANNING FOR
THE BIG EVENT

"Whatever you can do, begin it. Boldness has
genuine power, success, and magic in it."

—GOETHE

After deciding on the kind of event your organization wants and
choosing a team to put it all together, it's time to select a date and
a place. Then you will need to establish a theme and begin thinking
about an honoree, the program, and/or entertainment. Flexibility is
important throughout this early planning process.

As chairperson of a big event, you must take the lead and work
directly with each appropriate subcommittee chair to get major decisions made at the earliest possible time. Whether the decision is about
choosing a venue, planning a theme, nominating an honoree, or determining the amount of the ticket prices, make a decision and stand by
it. The process of going from one committee member to another
before making a decision can be defeating to the morale of the group.
Too much committee talk can dampen everyone's enthusiasm.

FINDING A VENUE AND SELECTING FOOD AND
BEVERAGE PROVIDERS

Select a venue where you have room to grow. For example, for a
gala, you'll want a space that will work as well for 500 guests as it

will for a thousand. (And even if there are only 250 guests, the room can be scaled down proportionately.) Choose a configuration that will accommodate everyone in the room. A long rectangular space is difficult for unifying a group, because the shape literally divides the room in half. Some guests will have difficulty viewing the program. If the event includes a pre-reception and silent auction, check to see if there is adequate space available outside the ballroom in the foyer. To be sure all necessary elements are taken into consideration, ask the decorations and auction chairs to be part of the venue selection process.

The committee can determine whether the space is adequate to display auction items and assess the flow of the crowd during the silent auction reception. Also, you'll want to check on any other activities that will be taking place in an adjacent ballroom at the same time as your event. If there is another function, venue staff and volunteers will have to direct guests to the proper event. Security needs to be aware that another function is taking place to ensure the protection of auction items. You'll also want to make certain that the sound from the adjacent ballroom doesn't interfere with your program.

If a hotel, private club, or resort is involved in your event, discuss in advance just what your expectations are and what their responsibilities will be. Ask representatives from the venue to join the event planning committee for an on-site meeting so they will be aware of all of the important elements involved in the event. Ask the venue representatives to provide rooms for committee meetings, and see if they might offer coffee, water, and cold drinks. Inquire about special packages, like weekend getaways at one of their resort destinations that could be donated by the venue as an auction item. In this way the people at the venue become actively involved with your fundraiser and will understand that good public relations mutually benefit their organization and the charity.

Try to negotiate a discounted room rate and other perks that would provide an incentive for out-of-town guests attending the event. Perhaps the in-house florist will provide complimentary flowers and/or fruit baskets. See if the hotel will sponsor a pre- or post-event function. Try to negotiate free or reduced valet parking or have the valet parking costs worked into the cost-per-person banquet charge.

See if the hotel or venue policy will allow you to serve donated wine from an outside vendor at the function. Each city and state has different laws regarding the serving of alcohol, so check with the banquet manager at the venue to see what is permissible. It is very challenging (and sometimes impossible) to get the wine and liquor donated, but there are a few options. Many wine connoisseurs have connections to a vineyard and might be willing to write on behalf of the organization. You should give them enough lead time to send out several requests. Or perhaps a nonprofit wine and food society would help the charitable organization by donating wine for the main course. Try negotiating a reduction in the corkage fee if you are successful in getting the wine donated.

Read the Fine Print

When you are negotiating a contract, many factors will come into play. If your organization has hosted an event at the hotel on several previous occasions, this may give you greater leverage in working out the fine points such as a pre-event hosted by the venue for major benefactors, reduced room rates and upgrades for out-of-town guests, complimentary tastings, and consideration in costs of food and beverages.

Know your minimum expenditure for food and beverage. Your minimum should be addressed clearly in the proposed contract under Banquet Terms and Conditions. When negotiating the minimum expenditure for food and beverage, clarify if the service charge is included. If the minimum is not met, the organization will be charged the difference as a room rental fee.

If under Deposit and Cancellation Terms, your contract reads, "the required non-refundable deposit of $1,000 will be held as part of but not limited to liquidate damages," it should be rewritten. State, "A deposit in the amount of $1,000 will be included with the signed contract. Said deposit is nonrefundable, but remains subject to the satisfactory fulfillment of the terms and conditions contained within this contract. In the event the hotel fails to meet its obligations as stipulated within, the deposit will be refunded in its entirety."

What's the Count?

Most hotels require notice of the number of guests attending seventy-two hours in advance. If you haven't heard from prepaid benefactors regarding their attendance, follow up with a call. You don't want to pay for food and services that will not be used or have empty tables. Generally the hotel will allow you to increase this number after the initial guarantee, but you cannot reduce the guarantee after this time period. Be prepared with extra meals for unexpected guests. The hotel usually sets up and prepares food for 5 percent over the guaranteed number of guests (or for no more than thirty extra attendees).

If a hotel applies a mandatory service charge, which is taxable by certain states, you can try and negotiate this charge for a lower percentage with the banquet manager. The range for service charges is anywhere from 15 to 25 percent.

Finding an Independent Caterer

If you are not having the event at a hotel, restaurant, or country club where the food is provided, you'll need to hire a caterer to provide the food. It is a good idea to contact several caterers and then make your decision according to the most reasonable bid and presentation.

Decide if the meal will be served buffet style or seated. Settle on the number of courses—an appetizer or salad as the first course, followed by an entrée and dessert. Make an alternative menu available for people with special dietary needs. Consider the cost of rentals and linens. Is it more economical to handle rentals as a committee task or to make this part of the off-site catering package? Should the committee arrange for flowers through the caterer or independently? Where is the off-site kitchen to be set up, and is there enough electricity to handle the equipment?

ESTABLISHING A THEME

To come up with a theme for your event, let the Internet or personal experiences spark your imagination. Your theme should be carried out throughout the printed materials, décor, menu, and pre-events. It's easier than you think to recreate another place, another time. Guests should be encouraged to dress creatively.

For example, if you're planning an evening around the music of Count Basie, you can research the jazz era on the Internet to see what people wore on a steamy night to the Cotton Club in Harlem. Refer to pictures of the club to get a sense of the décor. You may find a local group that collects jazz memorabilia as well as photographic images and borrow them to enhance the theme. A fog machine can recreate the smoky atmosphere. To bring a theme to life, your decorations committee can create a backdrop of a famous nightclub, add special lighting with colored gels, and tie the floral arrangements into your overall theme.

After visiting the Alhambra in Spain with a museum group, I was inspired by the architecture—columns, beautiful tiles, and arches. A tapestry of ideas began to take shape in my head for creating the theme "A Night at the Alhambra" for a gala benefiting the Houston Grand Opera. My memories of the Alhambra with its exotic mysticism and richness brought many thoughts to mind for the table coverings, pashminas, candelabras, overall décor, lighting, entertainment, and menu.

If the organization is celebrating an anniversary, you can build a theme around the symbolic number of years being celebrated. To underscore the history of a regional theater company, you can highlight past productions with silk-screened images that may stand out in the memories of past theatre patrons. During the pre-reception, have costumed actors move through the crowd reciting memorable lines from different performances. For a milestone celebration for the theater, honor distinguished theater alumni who have received national recognition with an award. The award could be named after a family of theater nobility such as the Barrymores or the Redgraves.

Give demonstrations to make your theme come alive. For example, when I chaired an event benefiting the College of Natural Sciences and Mathematics at the University of Houston, we selected as our theme the Quest for Excellence. This celebrated the achievements not only of the college, but of distinguished honoree Eckhard Pfeiffer, former president and CEO of Compaq Computer Corporation. During the reception guests participated in sophisticated scientific demonstrations. Educators offered a hands-on experience, allowing guests to explore a virtual-reality cave, be levitated by superconductivity magnets, and manipulate molecules. Members of the college alumni association made up the task force of volunteers. All of these demonstrations were the collaborative work of the scientists at the university, and their involvement brought other professors and students into the fundraising process. Through these thought-provoking exhibits, guests gained a sense of the college's accomplishments, met faculty and students, and received insight.

The Pink Ribbons Project—Dancers in Motion Against Breast Cancer—is a Houston dance organization that promotes awareness about breast cancer and raises money for breast cancer advocacy, research, and education. It has raised in excess of $700,000 through various fundraising activities, including dinners, dance performances, and bowl-a-thons. I thought of the Pink Ribbons Project when a high-end lingerie retailer relocated to an upscale shopping mall in the area and wanted to partner with a charitable organization for its formal opening. The retailer wanted to match its corporate philosophy with its targeted audience.

How do you put together a fundraiser and a store opening with a limited budget? First, seek the guidance of a respected volunteer chairperson who can guarantee a turnout. Top Drawer Lingerie called and asked me to recommend a cause that was compatible with both its product and its goal. I suggested the Pink Ribbons Project in support of breast cancer awareness and the medically underinsured women in our community. The timing of the opening was perfect; it was in October, which happens to be Breast Cancer Awareness Month. Instead of the typical stand up reception, we decided to create a theme-inspired evening titled "It's All About Pink." We priced the tickets at $75 per person, which we estimated to suit the occasion and the audience enough to ensure a good turnout. The next consideration was deciding what could we offer our prospective benefactors to entice them to support this worthwhile cause.

We visited the surrounding retailers in the shopping center and asked if they would participate in various aspects of the event. Most were receptive, so we were fortunate to have expenses partially underwritten. This combined effort helped promote the neighboring retailers and showed their community involvement. It proved to be a positive experience, and more than four hundred guests attended.

During the first part of the evening, the guests sampled sushi, Mexican fare, ice cream desserts, wines, and sparkling waters donated by the various retailers in the center. The Pink Martini station was a clever way to raise additional funds as guests purchased these drinks and were given an opportunity to draw for luxury items from the store. Entertainment was donated by local pianist Marshall Maxwell, who dressed all in pink for the occasion. Artists were asked to create bustiers for the silent auction, and each of the thirteen items was a work of art. We had a lingerie fashion show with a modern dance troupe performing during intervals while the models changed.

Commemorative objects such as inscribed letter openers and crystal or silver items that serve as mementos of a magical evening have enduring value. (Make sure that the recipient's name is inscribed correctly.) At the Houston Grand Opera Ball decorations such as the pashminas, candelabras, and centerpieces were sold at the end of the evening. This not only helped to increase the net, but also served as lasting mementos for the guests.

Expect your great ideas to be duplicated. An organization will always need to come up with fresh ideas or a "signature," such as the monumental cows that raised money in New York, Chicago, and Houston for children's causes. Miniature versions of the cows continue to make people smile in gift shops, and the philanthropy continues, as well.

CHOOSING ENTERTAINMENT

Imagine that you are on the charity circuit and have attended at least three to four events in a week. There are many people who maintain such hectic schedules. With this scenario in mind, make your event sensitive to the wear and tear that your donors may experience. Try to provide an evening of enjoyment and/or enlightenment.

Pure Enjoyment

If you want to add a little spontaneity, why not have a mime or marvelous magician work his way through the crowd doing simple slight-of-hand tricks during a silent auction reception? This will entertain your guests who are not participating in the auction. The performer can continue to roam throughout the ballroom as guests are being seated for dinner. A string ensemble can provide conversational background music during the reception, creating a relaxing atmosphere. The same group can add additional musicians and perform during dinner.

For the American Ballet Theatre's 50th Anniversary Gala in1990, the evening was presented in two acts and a finale. Selections from the first twenty-five years of the ballet company's repertoire were presented on film and in live performances by Rudolf Nureyev, Agnes de Mille, and Natalia Makarova. The finale included the entire cast and special guest performers.

For my Opera Ball 2001, A Night at the Alhambra, we utilized the entire lobby of the Hyatt Regency Hotel for our silent auction reception. After guests ascended the escalator to go into the ballroom, the silent auction was reorganized in the area outside the ballroom. Members of the World Wrestling Federation for Wrestle Mania Weekend were in Houston staying at the hotel and added to the magical mix of bagpipers, entertainers, and giant puppets.

Are you are thinking of hiring a dance band that rocks guests? Why not offer other entertainment in an adjacent area such as a casino? Guests are given a certain number of chips when they enter the casino, and after they amass a mini fortune, they cash in their chips and receive raffle tickets for a midnight drawing of prizes.

You may be able to entice a big-name musician to your city to perform for a major fundraising event. But if you are looking for inexpensive musical entertainment for your event, investigate resources close at hand. Local nightclubs feature young bands and individual performers who may be persuaded to donate their time for a worthy cause. University music departments can supply the names of talented students who will perform for a nominal fee or simply for the experience.

Your guests might enjoy a personal encounter with someone whom they have admired through seasons of outstanding ballet performances or symphony concerts. You might invite cast members of the city's repertory theater company or a university's drama department to perform.

Consider setting up a photo studio in one corner of the silent auction reception area with a backdrop that relates to the theme of the event. A commemorative photograph for your guests is a nice gesture and a pleasant way to pass the time.

Seeking Enlightenment

Many people enjoy nothing more than a fine dinner followed by a good speaker. If your speaker is an actor, performer, or author, celebrate with a mini–film festival or highlight her music or books. Readings from letters, journals, books, and screenplays can be both powerful and poignant. For example, former First Lady of Texas Nellie Connally captivated a group at an event reading from her journal about the day that President John F. Kennedy was assassinated. Guests were eager to hear her firsthand account of what transpired and to get that sense of closure.

If you have several authors at a "Book and Author" dinner, an underwriter is usually more inclined to sponsor a table if he gets the option of hosting one of the guest authors at the table. Provide the underwriter and his table guests with books signed prior to the event by the author sitting at that table. This concept works well for formats advocating literacy programs of the local public library or adopt-a-classroom projects.

If you are raising funds for a university performing arts building, having as your speaker a distinguished alumni who has gained notoriety in theater, dance, film, or music is guaranteed to create revenue. Invite corporate, individual, and foundation leaders in the community to put their name on a chair, row of seats, a rehearsal room, hall in a theater, or a dressing room. To coincide with your special event, ask if the performer would consider teaching a master class.

Distinguished alumni often participate in major fundraising events for the business and science colleges on the campuses of their respective universities. (For example, a few generous alumni I've worked

with who have lent their time to honoring their alma maters are
John F. Smith, former chairman of General Motors, and Dr. Paul
Chu, widely known as the father of superconductivity.)
Achievements like theirs serve to mentor and inspire others to
become involved. High schools as well as universities should maximize the impact of their distinguished alumni to the extent that these
people will allow. For example, encourage the alumni to participate
in leading a panel discussion that will coincide with the main event.

Secure a corporate sponsor to provide the funding for taping a
series of lecture events, which could be called, "Live From ..." or
"Conversations With. ..." See if the municipal channel or local cable
channel will air the tape at a designated time slot in the interest of
increasing community awareness and financial support for your
organization. Local stations always need to fill air time. Add to your
format each year by building on the original concept.

HONORING SOMEONE SPECIAL

When selecting guests of honor for a fundraising event, select individuals who are well regarded throughout the community, who will
create greater awareness for your cause, and who will actively
involve others through their personal commitment. Honorees can
offer lists of individual, corporate, or foundation contacts. They can
cosign or write special notes on specific benefactor letters. It is
important to have an honoree that is willing to attend most of the
pre-events, as well as the main event.

Always include a biographical sketch of an honoree, not only for
those who already may be familiar with the individual, but for those
who may not be aware of the honoree's involvement and accomplishments in the community.

Honorees can speak about their personal commitment on behalf
of causes such as breast or prostate cancer research, rehabilitative
drug and alcohol facilities, or the New York Firefighter Fund. Giving

your guests something to reflect on as they leave an event will reap a positive response. Perhaps the honoree has survived a life-threatening disaster like Dr. Jerry Nielsen, who bravely ministered her own chemotherapy treatments for breast cancer while stranded at the South Pole. Professional golfer Laura Baugh, who successfully overcame alcoholism, also has shared her story to give hope to others. A fearless fireman who, without concern for himself, saved lives at the World Trade Center is a great source of inspiration.

You might honor a local individual such as Houston Police Officer Michael W. Jones, who received the "Sylvan Rodriguez Role Model of the Year Award," named for the late Houston CBS television anchor. This award honors people who challenge young people to go beyond the status quo. Officer Jones has impacted the lives of four-and-a-half million young people through Soul Patrol, a police organization that carries the motto "Knowledge is Power." Presenting an award that has been named for someone keeps the individual's memory alive while recognizing deserving honorees.

I suggested we create an award and present it to an honoree for the "A Night at the Alhambra Gala." It needed to be someone who had distinguished herself in the world of opera, possibly as a director, composer, producer, or artist. I suggested artist and opera director Robert Wilson to David Gockley, the director of the opera. Robert Wilson had worked with the Houston Grand Opera and would bring international focus to the company. We agreed to present him with the newly created Andrea Palladio Award. Early in the campaign, I wrote Bob's friends and associates to let them know of this honor, hoping that their schedules would permit them to attend. It would be interesting for our guests if just one of his many notorious friends, such as famed soprano Jessye Norman, accepted. I asked them to write comments about their friendship and experiences in working with Bob. This would be included in the program as a special surprise for him.

If the unforeseen should happen such as the death of an honoree, you respectfully should go forward with the event. Ask the family for their suggestion of someone who could represent the individual. If your honoree is elderly or physically challenged, be considerate and offer beforehand to have a microphone taken to her table for acceptance remarks rather than have her maneuver the crowd to the podium. Also, make sure that the person is not left unattended during the pre-reception in a crowd of people. Assist her in advance of the other guests to the appropriate table in the main ballroom.

Eleanor Searle Whitney McCollum
Early 20th Century – 2002

Eleanor McCollum was our star. If we were to look up to the sky, we would see her twinkle from afar. She lived an extraordinary life of fascinating and varied experiences. She was a persuasive evangelist and a key supporter of many Christian ministries. She was an ageless regal woman who introduced beauty at every opportunity into the lives of people from all walks of life. Eleanor touched everyone she encountered from heads of state to native villagers.

Eleanor was born in Plymouth, Ohio to the delight of her parents Dr. and Mrs. George James Searle. After studies at Florida Southern College, she took voice lessons and became an opera singer.

Her first husband, Cornelius Vanderbilt Whitney, was the son of two notable American families. During their marriage, Eleanor became involved in numerous cultural and charitable activities while living in New York and later in Washington D.C. They had one son – her beloved Cornelius Searle Whitney. Eleanor was a leader of style and fashion and appeared regularly in the society pages. In a famous photo, she is featured on the cover of Life Magazine driving her "four-in-hand" coach and horse on their Long Island estate.

Her endurance and radiance astounded us with her many achievements and accomplishments. Eleanor never accepted "no" when she was pursuing with gusto one of the causes she believed in. Her causes were many – Orbis International, Flying Eye Hospital, Theater Under the Stars, Houston Grand Opera and The Eleanor McCollum Competition for Young Singers. Each year the awards and auditions program culminated in the Concert of Arias. When presenting awards to some of the world's best young opera singers, Eleanor did her famous twirl across the stage.

Eleanor served on Northwood's National Women's Board Houston chapter and was named a Northwood Distinguished Woman in 1989. She established the Bone Disease Program of Texas, a collaborative program of Baylor College of Medicine and The University of Texas M.D. Anderson Cancer Center.

Her autobiography, "Invitation to Joy" was published in 1971. During her singing career, she traveled the world performing for Billy Graham Ministries and sang as a soloist with the United States Air Force Band. At heart, Eleanor loved the simplicity in life – comfort foods – macaroni and cheese, hot chocolate and her favorite dessert rice pudding. Eleanor adored hats. She was named "Best Hatted" so many times that she was retired to the Hatter Hall of Fame.

Eleanor shared 18 wonderful years with legendary Houston oilman cattle breeder, banker and philanthropist, Leonard R. "Mc" McCollum. She continued the couple's tradition of service to the community after his death in 1993. She launched a historic restoration program in Plymouth, Ohio and created a museum as a lasting tribute to her cherished family in Ohio heritage.

We miss her slightly trilling falsetto voice, her warm smile, her elegance and her passion. She was a visionary that painted in broad stokes – there were no small pictures on her horizon. Her ability to laugh at herself when something went astray was another admirable trait. What was important for Eleanor is that you try. Even as she began to slow down, no one could keep up with her. Eleanor was larger than life – how blessed we are to have had her glide through our lives.

– *Carolyn Farb*

A written tribute in your event program is a good way to recognize an honoree who has passed away.

Remembering Past Supporters

Take time to remember those who have supported the organization in the past. This assures future honorees of the sincerity and earnestness of this recognition. People are sometimes reluctant to be recognized, but once they realize the positive impact it may have on others, they respond with enthusiasm. In an event program, a page remembering past honorees and their contributions imparts the message that your organization continues to appreciate and recognize them.

If you are going to honor the former chairs at an annual event, give some thought to how you want to recognize them. You could arrange for a local photographer to photograph them, and the photographs could be displayed during the reception hour of the gala. Be sure to list their names, the titles of the events they chaired, and the dates. You can also put the photographs in the program, which serves to highlight the photographer who generously committed to the sittings.

The honorees should be seated at tables throughout the venue. Recognize them as a group with remarks thanking them by the president of the board, event chair, or executive director during the program. Don't lose the opportunity to say "thank you" in a poignant way. Everyone wants to feel appreciated.

 *Chapter Nine*

CULTIVATING COMMUNITY INTEREST

"The best way to predict your future is to create it."
—STEPHEN COVEY

An event needs to have allure and offer a variety of reasons for others to want to become involved. The style and type of the event that is presented to the public reflects the credibility and image of the organization. Operate on the premise that there is potential interest in your cause and offer opportunities for others to become engaged in the story.

People form perceptions about nonprofits, just as they do about any organization. Hopefully, those perceptions are positive. Because donors buy into a perception they believe to be true, your organization's success depends on how it is perceived by the public. It takes hard work, energy, focus, money, and time to create and maintain that positive image. You'll want to create a strong image and use it for everything from fact sheets and benefactor letters to invitations.

FIRST IMPRESSIONS COUNT
The Internet has made information faster, more available, and easier to access, but never underestimate the power of the human voice, charisma, and sparkle. People will always prefer relating to people

rather than to a computerized telephone voice message system. We should never lose sight of the fact that the art of conversation is what sets us apart and makes the connection

When people attempt to reach a real person at a nonprofit organization, they should not have to listen to unpleasant music, punch at least five or six instructional buttons, or get disconnected. It is all too impersonal. People calling to RSVP will sometimes hang up in frustration. The lack of the personal touch creates an unfriendly environment

If your organization has a receptionist, keep him informed. Provide the receptionist with a fact sheet and other information about the organization and a schedule of upcoming events. This person is sometimes the first contact prospective donors and volunteers have with your organization. As a member of the team, the receptionist's attitude and knowledge can be a helpful resource—or a deterrent.

Take time to work with the organization's staff, or you could lose out on making contact with a prospective donor or volunteer. Training and orientation is essential. Callers don't like to be placed on hold before having the opportunity to express the nature of their call. If the receptionist doesn't have the answer, his best reply is, "I don't know, but I will find out and get back with you," or "I don't know, but I will transfer you to someone who can give you that information," or at the very least, "If I can have your phone number, I will have someone get back to you before the day's end." The receptionist needs to be upbeat, positive, and knowledgeable about the organization or the event.

Ask the receptionist to get the names and telephone numbers of individuals calling about the event to add to your database. She should direct them to the Web site but also should be prepared to mail, e-mail, or fax them the information as requested.

Make sure supporters can find special event locations or the organization's office. Have a map available for the receptionist to fax in addition to written directions to give over the phone. The receptionist should also have the information for alternative event dates should there be a cancellation due to weather.

Spell It Out

When tweaking fundraising plans, get the name out. A nonprofit identified only by its initials runs the risk of the public not recognizing its identity. Even when an organization has a strong track record and extensive public relations, prospective donors may not always recognize the organization by the initials. Do the initials JNF (Jewish National Fund), JDRF (Juvenile Diabetes Research Foundation), TNF Foundation (Texas Neurofibromatosis Foundation) ring familiar?

In an effort to communicate its mission more clearly, the Juvenile Diabetes Foundation (JDF) added the word "Research" to its name in the year 2000. They also make a point of clarifying the allocation of research money: All monies raised for research go into an international fund, and funds are awarded to the research efforts worldwide that are deemed most worthwhile. Two advisory boards (one of medical reviewers and one of lay persons) study grant proposals and present findings to the board of directors of the organization, which makes the final decision. Over the thirty-year span of JDRF's history, monies raised from annual fundraising efforts have gone from $10,000 to $410 million.

CREATING INTEREST IN YOUR EVENT

Design a Logo

You might consider developing a logo for your event. It should relate to your mission statement or event theme and, if well done, can be extremely effective. Secure a graphic artist who will agree to donate her service. Ask committee members, board members, and supporters for recommendations of an artist who might consider the project. Then submit a proposal in hopes that one of these prospects will bite. The individual artist or company can be recognized in the invitation as well as the program as an in-kind donor. The graphic artist or designer will create the logo and theme that should be used for the letterhead, media alerts, invitations, and programs. The purpose is to give the campaign an overall theme that donors and prospective supporters will identify and recognize.

For instance, the Loving Hearts Caring Hands logo is an angel with open arms and a light radiating to signify God's all-embracing glow. For an Egyptian-themed event, a Sphinx or a similar Egyptian symbol above the event's title might appear on the outside of the envelope to identify it. For a charitable golf tournament, one sponsor created the image of a bird with a cap and golf club. This image, combined with the words "Birdies for Charity," created a memorable logo.

A logo can help define the identity of your cause and/or event.

Save-the-Date Cards

To get your fundraising event on everyone's calendar, mail "Save-the-Date" cards two to six months in advance of the event to those on your mailing list. Inform invitees of special guests and celebrities who will be attending and the names of your honorary chairs and honorees. Giving your benefactors and prospective benefactors the opportunity to plan ahead helps them budget their charitable contributions for the year and organize a table of friends and colleagues for the event. Save-the-Date cards serve as a reminder to support your organization.

16th Annual Dinner

Guess who's coming to dinner?

Mark your calendar
Sunday, October 15, 1995

Westin Galleria
7:00 p.m.

In the past, prominent authors and celebrities have attended the annual Book & Author Dinner. This year's event promises to be even more exciting. Come out and be a part of it all. Look for your invitation soon!

For further information, call

Benefiting the Parent Reading Program of the Houston Public Library

An attention-getting save-the-date card is a great
way to kickoff early promotion of an event.

Toot Your Own Horn

To develop any project, promote your nonprofit's mission at every opportunity. Never grow tired of beating the drum. Always be prepared to give your personal testimonial as to why you are involved. Inform donors about your organization, how it differs from other similar groups and how the donated funds are being spent. Talk about upcoming fundraising events. Whether you're a chair, committee member, or volunteer, your knowledge builds confidence in prospective donors.

Use Your Newsletters

Let the organization's newsletter be a voice to spread the cause's message. Inform your readers about new staff members or how to reserve a raffle ticket on a unique auction item, such as a vintage Harley-Davidson. Include quotes from those who are benefiting from the programs you are helping to fund, like a "Dreamer" from the "I Have a Dream Foundation." Announce upcoming pre-events or new activities like corporate sports challenges, and encourage interested parties to sign up.

Your organization's newsletter is a natural outlet for promoting your events.

Profile new board members of the organization. Talk about the upcoming season and announce guest performers. Introduce a noteworthy director or production or discuss a touring success. Give school schedules, announce scholarship awards, and highlight pre-events leading up to the major fundraising gala. Keep your newsletter optimistic and interesting. Include photos of events.

Use the in-house public relations department of a hotel or venue where the event is being held to get the word out to their vendors about your event. See if they publish a newsletter that is placed in the guest rooms or public areas. For your event, have them run signage on one of the hotel electronic bulletin boards.

Develop Your Web Site

Develop a good Web site. See if a computer class or journalism organization at a local school might create your Web site free of charge as a project to support their volunteer commitment. All information pertinent to the organization and its upcoming events should be included. This can be your link with the community, as well as with your volunteers. Include your Web site address in your organization's newsletter. The Web site and other public relations sources should also include information on how to reach someone at the organization who can answer any questions, including that person's extension number and e-mail address.

Use your Web site as your satellite. Publish a wish list of the organization's needs and set up a pressroom with information for media contacts. You can also use your site to Web cast your special event to a global audience, promote lectureships by distinguished speakers, or sell ticket subscriptions or raffle opportunities online. You can even enable invited guests to RSVP to your events online.

Modern technology can allow individual or corporate donors to learn more about your nonprofit via a streaming, interactive virtual tour. Present compelling photographs and testimonials with photo galleries. Create city maps and provide directions to your event or nonprofit site location.

Don't miss the opportunity to capture any information about visitors to the nonprofit Web site—name, telephone number, address, or e-mail address. This way, you can build databases for mailing lists and e-mail blasts.

GETTING THE PR CAMPAIGN ROLLING

If people don't know about your organization, they can't lend their support. There are many worthwhile organizations that have been around for as long as forty years but that remain relatively unknown to the public. Fundraising and public relations go hand in hand. Creating awareness of your organization and its value gives donors reasons to support your cause.

Host a kickoff event before you begin a major fundraising campaign, and treat it like a press conference. Media coverage raises awareness and creates anticipation leading up to your big annual fundraising event. If a performer or well-known person, such as a high-profile CEO, politician, author, or sports figure, is the guest of honor or distinguished speaker at your event, host a pre-event reception to enable photographers and reporters to get photos and quotes from this individual. An event chair can use this opportunity to thank cochairs, committee members, board members, distinguished guests, major benefactors, and volunteers who would appreciate being included in the smaller reception.

Preview parties are important ingredients in the launching of your public campaign. They provide the perfect opportunity for announcing honorees, acknowledging benefactors, and previewing such features of your main event as a sampling of auction items.

Develop a Media Plan

It is wise to create a media plan that captures the spirit of the event. Some large organizations employ a public relations firm or have an in-house director of marketing and communication who is responsible for creating this plan. Everyone developing the media plan should work closely with the chair of the event to plan the strategy of the overall media campaign. The public relations team should be involved in the process beginning with the selection of a graphic designer and following through to the production of the invitation, event program, and, if applicable, auction catalog or award presentation.

Press Releases

Be sure to keep your event in front of the public. Send out press alerts and media releases about any interesting stories, high profile-visitors or guests at your events, or upcoming performances. Pre-event fact sheets and press releases are important to the success of any fundraising event. Keep updating press releases and fact sheets that are mailed to benefactors as new and exciting elements are added to the event. The executive director or communications director should write a skeletal post-event press release prior to the event leaving spaces to fill in last-minute details—important names, distinguished or mystery guests, décor, a special concert, the high bidder on an auction item, and any other newsworthy item.

When writing a press release, be sure to include the basics: who, what, when, where, and why. Describe the reason for the special event, information about the organization, the mission, the different levels of sponsorship, the recipient of the proceeds, the goal, the guest of honor, and specific directions. Your event should be regarded as more than a party, and the release needs to be well written in order to inform the public of the reason for the event. Just dropping off a press release doesn't insure that your information will go directly to whomever it is intended. E-mail is a sure shot, but you should still follow up. Ask a volunteer to meet key representatives at each of the various media when delivering tapes, press releases, or photos.

For Immediate Release

Media Contact:

Name	Date
Title	Time
Phone/fax number	Place
Email address	

Young Audiences of Houston

11th ANNUAL YOUNG AUDIENCES AWARDS LUNCHEON A BRILLIANT SUCCESS!
April 8, 2002

HOUSTON – On Tuesday, May 7, 2002, Young Audiences of Houston hosted its 11th Annual Awards Luncheon, Learning through the Arts, at River Oaks Country Club. This years luncheon honored Houston philanthropists Susan and Eugene Vaughan with the Outstanding Civic Leadership Award, The Arts in Medicine Program at Texas Children's Hospital created by Dr. David G. Poplack with the Community Leadership Award, and devoted Houston Symphony League volunteer Terry Ann Brown with the prestigious Fredell Lack Award, each for their dedication to education and arts in the Houston Community.

The elegant event was cochaired by Carolyn Farb, philanthropist and author, and Joe Hafner, President and CEO of Riviana Foods, Inc. The event was a grand success with a turnout of more than 350 supporters and friends of Young Audiences. Dave Ward, ABC Channel 13 Anchor, served as the Master of Ceremonies. The event introduced the silent auction element for the first time, showcasing a wide array of items: an upholstered chair from Shabby Slips, Oriental Soumack from Stark Carpet, Cartier Must Tank Watch, gold earrings from Theresa Ranzau Jewels, and a beautiful silver lariat necklace designed by Luci V, the silent auction chair, Lucinda Loya.

continued

The Blue Gnus Trio, one of the Young Audiences performers, played during the reception giving guests an idea of what Young Audiences has to offer to the children of Houston. Benefactor favors were provided by Bob Devlin of Neiman Marcus. The program began after the first course had been served, and during dessert, the Marian Anderson String Quartet provided enlightening entertainment. Departing guests received gift bags containing a generous assortment of Success Rice and Kid's Recipes for Success from Riviana Foods, Inc.

Those in attendance at the luncheon included Molly and Jim Crownover, Joe Davis and Janet Swikard, Dr. Grady and Martha Hallman, Jan and Tom Barrow, David Hill and Sylvia Forsythe of the Hotel Derek, David Nelson, Young Audiences founder violinist Fredell Lack, Young Audiences Board President Herb Karpicke, Lilly and Charles Foster, Wendy Hines, John and Marilyn Holstead, Lynda Transier, Bill Hill, Ginya Trier, Jeff Love, and Bill Wright to name a few.

Young Audiences of Houston has been an active member of the community for 45 years and reaches over 300,000 children each year through fine arts performances, workshops, and residencies at schools, libraries, and community centers. As one of the largest chapters of a nationwide network, Young Audiences of Houston uses the arts to bolster academic achievement and connect students to their communities. The Annual Young Audiences Awards Luncheon raises funds to support Young Audiences of Houston's mission to educate children through the arts and to make the arts an integral part of every child's learning experience.

Notice how this press release clearly states who, what, when, where, and why.

Newspapers

Get to know the social column writers so they will be aware of your organization's upcoming events. Send the lifestyle section editor at your local newspaper column items throughout your fundraising campaign—from pre-events through your big annual event. You also should submit to have your event listed in the social calendar in a newspaper column that lists charitable events in the area. Usually, you are limited to about ten to twenty lines, so make each one count. State the name of the hosting organization, honoree, where and when, specifics about the benefit, event chairs, those who benefit, lowest priced individual ticket, as well as an e-mail, telephone number, and fax number for reservations. These calendar articles usually appear in the newspaper the month of the event or a week prior to the event. For example, Shelby Hodge of the *Houston Chronicle* puts together a calendar annually, and event planners use it as a reference to schedule their fundraising activities.

The media give you the opportunity to reach individuals, groups, or businesses who may not be on your current mailing list and would like to be. Always be on the lookout for ways in which your organization might be featured by local media outlets. Then submit your ideas, including as much information as possible. Such mentions may help sell your event to the public.

THE SOCIAL BOOK • A CALENDAR & RESOURCE GUIDE
2002 SOCIAL EVENTS   Dec 2001

DATE	EVENT	BENEFICIARY/ORG.
Jan 1	New Year's Day	
Jan 8	The Social Book 2002 Launch Party	
Jan 10	2002 Kipp Academy Gala	Kipp Academy
Jan 12	Winter Ball	Crohn's & Colitis Found.
Jan 17	Paul Bryant "Coach of the Year " Award	American Heart Assoc.
Jan 21	Martin Luther King Day	
Jan 22	Rienzi Society Annual Meeting/Dinner	Museum of Fine Arts
Jan 24	Hou. Chap. of TX Society of CPA's Gala	Ronald McDonald House
Jan 31	"Girls Just Wanna Have Fun"	Ronald McDonald House
Feb 2	Groundhog Day	
Feb 2	Toast to Texas	Muscular Dystrophy
Feb 3	Wine Luncheon & Auction	American Diabetes Assoc.
Feb 7	Concert of Arias	Houston Grand Opera pgms.
Feb 7	Pearl Ball	Good Samaritan Found.
Feb 7-9	Houston Livestock Show & Rodeo BBQ	HLSR Scholarships
Feb 9	Houston Livestock Show/Rodeo Parade	HLSR Scholarships
Feb 9	"An Evening with Da Camera"	Da Camera of Houston
Feb 12	Lincoln's Birthday	
Feb 12	Mardi Gras begins	
Feb 12-Mar 3	Houston Livestock Show & Rodeo	HLSR Scholarships
Feb 13	Ash Wednesday	
Feb 14	Valentine's Day	
Feb 16	Heart Ball 2002 • "Heart & Soul"	American Heart Assoc.
Feb 16	The Poets and Writers Ball	Inprint, Inc.
Feb 16	Heart of the Park 5K Fun Run	Friends of Hermann Park
Feb 18	President's Day	
Feb 20	The Blue Bird Circle Fashion Show	Blue Bird Circle
Feb 20	The "Heart of Gold" Celebration	Neighborhood Centers
Feb 22	Washington's Birthday	
Feb 22	BRAVO! Gala	Houston Grand Opera
Feb 22	AVAYA Golf Classic	Junior Achievement
Feb 23	Houston Ballet Ball	Houston Ballet Found.
Feb 23	Children's Scholarship Ball	Jewish Community Center
Feb 28	Bo's Place Luncheon	Bo's Place
Mar 2	Museum of Natural Science Gala	Mus. of Nat. Science
Mar 2	A Night for the Children	Inner City Catholic Schools
Mar 4	SEARCH Swing for Success Golf Tour.	SEARCH
Mar 7	Urban Campout	Girl Scouts of San Jacinto
Mar 7	Neuhaus Benefit Luncheon	Neuhaus Education Center
Mar 8	Houston Symphony Ball 2002	Houston Symphony
Mar 9	River Performing & Visual Arts Gala	River Perf & Vis Arts Ctr

Submit information about your event to all
social events calendars in your region.

Don't overlook smaller media organizations, neighborhood week-lies, and periodicals to get your message across to diverse audiences. Keep your media list updated, as there are always changes in staff. Include a note with the release, and, if you are fortunate enough to get press, follow with a thank-you. Don't be afraid to send out information; someone will be interested.

Television and Radio

You must develop a "hook" to entice local television and radio sta-tions to give you air time. Some television talk show hosts prefer a straightforward pitch about your organization, what it has to offer to the community, what its needs are, upcoming events, and a video clip, if available, showing services that are provided. Invite your executive director, a long-time board member, or a prospective event chair to serve as your spokesperson.

If the talk show host is on the theatrical side, you might get more creative with your pitches. For example, if your charitable organiza-tion represents the High School for the Performing & Visual Arts or Young Audiences, you might suggest having one or two students give a brief performance to demonstrate what the school offers in music, dance, art, and theater.

Another approach is to invite a television reporter or weatherman for an on-site visit at one of your organization's projects or events.

You also should write a thirty- or sixty-second public service announcement (PSA) for radio or TV that tells your organization's story. Ask the public service director at your local TV station to cre-ate a public service message to support a worthwhile campaign. See if the station would make additional copies that can be hand-deliv-ered to other stations. Have the PSA ready should a station make air time available. Ask a volunteer to deliver the tapes and to introduce himself to the public affairs director at each station. The personal contact might make the difference in getting your PSA aired. People appreciate the extra effort that has been made on behalf of your organization.

If you are representing an arts group, make a presentation to the public television station about broadcasting live performances of the symphony, opera, or ballet. Take your patrons backstage. Let them experience what goes on there, from applying stage makeup and putting the costumes together to conversations with lighting and set designers.

Tips for Meeting with Public Service Directors

- Importance—They must understand and support your cause. Let them know that through the PSA you hope to reach a wider segment of the population.
- Timeliness—The campaign should be newsworthy. Inform them of what the organization does—its activities and goals.
- Quality—The PSA should be done in good taste.
- Pleasantly Persistent—A personal visit should be brief. Fifteen minutes should be enough time for you to cover the necessary points.
- Checklist—List target television and radio stations, newspapers, and magazines. When you are tying to get newspapers and magazines to run a PSA, have camera-ready art and a list of ad sizes. Be professional.
- Follow-up Thank You—Whether or not the media contact has agreed to participate in your project, send a thank you; there will always be another opportunity.

Billboards

Billboards can get your message out to a broad audience. By partnering with an ad agency, the Boy Scouts of America helped to create a scouting awareness campaign that had the potential to raise a significant amount of money. A billboard campaign is an excellent way to recruit and offer scouting to the public. One such billboard message read, "We teach boys the ropes—Boy Scouts of America." The billboard image depicted hand-tied knots at various angles covering a green board.

An outdoor advertising company may be willing to underwrite a fundraising campaign for a nonprofit organization. You generally have to pay for the cost of the paper, which is nominal compared to the overall cost. Keep your message short, usually twelve words or less, and treat your billboard design as a work of art.

Organize a small event around a billboard unveiling and invite the media. You never know who will turn up, especially if the cause benefits children or prevention of cruelty to animals.

This billboard was successful in promoting this charity benefit.

STAY FOCUSED ON THE CAUSE

Use media and public relations opportunities to highlight the cause and accomplishments of your organization. Recognize the individuals and organizations that make significant contributions to the success of that effort. Try to involve spokespersons who have been touched directly or indirectly by the organization's cause. For example, Helen Harris, president and founder of Theatre Vision, is blind and has two sons who are also losing their sight. While waiting for a cure for blindness to be found, she is developing ways for the blind to enjoy movies, stage shows, and television. Her project is the Movie Description for the Blind of the blockbuster film *Titanic*.

Be certain to state your mission clearly. If your mission is one of youth advocacy, identify basic resources you might provide, such as an ongoing relationship with a caring adult, a safe place, structured activities in after-school hours, the teaching of marketable skills through effective education, and encouraging giving back through community service. "A healthy start will lead to a productive and happy future" could describe a youth advocacy mission.

Enlisting the support of well-known individuals or celebrities will boost any project's media coverage and create greater public awareness for the cause. Having an actor or actress narrate or introduce an announcement or event—or simply be present—adds to the attendance and excitement of your message or event. Depending on the current news circumstances, having a well-known politician participate in a program will add additional media coverage for your event as well as for the cause. Also, the presence of luminaries enhances the effectiveness of a video or film clip.

For example, Houston's ABC Channel 13's "The Debra Duncan Show" had its highest rating when doing a program about thyroid disease in support of an upcoming fundraiser. Duncan interviewed the founder of The Thyroid Society and several high-profile individuals who gave testimonials about how the disease had affected their lives. Her audience was filled with other people with thyroid disease, volunteers, and individuals who wanted more information about the disease. The society received more than four hundred calls from the viewing audience as a result of the television show.

As a marketing tool to enlighten prospective donors about the cause, send a tape to potential sponsors who might consider participating in the event. For example, Knoll Laboratories manufactures thyroid medicine, so the company views its partnering with the Thyroid Society as a way of helping those who suffer with thyroid disease.

How to Work with a Public Relations Firm

If a public relations firm has generously offered to assist your organization in-kind, remember you are still the client. When getting together for that initial meeting, make certain the agency has a full understanding of your organization's mission, the expectations you have for the event, and the anticipated net result.

At the initial meeting, invite key committee members to share their ideas. One of your goals might be to reach as many new benefactors as possible on a national level. Discuss how and why to make it happen—does the organization need stronger identity, would a logo help, do we stand out from the crowd, what innovations can we bring to the organization? Determine the most effective course— to appear on talk shows, travel to nearby cities, plan a retreat, or bring in a speaker? Once the media plan is in place, it is important to stay in regular contact with the agency to get updates and assess how the agreed upon plan is working.

An enthusiastic staff member or committee volunteer who has some journalistic talent can help generate public awareness in the local newspapers, periodicals, magazines, radio, and television news. Such a media volunteer can create a pitch with a basic script about the organization. She should be able to express it verbally as well as present it in writing to the media. The media volunteer should give each media group a different point on which to focus. When writing a press release, liken it to a road map—go off the path, but stay on the main road. For instance, you might discuss the importance of supporting the cause, as well as how commitment can bring about change. Make the media believe in your cause through your enthusiasm, and the media will reach a mass audience with your organization's message. Write the way you speak. If you get blocked, talk into a recorder and then transcribe. Turn nonbelievers into benefactors and in-kind donors.

A benefit of using an advertising agency or public relations firm is its ability to gain national recognition for your event. Philanthropy endeavors are often featured in *Town & Country* magazine, *The New York Times*, *W* magazine, *Philanthropy World*, and *Brilliant*, to name a few.

Encourage the staff at the public relations firm to be a part of the event. Perhaps the firm could loan your organization a staff member to work with you and your committees on event publicity, further bonding the firm to your organization.

Frequently Asked Questions About Public Relations

- **Who needs public relations and why?** An organization may apply public relations strategies to support specific objectives, such as establishing awareness, increasing revenue, communicating a message, or influencing community behavior.
- **How does public relations differ from advertising and marketing?** Your marketing program should encompass many disciplines, such as advertising, public relations, direct sales, and sales promotions to meet your short- and long-term goals. Advertising is paid communication from an identified sponsor using mass media to persuade or influence an audience. This usually involves the creation and placement of advertising campaigns in a variety of media, such as billboards, newspapers, magazines, television, the Internet, and radio.

continued

Frequently Asked Questions About Public Relations (continued)

Typically, public relations programs do not use paid media, but the goal (to persuade or influence a target audience) is the same. Make a proposal to a public relations firm for its services pro-bono. Public relations programs can be implemented to support marketing, advertising, and sales initiatives.

- **If public relations is not advertising, how does it work?** Public relations programs support your marketing goals by identifying specific opportunities to reach your key target audiences. Programs vary depending upon goals, time, budget, and resources. Specific strategies are extremely varied and include press releases to the media, newsletters to key target audiences, speaking opportunities, special events, and cross promotions.

- **How do you guarantee results?** Results are not guaranteed. The client and the public relations firm agree on specific goals, objectives, and actions. These are implemented and then evaluated. Much like visiting a physician, a diagnosis and recommendations are made, but treatment options vary. Public relation firms work with you to accomplish the desired results. The best way to achieve success is through consistent communication and clear goals.

- **How much does public relations cost?** Public relations professionals charge for their services, like any other professionals do. These fees can be assessed as a retainer, special project, or hourly rate. Typically, a letter of agreement detailing the arrangement clarifies the relationship. In such an arrangement, out-of-pocket expenses also are reimbursed.

PHOTOGRAPHY AND VIDEOGRAPHY

For pre-events and the main event, prepare a "shot list" in advance of the event so the professional, staff, or talented volunteer photographer will know whose images to capture. If a volunteer or staff member is not available to escort a photographer, you might ask the photographer to carry a small recorder to capture the names of those being photographed. Request the photographer to shoot both color and black-and-white images, and to have the contact sheets or prints back as soon as possible in order to meet various press deadlines. (In addition to arranging for your organization's own photographs of the event, you should assign a volunteer to members of the press or media photographers covering the event to point out key supporters and distinguished guests. Walk all members of the media through your event so they are familiar with all of the elements.)

As soon as the photos are developed, you need to identify the subjects in the photographs. Members of the organization staff, fellow chairpersons, and the publicity/media chairman can assist you in getting the photographs identified and to the press.

Forward the photographs of the event chair, committee chairs, honoree, high-profile guests, volunteers, major benefactors, and in-kind donors, along with a post-event press release, to local print media. Follow-up with a phone call to make certain that they have received everything they need by print deadline. Always have the subject(s) name, title, and any other pertinent data (such as event title and date) labeled from left to right on the back of the photograph. If you want the photos returned, include a self-addressed stamped envelope.

VIPs and major benefactors will enjoy being included for a photo opportunity with the guest speaker at a pre-reception before a luncheon, tea, or dinner event. These same photographs can be sent to benefactors with a nice note, kept in the organization's archives, or used in a monthly newsletter. This is a nice way of saying thank-you to those benefactors, who will remember the event when they receive their photo with the honored guest.

Taking candid shots at an event is okay, but most people prefer their best angle if a photograph is being sent to magazines or newspapers. You want pictures to say something about the event. For instance, you can set up a shot of event-goers standing by an auction exhibit, holding an award, standing by a centerpiece, or with the emcee at the podium. These photos help to share your event with others.

A new trend is for photographers who cover special events to set up their own Web sites that feature photos and contact sheets by event and date. Individuals, as well as organizations, can order the shots they want online. This saves time and is cost efficient for the organization since benefactors can review and order shots directly. Also, the media can view the photos and make their choices. The media make their selections and give requests directly to the organization. However, this method is more difficult as there are many pages of photographs, and they may not be identified in detail. Another option is to order the photographs on CD. Or, you may prefer the standard way of receiving the proofs or contact sheets so you can identify subjects in photos and place orders at the same time.

Ways of Gathering Potential Support

- Positive organization staff support
- Letter writing campaign
- Articulate spokesperson
- Press releases
- Newsletters
- Calendar listing of event in print media
- Press conference
- Radio and television coverage, including news or talk show host programs
- Web site
- Compelling video

 *Chapter Ten*

BRINGING BENEFACTORS ON BOARD

*"We are each of us angels with only one wing, and
we can only fly by embracing one another."*
—LUCIANO DE CRESCENZO

All events need seed money to initially fund an event, whether it's for buying crepe paper for an elementary school carnival or making a deposit on a hotel venue for a lavish gala. Finding potential underwriters is the way to begin. At this time, your current benefactors come into play, and efforts to find new people to support the cause are begun.

Don't knock on the same donor door for every fund drive, special event, and campaign that the organization sponsors. You can't rely on the same list for every mailing. Instead, cultivate new prospects for each event. Find a program to match a donor's interest. If you're courting a sports-fan donor, he could enjoy fundraising that's aimed at building a new stadium, improving the level of professors at a college, or growing a college's national prestige.

BENEFACTOR PACKAGES

Benefactor Letter
The benefactor letter is a conversation with prospective donors explaining why it is important for them to support your organiza-

tion's cause and fundraising efforts. Make the letters as personable as possible. Have the "you's" outnumber the "we's." Touch their hearts. Be specific about the ask, but leave an option. Write the way you talk. Visualize someone with whom you feel comfortable, and imagine you're directing your appeal to that one person. Make the prospective benefactor understand the importance of the cause. Remember, no matter how many letters you write, view each one as a personal communication between you and the reader.

Don't send letters with the "Dear Friend" salutation. People tend to disregard form letters. To personally involve the reader, your letter needs to create an emotional bond between the reader's giving and the mission of the organization. Psychologically, the readers must feel the success of the campaign rests on their participation. Let them know you will be calling them to follow up on the letter and that you look forward to talking with them personally about subjects of mutual interest and concern.

People are not going to give simply because they're asked. If possible, tailor your letter to your reader's level of interest. Use words and expressions to help readers visualize your cause and to let your readers know exactly what you want them to do. Put action into your verbs. Your appeal should take into consideration why people give.

The letter should be no more than one to one-and-a-half pages in length. The first two paragraphs are important. Discuss the cause and enthusiastically share the organization's mission. Explain the goals of the organization's community outreach and illustrate its individual effectiveness. Let them know how the funds will be used.

Personally sign every letter. To emphasize to the readers of your benefactor letters that you have personally signed each one, use ink of a different color for your signature. If the letters are printed in black ink, then use a blue pen. Your willingness to sign several hundred letters and write personal notes indicates to the reader your strong commitment to the project.

August 11, 2003

Dear _____,

As President of the University of Houston Architecture Alumni Association (UHAAA), I have had the opportunity to work with many talented and enthusiastic people throughout the year to promote the greatness of the University of Houston and the Gerald D. Hines College of Architecture. Our premier annual event is at hand once again, and it is my pleasure to invite you to join Honorary Chair Carolyn Farb and the UHAAA for another special evening at this year's Blueprint Ball to be held on Saturday, October 18, 2003.

The Gerald D. Hines College of Architecture has remained focused on design as the fundamental activity of its discipline. Its 50 plus year history now includes the first cutting edge program in Industrial Design in Texas and the Southwestern United States. We are fortunate, with the college's long history of faculty expertise and world recognized lecturers, to have produced many exceptional architects and nationally recognized programs in design education. We are asking for your generosity in supporting the continued success of the College of Architecture and the Philip Johnson Endowment.

The Blueprint Ball will be held in the atrium of the College of Architecture, designed by renowned architect, Philip Johnson. To quote Johnson, "Architecture is sculpture that is inhabited." We will be honoring architect, Michael Rotondi, FAIA, a principal in RoTo Architects for his outstanding contributions to architecture and architectural education. Mr. Rotondi is co-recipient of the American Academy and Institute of Arts and Letters Award in Architecture.

In addition to our cocktail reception, silent auction, program, outstanding cuisine, and entertainment, we will have the drawing for the Porsche Cayenne that has been generously donated by Momentum Motors and Ricardo and Martine Weitz. We are presently offering raffle tickets at $100 per ticket for this exciting

continued

automobile. Only 1000 tickets will be sold. Should you wish to purchase tickets, please contact me at the numbers found on the enclosed fact sheet.

News 2 Anchor, Dominique Sachse will serve as our Mistress of Ceremonies. The funds raised will benefit the College of Architecture and the Philip Johnson Endowment. We hope we can count on your support and commitment to the College of Architecture. We anticipate a sell-out crowd of 500 guests, and encourage you to review the enclosed fact sheet and respond with the enclosed donor form at your earliest convenience.

We welcome your interest, so please feel free to contact Dean Joe Mashburn or me at the numbers available on the fact sheet. We would be happy to meet with you personally as well.

Best Regards,

Carl E. Penland, AIA
Blueprint Ball Chair

This is a good example of an effective benefactor letter.

Make your first sentence in a benefactor letter one that captures everyone's attention. "Share an evening with champions..." or "Honor a legend...." Announce a new and exciting venue that has never before been used. Celebrate a retail store opening. Showcase a couple of stellar auction items that will peak donors' interest. Let them know that additional information on the exciting silent and live auction items will be mailed soon.

Share the dates for pre-event activities. Talk about the honorees. Describe the cuisine the caterer will prepare for the event. Highlight the orchestra, dancing, or other special entertainment. Include a fact sheet and a brochure, if available, or any other supportive literature. Invite them to join you for coffee and a site visit if that would spark their enthusiasm.

March 8, 1996

Dear _____,

We'd like to share with you some information about a very special event, "Marvin's Million Dollar Dream" which will take place on Saturday evening August 24, 1996. This once in a life time event will jointly celebrate the grand occasion of Marvin Zindler's 75th birthday and the remarkable tenure of retiring M. D. Anderson Cancer Center President Dr. Charles A. LeMaistre. Dr. LeMaistre is a true visionary dedicated leader who has made lasting impressions wherever he has been. We stand in amazement at the commitment from one such great individual. Through his extraordinary leadership, M. D. Anderson Cancer Center has become the world's premiere Comprehensive Cancer Center. To put it briefly, Dr. LeMaistre has accomplished major miracles. We must continue his legacy.

We are privileged to have been asked to lead this challenging event! We are totally dedicated to our goal of raising $1 million for prostate and breast cancer research—two programs that may affect us all. The money that we will raise at this million-dollar event will strengthen research initiatives at M. D. Anderson and facilitate bold new healthcare solutions to improve the outcome for all men and women who are diagnosed with the devastating diseases of prostate or breast cancer.

We have set our goal high because the facts about cancer are so frightening and the research is so costly. Every minute counts—in the United States, 3 men are diagnosed with prostate cancer every 5 minutes and more that 47,000 will die from the disease in 1996 alone. Conversely, a woman is diagnosed with breast cancer every 3 minutes and every 11 minutes a woman dies from the disease. With your financial commitment we can make "Marvin's Million Dollar Dream" a reality.

The Hyatt Regency Grand Ballroom will be the venue for the event. The star-studded evening and audience will be expertly coproduced by Pace Entertainment and KTRK-Channel 13. As plans take shape,

continued

the festivities will begin at 7p.m. with a "dream" auction of 100 items and a reception in the foyer of the Grand Ballroom. Harry Sheppard, Vibraphonist, will provide the music during the reception. An exquisite dinner will be the prelude to an evening of entertainment with a world renowned performer. A number of celebrities and dignitaries are invited to attend, many who have been directly or indirectly touched by this disease, and we look forward to their participation. We have enclosed an event fact sheet to familiarize you with our plans, and hopefully you'll be inspired to make an underwriting commitment at this time. We will be practicing Carolyn's "zero budget" philosophy so that all of our funds go directly into research and not expenses.

We all have our causes to contemplate, but the research work at M. D. Anderson is monumental and deserves careful consideration. Cancer is a life and death matter. We hope you will respond affirmatively to our appeal for underwriting support and join us as we begin our journey of raising $1 million for prostate and breast cancer research. A description of benefits at the various underwriting levels is included. If you have any questions please call Carolyn at (555) 555-5555. Mary Kathryn Cooper or Laurie Selzer of M. D. Anderson Cancer Center's Development Office may also answer any questions you may have and can be reached at (555) 555-5555.

We thank you for your thoughtful consideration. We hope you will be joining us in fullfilling "Marvin's Million Dollar Dream." Your involvement will be a treasured gift to M. D. Anderson Cancer Center. We eagerly await your decision in joining us in this battle against cancer and thank you for your thoughtful consideration.

Sincerely,

Carolyn Farb   Marvin Zindler   John Doe
Chairman   Birthday Boy   Honorary "Dollar
                                              Dream" Committee
                                              Chair

The strong appeal in this benefactor letter can serve as a good model for your own.

Be sure to include the statistics. For example, when discussing fundraising to combat a disease, donors want to know the number of people who suffer from this illness, your goal (such as research to find a cure), and how lives of people affected by the disease can be improved. For example: "One in every three thousand babies is born with Neurofibromatosis. NF is the most common neurological disease caused by a single gene. Fifty percent of children inherit the disease from a parent. The other 50 percent are the result of a spontaneous mutation. Three ways the Texas Neurofibromatosis Foundation uses your donations are to enhance patient outreach programs, to fund vital research programs to find a treatment and a cure, and to provide support."

Describe the substance of your organization's work. The readers will want to know what your organization does, who sponsors and supports it, and who benefits from it and how they benefit. New prospective benefactors need enough information to appreciate the worthiness, need, and value of your cause. Demonstrate to the readers that your organization has widespread support. Let them know of individual and corporate support that your organization receives. Include a brochure, newsletter, or piece of media coverage that illustrates programs and services being offered as well as success stories. Show what their gift will accomplish and tell them why your organization is deserving of their support.

Any benefactor letter, save-the-date card, or pre-event invitation encouraging support should include a personal note from the chairperson. This will get a donor's attention and further share your commitment to the project. Mention how your organization will create a better quality of life for an individual or group, and discuss the programs that will be funded as a result of their contribution at this event. Let donors know how they can share in resolving the problem and how much the organization is relying on their support. You might also provide a simple breakdown of what each dollar amount donated will provide.

A note from the chairperson can strengthen your message.

When sending a written request to a corporate contact, be sure you know who should receive the correspondence and verify the individual's proper title. There can be a shifting of job positions in large companies, and last year's contact may have moved up the corporate ladder or moved on. It's worth doing the research to determine which representative of the organization should sign the letter making the donation request to the company's decision-making board. A follow-up call to that contact is essential in showing your commitment to the cause. The recipient will consider the request and also the professional manner in which it has been made. The letter may then be forwarded to a corporation's contribution committee for consideration.

Goals For Your Fundraising Letter Appeal

- Motivate—Include incentives or facts of interest to inspire people to support the cause and attend the event.
- Congregate—Network with friends, associates, and high-profile personalities from the city's civic, sports, corporate, medical, and socio-economic communities.
- Salivate—Mention inspiring speakers, exciting high-profile personalities, sterling programs, entertainment, music, great food and wine, and favors.
- Stimulate—Include video presentations containing motivating speeches and footage of your events, complete with any entertainment and unusual decorations.
- Congratulate—Highlight honorees, outstanding awards presentations, outstanding benefactors, good deeds, and winning volunteers.
- Initiate—Recognize positive role models from corporate and philanthropic America.
- Illuminate—Highlight categories of generosity in relation to the overall theme and goal of the campaign. Create imaginative names for the categories of giving, and offer reasonable perks.
- Agitate—Get the energy going; get the adrenaline flowing.
- Activate—Make your reservation to sponsor a table or buy individual tickets, and encourage others to do the same.

Fact Sheet

A fact sheet should be included with your letter in the benefactor package. This provides a detailed, one-page account of the upcoming event. Update the fact sheet with new details and information as the event progresses, giving names of major benefactors, special guests and celebrities, and donors of auction items or other services. Keep the information fresh.

HoustonPBS
50th Anniversary Gala
Honoring the Legacy of Hugh Roy Cullen

Join us as we celebrate 50 years of excellence in broadcasting,
while we "Set the Stage" for the future of HoustonPBS/Channel 8!

Who, What, Where, When, & Why...

Who
- Honoring the legacy of the late Hugh Roy Cullen, the original founder and benefactor of public television in Houston
- Mary Lou Retton-Kelley, Honorary Chair
- Sara and Brad Howell, Gala Co-Chairs

What
- Chic sound-studio décor including authentically reproduced set stages from PBS shows
- Vignette performances by noted PBS television and recording artists - guaranteed to delight and entertain!
- Cocktail Reception with HoustonPBS Celebrity Chefs
- Elegant, seated black-tie dinner by Connoisseur
- Show and Dinner in our specially-designed "Sound Stage" Ballroom
- After-dinner dancing

When
- Saturday, May 17th, 2003
- Reception: 6:00
- Dinner and Show: 7:30
- Dancing after the Show

Where
- The fabulous new Reliant Center

Why
- To support on-going quality educational programming to over 1,000,000 households in the Houston area (at least $8M per year);
- Assist with the digital conversion mandated by the federal government
- Purchase software integral to contributor relationship management.
- Community Education & Outreach

Need additional information? Contact Jane Doe, 555-555-5555, jane@doe.com

A good fact sheet is concise but packed with information.

Fact Sheet Components

- **What:** Format of the event—"black tie fundraising gala," honoree, auction, name of chair.
- **Why:** Purpose—"to extend outreach programs benefiting the community and broaden opera audiences."
- **Who:** Who will be attending—"group of cultural and philanthropic benefactors, both corporations and individuals."
- **When:** Date, also add schedule of evening—"Reception 7:00 p.m.–8:30 p.m., Dinner 8:30 p.m., Dancing 10:30 p.m."
- **Where:** Location, valet instructions.
- **Underwriting Levels:** Table sponsorship levels plus individual levels.
- **For more information contact:** Name of chair or director of special events.

MAKING THE PERSONAL CONTACT

To help make your event a success, the event's chairperson or an underwriting committee chair should personally contact potential underwriters and table sponsors after the benefactor packages have been sent. Never rely on invitations that are mailed six weeks in advance of an event to sell out your event. Invitations won't ensure success! The event needs to be at least three-quarters sold out before the invitations are even dropped in the mail. Work at least six months—and preferably a year—in advance of your event to achieve your goal. You should begin planning shortly after the previous year's big event has taken place.

Prospective benefactors and, in particular, those who give to other causes receive many requests for funding from nonprofit organizations. A personal call can make the difference. The event chair should organize the call list and determine which calls she will be making personally and the ones that will be made by committee members. If someone on the event committee has a personal or business relationship with a prospective benefactor, then he should make the call.

Make it easy for your volunteer committee members to make those follow-up calls for funding requests. Provide them with pertinent information about each of their contacts in advance of their call. Provide a record of previous support—the amount and time of the contact's last donation (if known). Instruct them not to be timid when asking for the contribution and to make the "ask" clear. Remind them to show appreciation and gratitude on behalf of the cause or individuals being served by their contribution. They should accept a negative response in a gracious and hopeful manner.

In the future, the organization will be able to build on the relationship that you and your team of volunteers initiate if you handled such calls properly. Be serious about your ask and sincere in your thank you.

Written Confirmations

If your follow-up phone call on the benefactor letter results in an affirmative agreement, write a thank-you letter at your earliest convenience acknowledging the benefactor's commitment. Your benefactor may decide to wait until he gets a formal invitation in the mail before sending a check or credit card payment. A verbal commitment prior to the printing deadline will allow you to include that individual's name or company in the invitation.

You may go ahead and send an invoice acknowledging the commitment; just bear in mind that your donor may choose not to pay prior to the event. Inform your donor about important pre-event dates to schedule on her calendar. Emphasize how meaningful her attendance is for pre-event activities as well as the gala event. Options for payment include payment prior to the event or payment afterward (or even, for tax purposes, by a certain date in the next year).

 *Chapter Eleven*

PRE-EVENTS

"If opportunity doesn't knock, build a door."
—MILTON BERLE

Once the time, place, theme, and entertainment for the main event are in place, you should begin planning one or more pre-events for the people who have committed to support your cause and as a means of attracting new supporters. Begin by simply putting your ideas on paper. Think about the reason you are hosting a function and the message you are trying to impart to those who will be attending. Is your goal to acknowledge the generosity of key individuals or corporate donors? Is it to build enthusiasm and heighten awareness for the upcoming event?

MAKING THE PARTIES PURPOSEFUL

Take time to create the content and theme of the pre-event. Take into consideration that most people receive too many invitations and have too little time. Make their commitment to your organization a meaningful decision for them.

Benefactor receptions bring individuals together in support of a common cause and offer the opportunity to recognize outstanding individuals and corporations with words of appreciation and grati-

tude. This is the perfect occasion to present underwriters with benefactor gifts. It's important to include key committee members and
dedicated volunteers in the circle of philanthropy. A reception builds
momentum for the upcoming event as well as awareness of your
organization. Reinforce your cause at any gathering, and always try
to leave supporters encouraged and motivated.

With a series of pre-events leading up to a major fundraiser, try to
schedule some of the events relating to the cause on-site (on campus,
at the performance hall, or in the museum for instance). Any opportunity you have to reinforce the mission and purpose of your organization (inviting benefactors to a performance, introducing them to a
student benefiting from a scholarship, or showing them how medical
research is creating a better quality of life for patients) benefits your
organization's goals.

Benefactors who have made early commitments to your main event
should be invited to every pre-event and included in any pre-publicity
to recognize their philanthropy and generosity. Suggest to benefactors
that they invite to the pre-party friends and associates who might be
interested and want to know more about the cause. At pre-events, in-
kind donors (caterer, florist, Web designer, printer, or retailer) can be
verbally thanked. This will make them feel appreciated and ready to
say yes to the next event. The chair also should take this opportunity
to give an update on lead sponsors, table sales, exciting auction items,
Web site progress, new information regarding the event, or any
impending deadlines (for printing, auction items, etc.). Explain how
early credit card registration will make check-in a breeze and will
facilitate checkout at the actual function. Your guests will appreciate
not having to wait in line to take home their purchases.

A pre-event gives guests an idea of what to anticipate at the main
event and helps you and your organization to recognize areas in
which the event needs to be fine-tuned. For example, if your big
event is an auction and you are planning to preview auction items at
the pre-event, this will give you a sense of any issues that may have

to be addressed. If you have jewelry as auction items, for instance, you'll discover that you need good lighting and forms to properly display them. This is a perfect way for auction volunteers to understand what their responsibilities will be, especially if any early bids on the previewed auction items are being made or if centerpieces or raffle tickets are being sold at the pre-event.

Since many of the guests invited may not know the venue host, the honoree, or the key members of the organization, name tags will make introductions easier. Keep the entertainment at a conversational level, as functions like this are conducive to networking. These events give people a great opportunity to bond with one another and at the same time make a commitment to your organization.

If the invitations for the main event are already printed at the time of the pre-event, give guests a handful, along with information about the organization. It's a good way to get the message out to prospective attendees. Don't be afraid to reach out. People want to be involved and are waiting to be asked.

Pre-event invitations can be informal. This is especially true when the event is held in someone's home. The invitation should inform guests of the nature of the event, when and where the event will be held, and what the attire will be. You also should provide a contact number or e-mail address at the nonprofit to take the RSVPs.

BUILDING EXCITEMENT

Introduce the Theme
Once you decide on the theme for your main event, you can begin layering that theme with the type of music, entertainment, or menu for your pre-events. With subsequent pre-events, continue to build your theme, and excitement will increase with each one. For example, if the main event has a Latin theme, bring in strolling mariachis at a pre-event reception.

When I chaired "Night at the Alhambra," we had a flamenco guitarist at one pre-event, displayed Moorish-style candelabra centerpieces that were part of the ball décor with pashminas that complimented the gala's table coverings at another, and had a flamenco dance troop performing at a third. These nuances and details go a long way toward making pre-events successful and fun. For another pre-event, a reception at a new restaurant was hosted on a Sunday so that full attention could be given to the organization. The menu reflected the spirit of Alhambra with tapas and sangria with fresh peaches. For the business owner, it was a chance to introduce his restaurant to a new group of patrons. This is what I call layering.

The Rogelio Rodriquez Flamenco Dance Company at this "A Night at the Alhambra" pre-event brought the theme to life.

A Grown-up's Scavenger Hunt

Another idea for an unusual pre-event is to pile guests into cars for a scavenger hunt. You might even look into getting fancy cars supplied by a local auto dealer for the occasion. Approach specialty stores about participating in your event; for retailers to partner with a charitable organization is good for the pre-event budget. Guests can then look for clues that lead from one store to another. Retailers can have a fish bowl of clues from which each guest selects one and moves about the store to solve the riddle. Whoever finds the prize keeps it.

An Event at an Art Gallery

When your organization partners with an artist and/or gallery for a pre-event, see if the artist or gallery will consider donating a percentage of sales—10 percent might be an appropriate donation, for instance. Signage in the gallery should acknowledge the percent contribution being donated to the nonprofit. It is also helpful to have volunteers and staff circulating throughout the crowd with information sheets about the art. They can answer questions about the artwork, arrange an introduction with the artist, and post a sale-pending sticker on an item that may be under serious consideration. If there is a large crowd, volunteers can assist with locating individuals for photo opportunities.

People need to be motivated to participate on behalf of the cause. In the brief pre-event program, acknowledge all of the individuals who made the evening possible. The master of ceremonies should introduce the artist, the gallery owner, the chair of the special event, and a representative from the nonprofit organization.

Pre-Events in Other Cities

When trying to raise awareness for an organization that is based in another city or state, e.g. the American Film Institute in Los Angeles, California, a pre-event can be held to help potential benefactors learn about the organization. The development director of the organization should travel to cities that are in close proximity within a state—such as Houston, Dallas/Fort Worth, and Austin—to enlist a chair/coordinator in each city. In this example, through mutual friends, John Campbell, the Development Director of the American Film Institute, decided this would be a way to broaden the donor base for the organization. Generally, the AFI's pre-events at other locations are hosted in a private home with a member of AFI's board of trustees as the guest speaker. Such events help introduce potential donors to the AFI Life Achievement Award, which is given annually to honor excellence in a career through the conferral of Honorary Degrees in Fine Arts, Humane Letters, and Communication Arts. Visitors then learn how the AFI further catalogs and preserves American films produced during various time frames, hosts the International Film Festival, and innovates new media ventures. At the benefactor table level of $35,000, guests are seated with actors

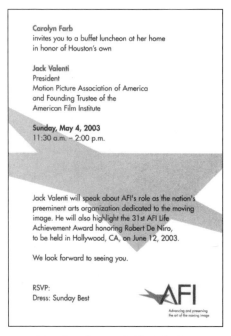

Carolyn Farb
invites you to a buffet luncheon at her home
in honor of Houston's own

Jack Valenti
President
Motion Picture Association of America
and Founding Trustee of the
American Film Institute

Sunday, May 4, 2003
11:30 a.m. – 2:00 p.m.

Jack Valenti will speak about AFI's role as the nation's preeminent arts organization dedicated to the moving image. He will also highlight the 31st AFI Life Achievement Award honoring Robert De Niro, to be held in Hollywood, CA, on June 12, 2003.

We look forward to seeing you.

RSVP:
Dress: Sunday Best

AFI

Advancing and preserving
the art of the moving image

The clean format of this invitation
worked well for this pre-event.

or other distinguished industry individuals. Those who make the commitment to AFI are invited to attend additional events throughout the year in various cities.

Pre-events as PR Opportunities

Use your pre-parties to generate additional community interest. Hire a photographer and send photos to local media with a press release. See what kind of press you might generate from this event. This keeps your event and cause before the public. The photos then can be put together in a collage format thanking the host or restaurant on a page in the event program or newsletter. Scanning the event

A pre-event photo collage like this one can
enhance your event program or newsletter.

photographs and press releases to send electronically will eliminate steps in getting information to the media. Be aware that you don't want to eclipse your media coverage for the main event by scheduling a pre-event too close to that date. The media could feel that they're already given your organization sufficient coverage, when in fact the best news is yet to come.

ACKNOWLEDGING YOUR IN-KIND DONORS

Whenever there is an opportunity, acknowledge the appropriate in-kind donors on the outside of a mailing piece such as a newsletter, back flap of an invitation, or in the surtitles at an opera before and/or during intermission. A specified number of tickets to a concert, reserved orchestra-level setting, a full-page ad in concert program, or an announcement from the stage at the performance are other gestures of appreciation. Recognize benefactors on a CD cover as underwriters or give them complimentary CDs. Celebrate a corporate gift with a donor profile in your newsletter or playbill. You can never thank donors enough.

It truly would not be possible to put on gala fundraising events without the in-kind support of floral designers, retailers who donate to the silent and live auctions, and printing and paper companies that print invitations, programs, and newsletters. Show your personal appreciation by giving those donors your patronage and support throughout the year. For example, if a caterer or restaurant group has offered to underwrite a benefactor dinner, you can repay their generosity by recommending them to your friends or associates. If a restaurant hosts an evening or donates a wine cellar dinner for an auction, gather a group of friends and patronize that establishment. Showing your appreciation in this way will help build long-lasting relationships with in-kind donors.

A corporate donor will want to know the ways in which the company will be acknowledged. Have these points of appreciation clearly defined in your letter before your meeting or telephone conversation. You can always create ways to recognize donors depending on the size of their gift. Be prepared to meet several times when making a proposal for a large gift.

A formal thank-you letter can serve a dual purpose when it includes the date and amount of a gift and the estimated value of benefits for federal income tax purposes. In thank-you letters you should acknowledge tax-deductible contributions, let your donors know exactly how their gift will be used, and reiterate the cause their gift will support. Send a centerpiece, event photos, or favors that may be held in reserve to show appreciation to in-kind donors.

 *Chapter Twelve*

PLANNING AN AUCTION

"The man who has no imagination has no wings."
—MUHAMMAD ALI

Some cities respond to auctions; others don't. What works well in Dallas might not fly in Seattle. While some people like silent auctions, others might prefer live auctions, especially if the auctioneer is a sports figure, an actor, or a popular politician. My friend Robin Leach, former host of the television series *Lifestyles of the Rich and Famous*, added his magic to one of my fundraisers as he challenged guests to bid on luxurious items and auctioned in his inimitable style. You could create the same effect in your own community by asking your mayor or a local sports hero to help host your event.

ACQUIRING AUCTION ITEMS

To boost your list of prospective donors and provide additional ideas for auction packages, your organization's executive director, board members, and chairs should attend other organizations' events. This will give your group a good indication of who is donating auction items (as well as who is buying them) and which items have the most bidder appeal. You can also scan media coverage of such events for major donors and attendees.

Donor Letters

Be creative in preparing letters to your prospective auction donors. Inform them of the innovative ways you will highlight their giving—Web site; online bidding; auction catalog; recognition in the invitation, program, and print and electronic media; and invitations to pre-events where their in-kind generosity will be recognized. Increased publicity on the Web site may encourage in-kind donors to commit their auction items early.

Don't forget to ask auction donors to supply any logos or letterhead designs they may want to incorporate into their auction item presentation. On your donor form, it is important to specify that the charitable contribution becomes the property of the organization—including all rights, title, and interest, once the contribution has been made.

March 8, 1996

Mrs. John Doe
123 Any Street
Houston, TX

Dear Mr. Doe,

Marvin's Million Dollar Dream is a "once in a life time" fundraising effort that will raise funds to support prostate and breast research programs at M. D. Anderson Cancer Center. This event celebrates the occasion of Marvin's 75th birthday and the remarkable tenure of Dr. Charles A. LeMaistre. Our dream is to raise one million dollars.

We have set our goal high because the facts about cancer are so frightening and research is so costly. Every minute counts—in the United States 3 men are diagnosed with prostate cancer every 5 minutes and more than 47,000 will die from the disease in 1996 alone. Conversely, a woman is diagnosed with breast cancer every 3

continued

---

minutes and every 11 minutes a women dies from the disease. With your in-kind donation of an item or service to our silent auction, we can make "Marvin's Million Dollar Dream" a reality.

We are holding the event in the Hyatt Regency Grand Ballroom and through the collaboration of Pace Entertainment and KTRK Channel 13, we will have a world renowned performer. A number of celebrities and dignities are invited to attend, many who have been directly or indirectly touched by cancer. An event fact sheet is enclosed to inform you about our plans and hopefully inspire you to be a part of our auction of 100 items. The bidding on each item or service will begin at one-half of the retail value of the item or service. We will be practicing the "zero budget philosophy" so that all funds go to research and not expenses.

We are planning to mail 5,000 invitations. You and your company will be recognized in the invitation, official extravaganza program, and other printed material. Without donors such as yourself, our goal would be impossible to reach. Other plans for recognition through KTRK - Channel 13 are under consideration and you will be informed as soon as they are finalized.

We sincerely hope you will join us in fulfilling "Marvin's Million Dollar Dream," our salute to Dr. Charles A. LeMaistre, and the funding of breast and prostate cancer research programs. You may contact Connie Cooke at 555-1234.

Warmest regards,

Carolyn Farb

A simple, innovative donor letter can go a long way.

Follow-up Calls

Give potential in-kind donors a reasonable amount of time to respond to your letter before following up with a call. The follow-up call to the prospective donor can bring results. Making the call shows your level of commitment to the cause and makes that prospective donor feel important to the success of the event. Showing your appreciation and personal involvement is meaningful to others and will encourage their donation. You can develop an ongoing relationship with the donor who will support the cause.

DONORS' EXPECTATIONS

When picking up auction items from donors, remember you represent the organization, so be courteous and appreciative. Items should be picked up by a committee member, not a courier or delivery service—unless, of course, the item is a piano or something equally heavy or bulky. Using a courier service to pick up auction items gives the wrong message, as well as creating a potential security situation. Donors may perceive that you are spending funds needlessly rather than focusing on raising them. The hands-on approach is always a plus. If an intermediary is involved in the transfer, an item could be lost or stolen without anyone having an explanation.

In preparing for one auction I was involved with, a volunteer on an auction committee picked up an expensive watch that had been donated to an event by a jeweler. The volunteer gave the donated item to the concierge in the building where she lived to be picked up by a delivery service. She should have taken the item to the storage herself or hand-delivered it to the silent auction co-chair, because the watch never made it to the intended destination. No one had the answer, and the disappearance was a mystery. The chairman of the event had to explain this loss to the donor. The only way to avoid such problems is to deliver the item in person to the auction committee chair. It is the unspoken agreement to the donor who made the donation, as well as to the charitable organization. Don't take shortcuts.

Secure Your Treasures

If there are a reasonable amount of auction items, they can be stored securely at a volunteer's home until the event. With auction items that require more space and delicate handling, you need to arrange for a climate-controlled storage space and carefully move the items, after first wrapping and labeling them.

A storage facility may consider giving your nonprofit a discounted rate since you will be using it for a limited time period. If possible, find a professional moving company that will donate its services to pick up items from a central location, transport the items to the storage space, and later move them to the venue destination. Make certain that auction items reach the auction destination at the venue in the condition in which they were originally received. No one wants to take home damaged porcelain, a painting that has been scratched, or chipped picture frames; every item needs to be in mint condition.

Consider placing ushers at strategic locations during the silent auction reception to keep an eye on the auction items. Although you trust your guests, most events are held in public locations where things might disappear. An extra pair of eyes will help prevent loss. Be sure to keep all original packing and crating materials and store them at the event under the display tables or in a storage space designated by the venue. The original box or wrappings makes it easy for the bidders to transport items home.

Preview the Goods

Include auction items at pre-events where auction donors will be present and you can acknowledge their in-kind generosity. In-kind donors generally are not invited to attend the main event unless they are donating a major item such as a car, an exotic trip, or an extravagant piece of jewelry. Try to include the event's auction donors in at least one or more of the pre-events as a thank you. The more visibility and greater exposure you give in-kind donors, the more appreciated they feel and the more they will want to participate. A donor may have special requests, especially if the item is a car. The car dealership may ask to have the car on view at different pre-events, displayed in front of the venue site, and featured on slides projected before and during the live auction. The auction chair needs to handle these requests. Always be thinking of creative ways to present each of the items at your auction.

Multicultural Events

Be considerate of cultural differences. When your event draws a diverse, multicultural crowd, you may need to make arrangements to offer your auction rules in a second language. It would be helpful to provide your international guests with a brief explanation of how the auctions work and instructions for participation that have been translated into their language. This can be included in the event program. Sometimes the rapid-fire action during a live auction or the noise in the room makes it difficult for everyone to understand and participate. You never know who your high bidder will be, and you want to welcome every opportunity.

E-Auctions

Technology plays an important role when there is a silent or live action component to an event. Your Web site design and layout should reflect the overall theme of the actual event. Offer donor-friendly information for registering and bidding online. For those who might not be on the mailing list of the organization and would like to preview a printed catalog, offer instructions on how to obtain one.

Use the Internet to allow the public to preview your auction items, as well to place early bids. Have all of the prebids sent to a designated e-mail address, phone, or fax number. Enter all of the prebids on the bid sheets at the event by a determined cutoff time.

Recognizing the value of the Web and the potential for increased visibility for the event, I approached a firm called Idea Integration with a proposal on behalf of Houston Grand Opera (HGO) asking them to support "A Night at the Alhambra" by creating and underwriting an online auction component. My goal was to raise $1.4 million for the fifty-year old program, which was recently called "the world's leading presenter of new operas." To do it, I had to challenge myself and think beyond traditional methods.

I met with Idea's Web designer, the HGO development director, and other stakeholders to create a Web site, www.operaball2001.idea.com, which featured a mini eBay site allowing online bids. One of the featured auction items was a guitar from musician Don Henley, autographed by all the members of The Eagles. The site offered multiple views of the items, real-time bidding, event registration, and online donations to HGO. We used a cutting-edge Web presence to draw attention to the event and drive bids up for the 150 auction items that were separated into designated categories for bidding. The site allowed us to extend the event to a broader audience, as indicated by the 73,708 hits the site generated over one month prior to the event.

Idea Integration designed, built, and maintained the custom HGO auction site in a presentation that was consistent with the printed invitations and programs. Idea even created a looping video using the colors, tone, and brand established on the Web site. This video was available online and also played with audio throughout the event on flat-panel monitors mounted in the corners of the ballroom. The high-tech touches created another expanded dimension to the most successful ball in the history of Houston Grand Opera.

If your online bidding continues until the auction begins at the actual event, you need to have a computer set up with several bid runners to post the online bids onto the bid sheets. The number of computers you would need depends on the number of active online bidders already registered and those you anticipate, but you will usually require only one. Check to see if the venue for your event has an Internet connection available for your organization's use. Don't wait until the last minute to work out these details.

With the popularity of Web sites, registering and bidding online gives auction donors additional visibility and encourages early commitment of items to be put up for auction. Knowing that the lucky high bidders will be posted on the Web site after the event offers an additional incentive as donors become aware of the increased publicity they will receive for their generosity. Again, don't miss the opportunity to capture the number of hits and any information about visitors to the nonprofit Web site—name, telephone number, address, or e-mail address. This will help you expand your mailing lists and e-mail blasts.

TREASURE TROVE

Instead of presenting merchandise in an auction format, a new twist—one that falls somewhere between an auction and a raffle—is to set up a "treasure trove." First, approach potential in-kind donors to gather items similar to those that might be donated for an auction. These items then will be locked in individual treasure chests at your event. Guests can purchase keys—which are chances to open the treasure chest and win what's inside—in advance through a mailing, online, or by calling the nonprofit office. When guests arrive at the event, their names will have been registered, and they may exchange the replica key they received in the mail for one that could actually be the lucky key that opens a chest. To get things moving, benefactor table hosts might purchase a treasure key in advance for each guest. Guests can also purchase keys the night of the event. The advantage of preselling keys is to give the event's chairperson an idea of how well the concept is being received.

Retailers partnering with your organization could offer to host an in-store preview to create interest in buying keys to the treasure trove. You can organize a task force of volunteers to sell keys in advance by contacting guests who have made table reservations.

Keep the rules simple so guests will understand how a treasure trove works. Guests receive only one try with their key at any one of the available display cases. Once a key works or doesn't work, it is then given back to a volunteer in charge of the game. If a guest's key has opened the case, she wins what's inside or has the choice of one of several envelopes, inside each of which contains a description of a gift.

The gifts are available on site and are the winners' to take home. Items may not be returned to donors. In your event literature, be sure to inform your prospective guests of how many keys are being produced and their odds for winning. A thousand keys given out to open one of ten treasure chests will give you a ten-in-a-thousand chance of winning a fabulous gift from one of the generous contributors.

RAFFLES

Everyone enjoys the game of chance and the opportunity to win a lovely prize. Ask retailers such as jewelers, wine merchants, or local car dealers to participate by donating items. Drafting a letter that introduces the raffle, with an explanation of how it will work, helps sell this clever idea.

To offer raffle tickets on a large prize such as an automobile for a fundraiser, set up a hotline for information and ticket orders. In your correspondence and media promotion, let ticket purchasers know the total number of tickets being sold, because this allows them to evaluate the odds.

Note that raffle tickets are not tax-deductible. Items valued at $5,000 or more are subject to a 28 percent withholding tax. In the case of automobiles, specify if tax, title, and license are included.

You might place an ad to promote your raffle.

Tips for a Successful Raffle

- To defer mailing costs, hold raffle ticket stubs at the organization's office until the raffle drawing. If the number of tickets sold isn't too unwieldy, delivery may be an option. Have individuals' ticket numbers available in case a buyer calls the hotline with a question about his ticket.
- Make sure that volunteers return all unsold raffle tickets to the organization's office.
- Have volunteers write their name on the back of the raffle tickets they sell in case a discrepancy arises.
- Offer raffle ticket sellers a bonus for top sales—incentives might include an overnight stay at a luxury hotel, a spa day, a portrait photograph, or a $50 gift certificate to a smoothie shop.

 *Chapter Thirteen*

SILENT OR LIVE?

"We make a living by what we get.
We make a life by what we give."
—WINSTON CHURCHILL

An auction can stand alone as a major event or can serve as part of a larger-scale gala. When you are considering planning an auction to benefit your cause, you must carefully consider whether a silent or live auction would be best.

SILENT AUCTIONS

A silent auction is a very effective fundraising device, but you'll need to do everything you can to publicize this event in advance to make it successful. When a silent auction is planned as part of a major event, give potential bidders the opportunity to preview what you are offering—at pre-events, in the invitation mailing, in a catalog, via chair and committee member interviews on local talk shows, or in special listings in regional publications.

Make certain all bidders are aware of silent auction rules—if there is an identical bid, for example, the first bid received will get the item. Successful absentee bidders are notified by phone.

Allow plenty of time for a silent auction. By the time guests valet park and register to bid, if they haven't already done so online, the length of the reception has already been reduced for them. You'll want them to have plenty of bidding time, as well as time to socialize.

Get Creative with Your Catalog

Use your creativity to distinguish the different categories of silent auction items in your Silent Auction Catalog with interesting, eye-catching titles. If they are "Priceless Objects D'Art," make certain the objects are representative of the titles they are given. Items worthy of such a category might include jewelry designed by well-known jewelers, art by famous artists, a beautiful Faberge-styled evening bag, or a Chanticleer clock created by Vivian Tullos of Vivian Alexander. If you use titles in a language foreign to most of your guests, such as "Autres Bons Pour Vous," make sure they understand your meaning.

Your live or silent auction catalog should spotlight
the items both in picture and in words.

Luxury auction items, such as a trip to a vacation home, chateau in France, or condo in Colorado, have specific time periods and restrictions on air travel and blackout periods for hotel reservations. Your bidders need to understand that these terms are nonnegotiable. Don't forget to list your auction rules in the catalog. Have a volunteer available to work out any discrepancies or issues.

Rules for Happy Bidding and Happy Bidders

- State the time that the silent auction will begin and end. (Announcements will be made throughout the evening to indicate the closing of the auction.)
- An authorized official of the nonprofit organization is the only one who may alter or nullify a bid.
- All sales are final and no exchanges or refunds on auction items will be permitted unless specified in the catalog listing.
- All items offered in a silent auction will be sold "as is."
- Each item will have a bid sheet with a minimum bid specified. Each bid must follow the minimum bid specified for the item and be accompanied by the bidder's name and bidder number, telephone number, or table number. (Note: The information requested depends on the requirements of the organization.) If a bidder writes in a bid below the minimum bid, the bid is disqualified.
- The payment must be made by the successful bidder on the night of the auction either by cash, check, or credit card at the cashier's table or check-out station. When payment is not received by the nonprofit on that evening, the next higher bidder will be contacted and offered the item.
- All bids (excluding those bids for motor vehicles) will include state sales tax, if applicable.
- All items must be claimed the night of the auction unless size or

continued

Rules for Happy Bidding and Happy Bidders (continued)

quantity prevents their removal. Arrangements for large items can
be made through the nonprofit office. These arrangements and
expenses for delivery (unless specified) are the sole responsibility
of the purchaser.

- Deadlines are generally set on auction certificates relating to the
use of homes, airlines, hotels, transportation, restaurants, and so on.
Some of these items are subject to availability and restrictions with
dates mutually agreed upon by the donors. Tax, tips, and alcohol
are generally not included with some items unless noted on the
certificate.

- It is protective for the nonprofit to have some type of disclaimer
statement: "The nonprofit organization neither represents nor
assumes the responsibility for the correctness of description,
authenticity, authorship, or condition of items offered. The nonprofit
intends that most information be accurate; however, no statement in
this rule listing, program, or made orally at the sale or elsewhere will
be deemed an assumption of liability."

Setting Up Strategically

Plan your layout logically and strategically. By elevating the signage
above the crowd, you will help your guests locate specific items on
which they want to bid. Divide the items into categories such as jewelry, sports memorabilia, arts and antiques, and trips. Once bidders
locate the desired item, be sure they can easily read the information
on the clipboard. Surely some of your guests may wear glasses or
contact lenses.

Assess your auction inventory to determine the number of items
you will have per table. You can use eighteen-inch-wide, six- to eight-
foot-long tables to set up the silent auction display. If the items are
small, you could have anywhere from five to seven items per table.

When installing the silent auction at the venue, you might find that your original layout needs tweaking. The volunteers setting up the auction displays need to be flexible and ready to respond should any unexpected layout changes arise. Certain items may look better in different areas of the exhibition. Some may need additional lighting. If an auction item could bring in major dollars, place it in the center of the space, where the greatest number of people will see it.

For optimum viewing, art needs to be on temporary gallery walls or placed on easels with good lighting. Have the auction item information lighted, as well, and placed at the top or to the side, rather than on the bottom, of the work of art. Lights can be as simple as clamp-on fixtures, providing the venue has adequate electrical outlets. Display boards that highlight artwork also may be borrowed from a shopping mall, convention center, or fairground that hosts exhibits. It is always advisable to do a final lighting check.

With art, it is critical that the catalog number match the corresponding number on the bid sheet located adjacent to the artwork. A committee member who is familiar with the artist and his artwork needs to make certain there has not been a mix-up in donor's sheets.

A clear presentation makes your auction items more accessible to your bidders.

Imagine how the artist would feel if this happened. Having a volunteer who is an artist, gallery owner, or knowledgeable collector provide additional information about the art makes it more appealing for potential bidders.

Don't overdecorate or clutter the auction display lest your bidders miss the objects for the razzle-dazzle. Jewelry is best displayed on elevated pedestals and most secure in locked vitrines or glass enclosures. If you have a piece of furniture, be sure to elevate the table or chair so your guests do not mistake those items as part of the ballroom or hotel furniture. A beautiful or handsome model sitting or reclining on a piece of furniture is another way to set it apart. With a large crowd, you need to make your items stand out.

Elevating furniture can enhance its presentation.

A good way of identifying auction bidders is to furnish them with bidding labels, stating the individual name and assigned number, when they pre-register. This allows bidders to move through the auction more quickly, helps the volunteers identify the auction bidder, and facilitates the check out process.

Opera Ball 2001
A Night at the Alhambra
Silent Auction Pre-Registration Form

I hereby authorize Houston Grand Opera to pre-register me for the 2001 Opera Ball Auction.

Please type or print the following information:

Name _____

Address _____

City _____ State _____ Zip _____

Daytime Phone Number (_____)_____

Credit Card Type ____ Visa ____ MasterCard ____ American Express

Account Number _____ Expiration Date _____

Please mail or fax to:

Pre-registration streamlines the bidding process.

Dealing with Challenging Logistics

If you're in a venue that presents logistical challenges, it is important to have several site visits to familiarize volunteers and different crews (lighting, sound, technical) who will be working the event. This will help everyone involved know how the space flows and will ensure everyone is on the same page.

If you are planning to host the silent auction reception in an area of the facility other than where the event is being held (on another level of the venue, for instance), the auction volunteers need to transfer the bids to duplicate bid stations located at the other area once guests leave the silent auction reception area. The actual auction items will physically remain at the original location, as the checkout station and guest departure are located in the original reception area.

When trying new ideas with auction procedures and methods, test the new concept on a smaller event to work out any unforeseeable problems. Don't intimidate your bidders by giving them bid increments; let them increase their bids as they please. Offer the item at one-half or one-third of the actual value of the item, and let the bidders proceed from there.

Rehearsing Your Volunteers

Don't forget the importance of the volunteer orientation. Volunteers will make the difference in the success of your silent auction. Attitude is essential. A badge identifying auction volunteers or a T-shirt with the event logo is helpful, especially in a large crowd. The T-shirt also gives a coordinated look to the event and is a nice thank-you to the volunteers.

Create an "Auction Assignment Roster" for volunteers. This will help make the silent auction portion of an event flow smoothly. Things to consider are logistics, installation, storage, and teardown. Before assigning volunteers to monitor a particular item category, ask your volunteers what items they feel fall within their areas of interest or expertise. Would they be most motivated talking about jewelry, art, trips, or sports memorabilia?

When planning your installation, you have to allow for any situation, such as escalators not working, auction items that need to be steamed or freshened, or volunteers who don't show up, become ill, or abandon their assignments. An orientation at the venue prior to the event and a copy of the floor plan with specific station assignments will help keep everybody on track.

Offering early credit card registration will help avoid check-in and registration bottlenecks when guests arrive. You want to provide both your benefactors and your volunteers with a stress-free evening.

Tips for Auction Volunteers

- Volunteers should organize the display tables and make certain there are pens attached to the bid clipboards.
- Volunteers should monitor the bid sheets during the silent auction to determine if there are two competitive bidders and offer to place bids for both individuals.
- If there is a lull in the activities, volunteers should not leave the area. There is always something constructive that can be done, and forgetting their responsibilities could directly affect the outcome of the event.
- Volunteers should not fill an empty seat at a table reserved for dining unless the chair or a committee member has asked them to do so.
- Volunteers should remain at their auction stations during dinner to answer questions from those who leave the main hall to check their bids.

Seeing It on the Big Screen

In a large silent auction, there can be more than one hundred items plus, so make the auction interesting and appealing to your guests. Select your top twenty (or less) items and give bid updates on plasma screens or projectors during the silent auction reception and, later, in the main venue. This will serve as a reminder that the silent auction is ongoing, increase the excitement, and add energy and value to your auction.

No Bid?

If an item does not sell, don't panic and slash the price. You have an understood agreement with the in-kind donor to offer the donated item at 30 to 50 percent of the retail value. The event chair or auction chair makes the decision whether or not to take less than the reserve. It's good business not to give the items away, but negotiation is a possibility.

When there is not a bid or a minimum bid on a silent auction item, you have several options. You can reserve the item for your next event. You can reoffer it on the Web site. Or you can make it available at a reduced rate to your committee members and volunteers. The organization may decided to contact the donor and see if she would like the item returned, but this normally doesn't happen.

When certain items are offered at a silent auction and the bids are low, those in charge should not decide after the fact to put the same items into a live auction in hopes of raising more funds. Once a plan of action has been set into motion, it is unfair to your guests to change the game plan. You will confuse the bidders, and this could create an awkward situation for guests. If one person has already bid on the item in the silent auction, and another starts to bid on the same item when it is placed on the live auction, the original bidder should not be penalized by a last-minute change in the rules.

Don't despair if the highest bidder has a change of heart; simply contact the next highest bidder. Additionally, people sometimes will enter a bid far below the minimum. Those bids do not need to be recognized as valid.

At the Conclusion

Make it easy for guests to pay for their auction items. They shouldn't have to look for the checkout station. Payment in full must be made at the conclusion of the auction by cash, check, or credit card before bidders depart with the goods. The winning bidder must arrange for payment for the item on the evening of the event, or the item will be released to the next highest bidder.

Be sure to staff the checkout station with more than one credit card terminal. If people are in a hurry to leave and have to wait, they may change their minds about the item they have purchased and tell you to keep it. If someone in the organization knows the bidder, they can take the information and follow up the next day to get the credit card information and process the purchase. It's a good idea to have a separate line for people who want to pay with cash or by personal checks.

Never rely totally on technology, as electronic failures do occur. Always have a backup plan and equipment. Have a computer technician available to monitor any problems that may arise. When your credit card machine goes down, or someone forgets to bring the credit card machine, take the information by hand. Remember to think in the moment, or the silent auction sales will diminish if you are not prepared.

All items that can fit in a car must leave with the guests at the conclusion of the auction. The removal of large items must take place within a designated time period. If unusual items such as a miniature horse or donkey have been donated, the auction donor will usually take responsibility for delivering the animal and making certain that there are proper instructions for its care and comfort.

The sponsoring organization and the auction committee are not responsible for the condition of the items sold. There is no guarantee, except that of the manufacturer, expressed or implied. Items cannot be exchanged without donor approval.

LIVE AUCTIONS

The best thing about a live auction is that you don't need a lot of items to make a lot of money for your organization. You'll need to use your creativity and imagination to capture the interest of audience members who attend many other fundraising events. At the other end of the spectrum, you'll need to consider the demographics of your audience when auctioning a painting, an automobile, a trip with transportation included, or a designer piece of jewelry. Will those items be supported with the beginning bid and sell high?

Let your guests know beforehand that there will be a live auction and its importance in the overall financial success of the event. A live auction has the potential to help your event surpass its goal. Limit the number of live auction items to five or less; three is preferable.

Always be prepared when an item doesn't sell to have someone within the organization place a bid. This can prevent any embarrassment for your donor. Try to come up with creative live auction items that bidders could not obtain on their own. A walk-on part in a popular TV program or the opportunity to coanchor a local sporting event are examples of items that add excitement and energy to a live auction.

Spotlight the Items

For a live auction, you need to visually stimulate the audience so they are motivated to bid. Try to preview auction items, such as a car or piece of jewelry, at every scheduled pre-event as well as in the printed material. Post images of the items on your Web site and include them in any videos that are done in conjunction with the event. Stage a pre-event around a new car that everybody wants but that is unavailable because it is in such demand. You'll also want to display the car in front of the venue or in the ballroom where the event is taking place.

Another unique way to spotlight an auction item is to be the first to offer an item that is just coming into the marketplace. In 1999, for the Quest for Excellence "Only The Best" Cyber Live Auction, General Motors Foundation generously donated in full an Escalade Sports Utility Vehicle that had just been introduced. The lucky winner was able to select his own favorite color.

It is helpful to the auctioneer if the items are displayed on screens while they are being auctioned. Depending on the size of the crowd and the room, you can place the screens on either side of the auctioneer and throughout the room so the tables in the back of the room will have a view of the items.

Paintings, sculptures, and jewels can be moved through the audience for a closer view during the auction to further entice bidders. Models from a local agency can add glamour. An artist donating a painting may want to be brought on stage to say a few words prior to the auctioning of her work. The presentation is everything.

Let the Pros Handle It

If the live auction at your fundraiser has significant offerings, consider inviting a professional auctioneer from Christie's, Sotheby's, or Phillip's to enhance the success of the auction. Professionals bring an element of sophistication, but local auctioneers or individuals with that special talent are very effective, as well. Good auctioneers ramp-up the level of excitement when they take over the podium.

It is important that the auctioneer is sent a listing of the live auction items in advance and knows the order in which they are to be auctioned and the minimum bids the organization has in mind. A professional auctioneer may want to start the bids lower and be unaware of an arrangement between the presenting organization and the donor concerning the starting bid. It is helpful to give the auctioneer the revenue goal for the live auction. In rare situations, you may be lucky and have two serious bidders for the same item at a high-dollar level. A clever auctioneer will ask the donor, if present, if he might consider donating twice—two trips or two sculptures, for instance.

Auctioneers have their own preferences as to which signal they need from the spotters—red napkins, flashlights, or voices. The lighting in the venue has to be brought up to a certain level during the live auction for the auctioneer to see the spotters as well as any bidders the spotters may miss. Auctioneers always appreciate having someone stand by their side to keep up with the bidders and the bidding. Have a wireless hand microphone available for someone who might be assisting during a live auction.

You'll Need Spotters

A spotter is someone whose job is to help the auctioneer acknowledge all bids during a live auction. Each spotter is assigned and responsible for a certain number of tables. Depending on the size of the event, the number of tables can vary from two to five per spotter. During a live auction, the bidding is very fast and frantic. The spotter uses a flashlight, glow sticks, or a red handkerchief to catch the auctioneer's eye. An additional spotter may stand to the side of the auctioneer to point out someone bidding who may have been overlooked, as well as to identify the bidder by table, number, or paddle. When the bidding is completed, the spotter points out the high bidder to the individual assigned to get their information as to form of payment and inform them where to pick up and pay for their item. In certain events the spotter will take this information and give it to the auction committee. It is also a good idea that the second highest bidder's name and information be taken in the event of a default on a bid.

Spotters need to keep up with the auctioneer. If your spotters aren't focused on their task, the organization may loose its bidder. Make sure they understand their responsibilities. In addition to recognizing the bidders, good spotters also should encourage competition between the bidders.

Sometimes a spontaneous suggestion from the podium by an auctioneer can produce big bucks for the organization. You never know who in the audience will be motivated to make an additional commitment. At the Women's Home Annual Benefit, the honorary chair and the cochairmen came up with the idea of providing $5,000 scholarships for women needing to go through the program at the home. After the live auction, one man stepped up and issued a challenge for others in the audience to provide these scholarships. A dozen or more joined in, raising an additional $50,000 in support.

And Bid Runners, Too

Bid runners facilitate auction bidding and do the leg work for people who choose not to leave the table during an event. Bid runners give bidders a simple form that states they are willing to bid on an item which they confirm with their signature. This prevents an individual from declining the bid and serves as insurance for the organization.

For bid runners, enlist the support of a group of students. Ideal resources are a high school's organizations, youth symphony, or other junior service organizations. Ask them to act as bid runners during the silent and live auction, once guests are seated for dinner. They accommodate guests by checking on their bids, especially when competitive bidding action is taking place. They can help bidders increase their bids and act as ambassadors of goodwill, finding answers to guests' questions about the auction, e.g. when the auction will close and where items are paid for and picked up. This is a good way to introduce young people to the concept of philanthropy as they support a worthy cause.

Their presence adds a youthful energy, and, for them, this will probably be an evening that will be long remembered. The students may find it fun to create their own costumes so they will stand out in the crowd. For example, they could wear mime makeup, funny hats, or boas around their necks. Each student would be responsible for five or six tables during the live auction. An orientation is always helpful, so the students will know what their duties are, when and where to take a break, the location of a changing room, if needed, and where to find refreshments.

What to Do in a Tie Bid?

How you handle a tie bid will be up to your organization's discretion. At the conclusion of the live auction, the tie bidders should be permitted to continue bidding for a limited amount of time until a successful bid is reached. Ideally, the auction donor might offer a duplicate item. If it is a work of art, the artist might be asked to consider offering an additional work from the same series. In one situation, a donor requested an added incentive to raise the bid. In the tie bid for a Lance Armstrong cycle shirt, the high bidder said he would take the bid to $100,000 if Lance would agree to visit a children's summer camp program sponsored by the bidder. Lance agreed, and M. D. Anderson Cancer Center was thrilled with this unexpected bonus.

Absentee Bids

Absentee bids can be handled by the sponsoring nonprofit organization. If someone wants to support your cause and can't be there to bid in person, an absentee bidder can be appointed. Arrangements can be made in advance for the credit card guarantee for all absentee bids. Be sure to get the bids in before the designated deadline. Phone bids, like all others, must be confirmed. It's worthwhile for the organization to try to accommodate someone who makes the effort to support the cause.

Quiet, Please

Don't let a person's poor manners disrupt a live auction. Have someone from your staff or committee diplomatically let that individual know that others are being disturbed and ask if he would like to step into another room. During one live auction I attended, a woman repeatedly insisted on bidding, breaking the momentum of the auction, and then backing off the bid. Don't let exhibitionists ruin the day for others and your charity.

Auction Planning Checklist

- Send out donor letters and response forms.
- Follow up with potential donors.
- Secure storage, moving, and security.
- Select volunteers and assign duties.
- Plan carefully for setup and teardown.
- Work out details of checkout and delivery.
- Design an auction catalog and make it available at pre-events.
- Create and distribute auction rules.

 *Chapter Fourteen*

PRINTED MATERIALS

"Reading without reflecting is like eating without digesting."
—EDMUND BURKE

Printed materials for pre-events and the main event are key parts of the overall impression. Make sure to think through what you are trying to convey before you create your printed materials. Lend consistency to all printed matter, showing a well-coordinated campaign. The overall design of printed materials can make a big difference. And, of course, use all of your contacts to keep the costs minimal.

Prepare your printed materials far in advance of the gala. Donors and benefactors appreciate having plenty of time to consider your cause and your request for funding.

GETTING STARTED

As chairman, when trying to develop the concept for your invitation and other documents (such as benefactor packages, invitations, auction catalogs, and programs) that make up your campaign material, getting started is the most difficult part. Sometimes an inspiring quote might be just the way to begin. It can help focus your thoughts.

Use the wisdom of the greatest thinkers to support your cause. An expressive quote helps to create an image or mental picture of what you are trying to say. Try sprinkling quotations that are inspirational, uplifting, and motivational as an added touch to your invitations, envelopes, programs, or speeches. The words of accomplished people with something to say can motivate others to pause and reflect about the true meaning of your cause.

If you decide to try this method, be careful not to select a quote that has been overused or that may already be associated with another organization. Unique quotes stand out and will remain in the thoughts of those you are trying to reach. Use the Internet or an inspirational book as a resource to help find the perfect quote to support and lend substance to the message you are trying to convey.

"Do all the good you can, by all the means you can, at all the times you can, as long as ever you can." I used this quote by John Wesley as a sidebar in the program for Marvin's Million Dollar Dream. For "A Night at the Alhambra," benefiting the Houston Grand Opera 2001, I chose the following quote for the back of the mailing envelope: "If music be the food of love, play on!" by William Shakespeare. For the Rainforest Gala 2002, I used a quote by Henry David Thoreau: "From the forest and wilderness comes the tonics and barks which brace mankind." For the front cover of a Rainforest gala invitation I selected a quote by Frank Lloyd Wright: "I believe in God, only I spell it nature."

Even after you have put your thoughts down to create blueprints for your printed materials, there will always be revisions. The sincerity of your mission should capture the interest of and elicit a reaction from others. I always create a mockup of the invitation and, later, of the program before meeting with the printer. In reality, the program is a larger, updated version of the invitation with the inclusion of the latest data.

INVITATIONS

An event of importance requires an invitation that has a presence and is distinctive. I view the invitation as an opportunity to share information that will appeal to many types of donors. To ensure that your invitation makes an attention-catching arrival, use an over-sized format, adding a design element to your envelope that relates to your theme. Consider all potential sources for information and ideas when researching your design—the Internet, your local library, photographs, and even movies. Look everywhere until you find a concept you want to develop.

The invitation is the first impression your potential guests will have of the event. When selecting the paper, consider how it feels to the touch and how it looks. Should you choose recyclable paper? What color palette should you use for the paper and the ink? Try to go one step further and find a distinctive stamp that reflects your organization's cause or event theme. Choose an envelope size that won't get lost in the mail—not too small and not too large. The return address should be printed on the envelope flap.

Command Attention

Give your readers something to think about and reflect upon when receiving the invitation, such as its message, beauty, or uniqueness. Every detail of an invitation should express an element of creativity, from the graphic design to the verbiage. For the invitations to "A Night at the Alhambra," to convey the aura of excitement, mystery, and old world European elegance, we identified the different levels of giving in exotic terms. We also named our ballroom "The Perfumed Garden."

You also can add a gold or crimson cord, a dried flower, a ribbon, or a special seal to your invitations, programs, or menu cards to give them a distinctive look and an attractive presentation. This is a fun task for volunteers. If you know you will be involved in planning a major event, it is helpful to save a stash of invitations that you or your friends and colleagues have received and admired. You can create a small library and refer to them for ideas and inspiration.

Think About the Wording

Think of the invitation as the quarterback for your special event. It delivers the purpose for the fundraising event; whom it will benefit; a list of the chairs and committees, benefactors and in-kind donors, special guests or honorees; and the details of what exactly will take place. A message in the invitation from the chairman sharing with others why she is involved makes the approach more personable.

In writing the text, the creative process can be likened to putting together the pieces of a puzzle. You may decide to move the different components of the invitation around several times until they fall into the right order.

Proof the Layout

No matter how many times you have read the copy of an invitation or other printed matter, there may be one name, one initial, one accent mark, or one detail that is not correct or has been over-looked. There will always be one person who will find that detail and inform you of this fact. The best way to avoid such errors is to have two or three pairs of eyes to review all your printed information before it is finalized.

When you proof your materials, don't just look at the copy, but also review the order of the pages and the spacing. Make sure a page has not been omitted, review the typeset text, and check the paper choice. Pay special attention to the placement of any accent marks and punctuation in names. A fresh pair of eyes might pick up mistakes that have been missed—an awkward phrase, subjects and verbs that don't agree. You can never have too many people proof-read your work!

What to Wear?

The invitations should clearly state the suggested dress code. Giving guests a clear idea of what to wear to an event will save you and your committee a lot of phone calls. Help guests avoid the "What do I wear?" dilemma. Having to think about what to wear only adds pressure and may downplay the reason for the support.

Suggested Attire Options	
When a man is wearing...	**A woman could wear...**
White Tie*	Long Gown, Long Gloves optional
Black Tie*	Long to Short Evening Gown
Business	Cocktail Dress, Designer Pant, or Skirt Suit
Sport Coat/Blazer	Day Dress, Pants, Blazer, Blouse
Shirt, No Jacket	Long Causal Dress, Pant and Jacket
Western Style Clothes	Designer Clothes with Western Flair
Event Golf Shirt, Shorts or Slacks	Knee-length Shorts or Long Pants
Casual Beach, Colorful Print Shirt, Linen Slacks or Shorts	Cover Up, Long Gauzy Dress, Hat

 * *Since most men do no have white or black tie attire in their personal wardrobes, they can easily rent an outfit for the occasion. You might include the name of a formal wear rental company with the invitation.*

Include a Map

Include a map with the invitation if the location of the event is difficult to find. If there is road construction, a map could suggest an alternate route. Have one or more committee members test the map route by driving it themselves before the map goes to print. If the parking in the event area is problematic, stating that you're offering complimentary valet parking might be an added incentive for a prospective supporter to attend.

About the Auction or Raffle

If your auction committee has worked far enough in advance, the silent auction catalog or a partial listing of auction items can be included with the invitation. If you are hosting a raffle for a major item such as a car, give information as to the number of tickets that will be printed and when the raffle will take place. Enclose a photo and description of the item, including any restrictions. This gives the donor greater acknowledgment and exposure in the community.

Bring the Family

When an event takes place during the daytime on a Saturday or Sunday, why not include children? Families find time to be together so precious these days. This provides the children with a good opportunity to learn about helping others and to realize how fortunate they are. If children are welcome, the invitation should make that clear.

Key Invitation Elements

- Theme or logo of the event
- Name of the organization benefiting from the fundraiser
- The chairman's message
- Invitation page
- Day, date, time, place (with full address and specific venue and/or room name)
- Entertainment and master of ceremonies
- Suggested attire
- Valet parking
- Honorary committee
- Underwriters
- Sponsors, patrons, and supporters
- Honoree(s) and short bio(s)
- Description of any award being presented
- Listing of benefactors and in-kind donors
- Organization's mission statement
- Response form and return envelope
- List of nearby hotels and special rates for out-of-town guests
- Map

RESPONSE CARDS

The response form should not be too complicated. Indicate levels of sponsorship and state the benefactor opportunities for each one. At the top of the response card, reiterate pertinent details: chairman, organization, guest of honor, date, time, and place.

By adding a few simple lines for guest seating on the reverse side of your response cards, you can enlarge your mailing list. Encourage table patrons to provide you with the names, addresses, and phone numbers of their guests. Offer to mail their guests invitations so that they will have the necessary information about the event, such as date, time, place, and directions. The host may prefer to mail them directly, but this thoughtful gesture will eliminate the host's having to go over these details with each guest, as well as add to the organization's prospect list.

Don't forget to direct potential donors to your Web site or to add a donation form with the invitation to give those individuals who will not be in attendance an opportunity to make a contribution and support the cause.

In order to encourage prospective donors to support your organization at various levels, select name categories that distinguish the different giving levels. For example, for a film festival, levels of giving might be identified as Studio Heads, Executive Producers, Producers, Directors, Best Actor/Actress, and Extras. Or how about a *Field of Dreams* Luncheon with a home-run underwriter and third-base sponsors?

Reasonable perks for a major underwriter might include two premier tables for ten with favors, invitations for ten guests to a benefactor dinner and other pre-events, commemorative gift for host couple, recognition in newsletter and other periodicals, place cards for guests at the gala, and prominent acknowledgement of sponsorship in the media coverage.

At the different levels, other donor opportunities could include the name and logo of a donor featured in a one-page, full-color ad in a program, name listed on a contributors' page, name in promotional material, charter membership in an organization, inscription on a plaque, recognition on the organization's Web site, complimentary valet parking, T-shirts, and posters.

The Visionaries of Science Benefits Package

The HIMALAYA - $100,000

• VIP Table of Ten at the Gala.
• A personal tour with Eckhard Pfeiffer, President and CEO of Compaq Computer Corporation, for the Host Couple and 10 friends, of Compaq's award winning headquarters, product demonstrations in the IT Solutions Center, and a post-tour dinner at the new Compaq Commons.
• Ten invitations to the Benefactors' Dinner at the Wortham House, hosted by Chancellor and Mrs. Arthur Smith, on Friday, March 26, 1999.
• Ten invitations to VIP reception which includes photo opportunities with the honoree and special guests and dignitaries.

The ALPHA - $50,000

• VIP Table of Ten at the Gala.
• The ARMADA, the latest high-tech Compaq computer, with tutorial by a Compaq product engineer on request.
• Eight invitations to the Benefactors' Dinner at the Wortham House, hosted by Chancellor and Mrs. Arthur Smith, on Friday, March 26, 1999.
• Eight invitations to VIP reception which includes photo opportunities with the honoree and special guests and dignitaries.

The PROLIANT - $25,000

• Preferred Table of Ten at the Gala.
• Two hand held Compaq PALMTOP computers.
• Six invitations to the Benefactors' Dinner at the Wortham House, hosted by Chancellor and Mrs. Arthur Smith, on Friday, March 26, 1999.
• Distinguished scientist or special guest seated at your table.
• Six invitations to VIP reception which includes photo opportunities with the honoree and special guests and dignitaries.

The DESKPRO - $10,000

• Preferred Table of Ten at the Gala.
• Four invitations to the Benefactors' Dinner at the Wortham House, hosted by Chancellor and Mrs. Arthur Smith, on Friday, March 26, 1999.
• A distinctive commemorative gift.
• Four invitations to VIP reception which includes photo opportunities with the honoree and special guests and dignitaries.

The ARMADA - $5,000

• Priority Table of Ten at the Gala.
• Two invitations to the Benefactors' Dinner at the Wortham House, hosted by Chancellor and Mrs. Arthur Smith, on Friday, March 26, 1999.
• A distinctive commemorative gift.
• Two invitations to VIP reception which includes photo opportunities with the honoree and special guests and dignitaries.

Benefactors will also Receive the Following Benefits

• Invitations to the Celebration Brunch at the Wortham House on Saturday, April, 10, 1999.
• Special acknowledgment & recognition with photo by noted photographer Evin Thayer in the official Gala program. **
• A distinguished scientist or special guest seated at your table.
• Luncheon and behind-the-scene tour of the University of Houston's laboratories of distinction.
• Special recognition in all pre- and post-event promotional materials and press releases. **

The Wortham House is the official residence of the Chancellor of the University of Houston.

Proceeds from the evening will endow a Chair in Eckhard Pfeiffer's honor, and provide funding for scholarships and faculty development grants to advance excellence in the sciences.

For information please contact University of Houston
Tel:
Fax:

** if commitment received by program printing deadline.

Giving levels should be clearly defined in your literature.

Fair Market Value

For tax purposes, the fair market value of goods and services provided to donors in exchange for their donation must be calculated and subtracted from the donation amount. If a charitable event ticket sells for $100 and the fair market value of the event is $40, then the amount of the charitable donation is $60.

The unique nature of most charitable fundraising events means the benefits have no commercial counterparts. The cost of rendering a service or benefit to members or attendees is not a prescribed measure of value. If there is no comparable market, the cost may be determinative. For example, a chance to play golf with a pro would be the benefit; the value assigned to it would be the price of the chance. A raffle or door prize ticket would be the benefit, and the value assigned would be the price paid for the ticket.

To address tax reporting issues, the wording on the response form might read: "For tax reporting purposes, the fair market value of each ticket or per person is ____." Or, "Contributions are fully deductible; all but $___ of each ticket is tax deductible." Listing the organization's tax ID number at the bottom of the response card saves the benefactor or supporter a call to the organization. (Be sure to state that the organization is a 501(c)(3) organization, when applicable.) You also

An Evening With Phyllis George at the River Oaks Country Club

Benefiting the Northwood University Texas Campus Expansion Campaign
"Building For Texas – Northwood Today and Into the Future"

April 22, 2003 * RSVP by April 15, 2003

Name _____

Address _____

City, State Zip _____

Phone _____ e-mail _____

Please reserve:

Tables		Individual Tickets	
___ Royal Amblance	@ $25,000	___ Royal Amblance	@ $2,500
___ Rossini	@ $10,000	___ Rossini	@ $1,000
___ Prelude	@ $ 5,000	___ Prelude	@ $ 500
___ Tango	@ $ 2,500	___ Tango	@ $ 250
___ Peek-A-Boo	@ $ 1,500	___ Peek-A-Boo	@ $ 150

All guests receive a copy of Phyllis George's book. Royal Amblance, Rossini, Prelude and Tango levels will be listed in the evening's program and will receive an invitation to a private photo opportunity with Ms. George. Royal Amblance levels will receive an invitation to a Presidential Reception (date and arrangements to be determined by Northwood University).

Tables of 10 please indicate seating on back.

Payment in excess of $100 per Peek-A-Boo, Tango, Prelude and Rossini ticket and $150 per Royal Amblance ticket is tax deductible.

I/We cannot attend but wish to make a tax deductible contribution of $_____

Please make checks payable to Northwood University or charge to ▢Visa ▢ MasterCard.

Name as it appears on Card: _____

Card Number: _____ Exp. Date _____ Amount: _____

Signature: _____

A standard response form would look something like this one.

might add a disclaimer that reads: "Contributions or gifts to political parties are nondeductible as charitable contributions for income tax purposes. Contributions from foreign nationals are prohibited."

For A Celebration of Reading in Dallas benefiting the Barbara Bush Foundation for Family Literacy, the response card stated that the fair market value of the dinner was $75, with the balance of the contribution being tax deductible. The individual tickets began at the $150 level, with the table sponsorship beginning at $5,000.

Response Card Elements

- Name of the organization
- Theme or name of the event with logo
- Day, date, time, and location
- Price of tables and individual tickets, and spaces to mark preference
- Blank spaces for name of donor, address, e-mail, and contact numbers
- Blank space for those unable to attend to make a contribution
- Response date to encourage early reservations
- Method of payment
- If by check, to whom the check should be made payable
- If by credit card, spaces for type of card, account number, date of expiration, signature, and amount to be charged
- How many guests are seated at a table (the standard is 10, but sizes can range)
- Reverse side of the card should have blank spaces to list guests' names (space for addresses should be provided but optional)
- Tax deductible statement
- For more information, contact person with number or e-mail
- Place to request special meal considerations
- The size of the card should be reasonable and spaces should be adequate for the information you are requesting

---

ENVELOPES

To ensure that your invitation makes a statement upon arrival, use an oversized format. Small envelopes can get lost in the mail or may be overlooked. Always check postal restrictions as to the size of an envelope in advance to avoid any delays, costly postage, or problems with your mailing. Once you have designed your invitation and have a sample, postal employees can check the weight and determine the amount of postage required. A square-shaped envelope will cost more for postage. If doing a bulk mailing, invitations should be sorted and grouped by Zip Codes.

Make It Personal

In this age of technology, there are some things that should still be done by hand whenever possible. Even though addressing invitations by hand is almost a lost art, the extra effort will catch the eye of whoever opens the envelope. However, when the invitation mailing is too large to be hand-addressed, select a calligraphy-type font, and print the addresses directly onto the envelopes. Choose one of the fonts from your word processor's tool bar, selecting one that mirrors the theme of the event. Take care to avoid something that looks good but is hard to read. Standard printed labels lack personal attention and can diminish a fundraising appeal. People won't be as eager to open the envelope and look inside.

Make certain that the return address on your mailing envelope lists an individual's name, such as the event or reservations chair. The name of an individual on the outside of the envelope makes the invitation more personal. Most of the time, recipients of an invitation will glance at the return address before opening it, and seeing the event chair's name may influence donors to open the invitation.

What Volunteers Need to Know

Explain the importance of the organization's image to the invitation committee. If an invitation arrives sealed with scotch tape and marked insufficient postage, the recipient gets a bad message about your organization, and the invitation lacks appeal. In extreme cases, a recipient may wonder who oversaw the mailing and call the non-profit executive director to let him know that someone needs to pay attention to the mailings that are sent out.

The invitation chair should meet personally with volunteers who are addressing, stuffing, sealing, and stamping invitations. Show them, by example, how you want the components assembled in the envelope, where to place the stamp, and the best way to seal the envelopes. Bulk mailings of invitations must be bundled by Zip Codes.

Postage

Excellence is always found in the details, and the invitation stamp is no exception. You would be surprised at the attention a small stamp will receive. Even if you're doing a large mailing of 2,500 pieces, always use postage stamps. Hand-stamped mail lets those on the receiving end know the extra steps and busy hands that were used to give the invitation impact.

Visit your main post office or go online to see which stamps are available at the time of your event. Try to relate the stamp to the theme of the event or to the mission of the organization. You also can customize metered mail for a relatively inexpensive amount, placing a message or logo next to the meter mark. Nonprofit organizations also can apply with the U.S. Postal Service for approval to mail at special nonprofit postage rates if budget or staff is limited. To do so, you have to qualify for a nonprofit rate. In qualifying for this status, there are restrictions on the amount and kind of advertising you can do. Begin by obtaining an application to mail at non-profit standard mail rates from the postmaster, and submit that application with the requested supporting documentation of your nonprofit status. Other than the restrictions on the content, mail sent at the nonprofit rates are handled the same as other metered mail.

Try to adhere to a "zero budget" by asking a corporate donor to sponsor the postage for a special event. On the page in the invitation where in-kind donors and special thanks are listed, the donor can be acknowledged with a line reading "the postage has been provided by." This is an example of cause-related marketing, and it can both help your organization and help create awareness for the company.

Look into the possibility of lobbying for a national stamp that would support your particular cause, like AIDS or breast cancer. Philanthropist Milton Murray lobbied hard to bring the philanthropy stamp to fruition—"Giving and Sharing an American Tradition." Philanthropy was both Murray's vocation and his avocation. His personal philosophy advised, "Keep in touch, educate, and encourage," and he was an individual who embodied the highest ethical standards. The result of Murray's efforts was a double run of 50 million stamps that helped raise the consciousness of Americans nationwide.

Returned Mail

When you receive returned mail, update the change of address information and, if possible, resend the mailing. People marry, divorce, move, change jobs, and die. If your list has not been updated in a long time, consider using one of the authorized Change of Address vendors from the U.S. Post Office. Check out their Web site at www.usps.com. This is especially helpful for organizations that bulk mail most of their information, because bulk rate mail is not usually returned for incorrect addresses.

When an invitation is returned undeliverable, and the event is close at hand, it might be too late to do another mailing. Try to contact the prospective donor by phone, e-mail, or fax to let her know that the invitation was returned, give her all the event details, and get her correct address. And, of course, correct the information on the organization's master list.

No Response?

For pre-events and galas, hosts and reservation committee chairs need to know the number of guests attending for the caterer, valet parking service, and party rentals. With so many fundraising invitations to entice benefactors and event patrons today, people tend to neglect to respond, even though the invitation includes an RSVP form. Often, people who are very busy and overly extended will simply forget.

If your organization is not receiving a timely response to an invitation, perhaps the mail arrived too late or not at all. Have you ever received an invitation on December 7 that had been postmarked November 20 for an event to be held on December 6? If you're concerned about the number of responses that should have been received, place calls to prospective donors in various postal Zip Codes to make sure that the invitations were received.

A committee may have to divide the list and follow up with calls to get an accurate count. If your volunteer group or organization staff is small, this is another task that keeps the organization from directing its energies directly toward its goal; however, you have to take these measures if the RSVPs are slow in coming.

Online Invitations

A way to include donors whose mail was returned at the last minute or who are not on your mailing list is to create an online invitation. An online invitation can be sent directly via e-mail or can be accessed via the organization's Web site. On the Web site, there can be a link that takes visitors to the invitation, which can be formatted as a duplicate of the actual invitation that will be mailed. Include the response form to be completed; it should be designed so that visitors can choose either to register online and submit an electronic credit card payment or to print the form and mail it to your organization's office with payment in the form of a check.

COMMEMORATIVE PROGRAMS

A special fundraising event should be remembered by supporters long after it is held. With this in mind, organizations always print a memento referred to as the printed program. If an ad journal is printed in conjunction with an event, the information generally found in the program is included on its pages, and an additional printed program is not necessary.

The invitation is the prelude to the event program. The program includes all of the elements of the invitation with updated information. It should be oversized and contain specifics on the event, listings of committee members, participants in the speaking program, and information about the honoree(s). Be sure to add the names of benefactors and in-kind donors who have come aboard after the

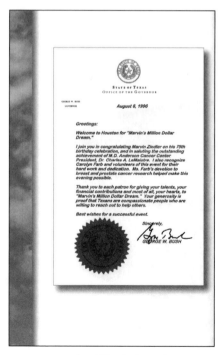

An event program should begin by welcoming guests.

invitation has gone to print. The program also should include biographies of honorees, broad descriptions of presentations or awards, the menu, the schedule of the evening, and expanded information on the cause or nonprofit organization.

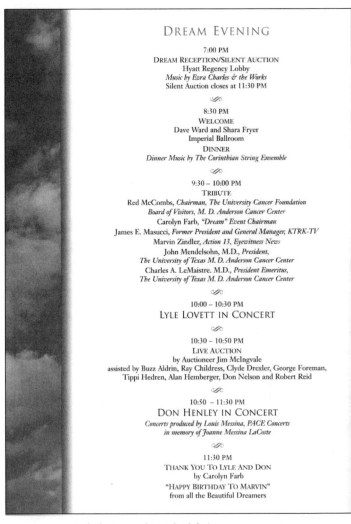

DREAM EVENING

7:00 PM
DREAM RECEPTION/SILENT AUCTION
Hyatt Regency Lobby
Music by Ezra Charles & the Works
Silent Auction closes at 11:30 PM

8:30 PM
WELCOME
Dave Ward and Shara Fryer
Imperial Ballroom
DINNER
Dinner Music by The Corinthian String Ensemble

9:30 – 10:00 PM
TRIBUTE
Red McCombs, *Chairman, The University Cancer Foundation
Board of Visitors, M. D. Anderson Cancer Center*
Carolyn Farb, *"Dream" Event Chairman*
James E. Masucci, *Former President and General Manager, KTRK-TV*
Marvin Zindler, *Action 13, Eyewitness News*
John Mendelsohn, M.D., *President,
The University of Texas M. D. Anderson Cancer Center*
Charles A. LeMaistre. M.D., *President Emeritus,
The University of Texas M. D. Anderson Cancer Center*

10:00 – 10:30 PM
LYLE LOVETT IN CONCERT

10:30 – 10:50 PM
LIVE AUCTION
by Auctioneer Jim McIngvale
assisted by Buzz Aldrin, Ray Childress, Clyde Drexler, George Foreman,
Tippi Hedren, Alan Hemberger, Don Nelson and Robert Reid

10:50 – 11:30 PM
DON HENLEY IN CONCERT
*Concerts produced by Louis Messina, PACE Concerts
in memory of Joanne Messina LaCoste*

11:30 PM
THANK YOU TO LYLE AND DON
by Carolyn Farb
"HAPPY BIRTHDAY TO MARVIN"
from all the Beautiful Dreamers

Include a complete schedule in your program.

Try to use creativity in your program's format. For example, describe the menu for a major gala in expressive terminology related to the theme of the event. For an opera gala, you might use "Overture" to introduce the first course, "Recitative" for your entrée, "Pavatina" for breads and vegetables, and "Pabaletta" for the dessert course. You might also want to intersperse quotations from famous composers, artists, and poets. It's the nuances, the details, and the theme that keep special events memorable, fun, well attended, and successful.

Design your menu to reflect your theme.

Another interesting approach is to include a page of photographs from pre-events. This helps to recognize and thank both hosts and benefactors who attended for their generosity. Before an opera gala I was involved with, for example, Saks Fifth Avenue hosted a cause-related marketing opera pre-event at the store with jeweler David Yurman and gave 20 percent of all sales that evening to benefit the charitable organization. The photographs from the evening were placed in the gala program to highlight Saks Fifth Avenue, jeweler David Yurman, and the other in-kind donors.

A rule of thumb is to add "as of printing deadline" at the bottom of the list of thank-yous and acknowledgments. (If it is listed at the top under the header, it distracts from the importance of the list.) Include the words "Our sincere apologies to those not listed due to printing deadline" to acknowledge commitments that come in after the printing deadline.

The invitation mailing may vary widely, depending on the size of your event. Generally, the number of printed programs is less than the number of invitations. Programs may be placed at every seat or every other seat in the venue. If your ballroom holds 500 guests, you would have 250 programs to be placed at every other seat or 500 if you choose to give one for every guest. People like to keep the program as a keepsake to be shared with others and capture ideas for their own philanthropic causes.

Check Your Facts

Just as good reporters checks facts and sources, fundraisers have the same responsibility to their donors to list their names correctly and recognize their gifts accurately. There's no quicker way to turn off a donor than to print her or his name incorrectly. It is easy for an error to occur when data is transferred from one person to another or from one computer program to another.

What do you do when you discover a major error after printing—say the honorary chairman's first name has been misspelled? Do you reprint all two thousand invitations that are ready to be put in the mail and already behind schedule? First, you call the honoree, tell her what has happened, apologize, and offer to amend the situation in an agreeable manner. There are newsletters and other subsequent printed material in which individuals may be recognized and the error corrected. As we are all committed volunteers and are working toward a common goal, the person will probably understand that this was an honest error. The point is that someone needs to double-check the copy before it goes to print.

Contact the donor if there's any doubt about the correct spelling of a name or the placement of an accent mark. Donors also have preferences on how they want to be recognized. For example, one individual may want his company listed with his name, while others may just want to list the company. Some gifts may be given in honor of another individual or anonymously. Don't forget titles—they have been earned.

Remember that computer "spell check" isn't infallible. Carefully check the auction catalogs because descriptions, donors, and bid amounts can be accidentally transposed and could cause a huge problem. For instance, when a performing arts group was acknowledging donors at an opening performance, a major sponsor's name was misspelled. Shell Oil Company was listed as Shall (acceptable in spell check) Oil Company, and it was no laughing matter. How embarrassing for both the sponsoring organization and the evening's benefactor.

WORKING WITH A PRINTER

Look for a printer who is community minded. This is no small feat. You may have to make several calls and send numerous packages of information before you find a printer who will consider the project.

Tips for Dealing Effectively with a Printer

- For your first meeting with the representative of a printing company, take along samples of past invitations and programs illustrating the different components you hope to assemble.
- Be clear about the scope of the project—the number of invitations, programs, or auction catalogs you will need.
- Ask the printer for names of vendors you can ask to donate the paper for printed materials.
- After you secure a printer, be considerate. Remember that his paying jobs take precedence over your project.
- If the printer does annual reports, anticipate a very congested spring schedule.
- Provide your material in a timely manner so that the printer can handle your job when the press is idle.
- Proof early and often. Every change you make creates extra time and costs for the printer and increases the possibility of introducing new typos. Be as accurate as possible.

 *Chapter Fifteen*

FINALIZING THE MENU, DECORATIONS, AND ENTERTAINMENT

*"Look at a day when you are supremely satisfied at the end.
It's not a day when you lounge around doing nothing;
it's when you've had everything to do, and you've done it."*
—MARGARET THATCHER

Once you've developed a theme and structure for your main event and extended invites to your donor pool, you need to be sure the event will deliver everything you've promised—and more. The decorations, food, beverages, and entertainment should work together to create an atmosphere that makes a strong and meaningful impression on your guests.

TESTING YOUR MENU CONCEPT

Sample the possible selections while there is still time to tweak the menu. Many times food tastes better "on paper" than in reality, which is one of the reasons a tasting is so important. The banquet manager, the chair of the event, the food and beverage committee chair, and the executive director should be included in the tasting. The fewer people, the better. A tasting should take place anywhere from three months to six weeks in advance of the event. There may be a charge for this service, so it is wise to ask.

The tasting group will offer its input on the selection as well as on different wines to be offered with several courses. The chef will bring

out three or four entreé choices, two or three vegetables to complement each of the entrées, and dessert options. After the chef has made
his presentation of the plating, he will then serve a portion of each
of the entrées, sauces, vegetables, starches, and desserts. The participants at the tasting will then make suggestions as to which sauce they
prefer with which entrée and the vegetables and starches of choice.
Participants also are at liberty to comment on the presentation.

For added media coverage, invite the food editor of a local newspaper or magazine to join the tasting group. See if you can turn the tasting into an opportunity to preview menu items that also can be
featured in the publication's food section. If you are planning a vegetarian meal, contact a local morning talk show or a PBS food program
and ask if they might be interested in doing a story on the creative
vegetarian menu and support the mission of your organization.

Presentation

It is important for the food to be visually pleasing. Your vision of a
pretty plate may not match another's palate. For an evening event, a
plate is more appealing if it has a lighter and more elegant look,
especially if guests are dressed in formal attire. Ask the chef or banquet manager to take a digital photograph of the final selection at
the tasting so you can be assured of getting the same meal and presentation you chose.

The Wines

When selecting wines, try to stick to your zero budget philosophy as
closely as possible. It is very challenging to get the wine and/or
liquor donated, but there are a few options. Seek the advice of good
friends or acquaintances for which wine has become a passion, or
someone who works for a vineyard or writes for a wine publication.
They can be helpful in advising which wines would go well with
your various courses and the best price per case. They also might be
willing to make a wine donation request to one of their contacts on

behalf of the organization. You should give your contact enough lead time to send the donation request. If the wines are donated or purchased elsewhere, work out the necessary delivery arrangements with the venue.

In the event you cannot get the wines donated, make certain you are getting the best value for your dollar. When obtaining a wine menu from a banquet manager, be sure to check the hotel's cost of the wine per bottle and per case with a local retailer. Hotel wines start at $25–$40 per bottle, which is reasonable for a decent wine.

It is surprising the difference a couple of ounces makes. Ask the hotel banquet manager for the ounce size of the glasses that will be used for the event. The size of the wine glass dictates the number of ounces. For example, if you are serving wine to a thousand people for dinner, fifteen to twenty-five cases should be sufficient, although this can vary according to your audience. Red or white wine with dinner served in five-ounce glasses calls for fifteen cases. Champagne with dessert served in a three-ounce glass calls for ten cases.

Ask the venue to set a water glass and an all purpose wine glass for either red or white. The wait staff can ask each guest her preference instead of offering both wines, thereby cutting down on the amount of wine used.

When guests pay top dollar to support your event, it is important to offer an open bar during the predinner reception. Guests at this level expect a choice. However, offering a choice of red or white wine with a cash bar is permissible for some events.

Hors d'oeuvres

When the reception time period is extended to an hour and a half, be prepared to offer your guests something to take the edge off their appetites, even if it's only nuts or chips. When passing hors d'oeuvres, be considerate of your guests. Serve bite-sized hors d'oeuvres that are not messy and are easy to manage. Just think, some women will be trying to hold a drink, handbag, auction catalog, and program.

In order for bar and wine service not to get out of hand, it is helpful to have waiters passing trays of wine during the reception. This will encourage guests to take a glass of wine, as opposed to going to the bar. Of course, you can't stop someone from going to the bar. If a pre-event is held in someone's home, many hosts offer only white wine. If there is an accident, it's easier to remove the spill than with a red wine.

Don't keep your guests at bay outside the doors to the venue. They may decide to resort to the bar when there is nothing else to capture their attention—silent auction, music, entertainment, or an exhibit relating to the purpose of the evening. Small talk only goes so far.

First Course

The first course sets the culinary tone and should complement the remainder of the meal. The season of the year could provide insight in determining your selection. In a warm climate, a cold soup like gazpacho or vichysoisse would be a good start. Tomato basil, served hot or cold, with croutons is a lovely soup. A very festive offering would be lobster bisque or Camembert champagne soup en croute.

For a cold appetizer, you might choose Scottish salmon with capers and delicate slivers of green onion. Garnish the plate with some greens lightly dressed, perhaps a crostini with chopped olives and cream cheese, and a wedge of Camembert. Think about whether or not to offer a sauce on the smoked salmon, what type of sauce for the greens, or the size of the crostini. Several giant prawns or lump crabmeat over lettuce or, perhaps, a cold seafood mélange would be equally delightful.

Don't overwhelm your guests with a large, hearty first course. Your choice of appetizer should be appealing to both the eye and the palate and promise more delicious surprises to follow.

Enter the Entrée

Choosing a pleasing entrée for a large number of people can be a challenge. If the chef knows in advance the number of guests that you anticipate, then he can build the ideal plate with that in mind and give the nonprofit his best recommendation. Ask the chef what foods for large groups will hold up best in the warming ovens. For example, in such instances it is better to cook chicken with the skin on to prevent it from drying out. Be considerate in planning a menu. Go exotic and you may lose your audience; save escargot and ostrich for a dinner for two.

We considered the following chef's choices at the tasting for the Quest for Excellence Gala, which hosted one thousand guests: a filet with truffle sauce and a crab cake combination with mushroom potatoes and a ring of asparagus; a grilled filet of beef with garlic roasted mashed potatoes and assorted baby vegetables; a grilled petite filet of beef with blackened crawfish and Creole mustard sauce, and a sautéed tiger prawn with lobster stuffing and sauce nantua with pommes dauphinoise and tomato provencal with wilted spinach and parmesan.

If you are planning a menu for a very special function, consider eliminating chicken unless it is a luncheon course of chicken salad or an entrée of chicken tettrazini. Some guests feel let down when they are served chicken. Offering beef or a combination of beef and seafood is an appealing combination. If a banquet manager tells you you're going to get a four-course meal, and one of those is chicken, eliminate one course or make another selection. If time and staffing permits, offer sauces and dressings passed instead of already on the plate.

Breads

Choose a selection of the best breads—variety tantalizes the palate. Many judge a meal or a restaurant by the quality of the bread that is served. For the Quest for Excellence event, the tasting committee chose the ever-popular house roll and a crustier herb roll. This made a nice combination and gave guests a choice. If you are planning a meal for a health conscious group, consider low-carb bread.

Just Desserts

For most people, the dessert course is the favorite. For the Quest for Excellence, we chose a chocolate mousse-filled globe showing the different parts of the world. The dessert reflected the global personality of our honoree and recognized his worldwide achievements. We further embellished the dessert plate with fresh fruit, a miniature pecan tart, and a sliver of flourless chocolate cake, thus accommodating all tastes.

To enhance the dessert presentation, the chef can create a design around the border of the plate or write a poetic line. A chocolate decal can be added to the dessert recognizing the honoree, corporation, or the nonprofit organization. When hosting a celebrity, why not name the dessert course in her honor (soufflé au chocolat Mitzi)? A glass of champagne adds to a festive toast or salute. If your budget allows, offer it with your dessert course.

Elegant Flourishes

Details, details. Why not add a slice of lemon, orange, or cucumber to the water for palate appeal? You can even add a flower or a spiraling lemon, lime, or orange rind. These tiny considerations give evidence to the details in planning. Serve chilled water rather than placing ice cubes in the glass, as they will cause the glass to sweat on the tablecloth and drip onto your guests' clothes.

A sugar and creamer add nothing to the table décor. My preference is to have them passed. It is also nice to have the butter pats done in a decorative style on the bread and butter plates. Napkin folds create part of the look, and there are lots of choices—bird of paradise, fan, candlestick, or the bishop's cap.

For any event where food is being served, make certain that cold items are served cold and hot items are served hot. You don't want room temperature smoked salmon when it's supposed to be chilled. Try not to overproduce your plate, and make sure that the foods that are selected are in harmony.

Don't forget to mention to the banquet manager that the food service should be completed before the program begins. It is important that all the tables be served the same course at the same time. For added flair at seated events, you can instruct the caterer to serve with white gloves and synchronized style: Waiters come out in one line with a plate in each hand, stand behind the ladies and serve them on the left, then serve the gentlemen on the right and exit. Synchronized service is like watching a ballet.

Look after your guests by avoiding bottlenecks. If the dinner is to be a buffet, have duplicate food stations. Make sure the food platters are replenished and look as they did when the first person went through the line. If a staff member sees someone holding up the line, she should attempt to remedy the situation. Create a plethora of foods spilling over with many different types of fruits, breads, cheeses, and vegetables. This makes for a lusty presentation.

Enhance the "Flavor"

Try to give the food items listed on your menu an international flare. It may sound more appealing if it's in Italian, for example—zamberetti con salsa verdi, tortellini alla pana, porchetta alla perrigini, insalata verde con brie, zuppa Inglese, and caffee.

You also can give the items on your menu pizzazz by naming them after the accomplishments of an honoree. At an event for author Phyllis George, the first course was named "Miss America," the main course, "Superbowl Sportcaster," and the dessert course, "First Lady of Kentucky."

If you are asked to provide a totally vegetarian menu for an environmental group event, enlist the assistance of a well-known food editor or a nutritionist to help you create a menu that all your guests will enjoy. Accept the challenge to create an interesting menu.

An Evening Highlighting
The Many Admirable Accomplishments of
Phyllis George

Spring Gala 2003 Menu
by
Chef Charles Carroll

"Miss America"

Wedge of Brie, Sliced Pears, and Toasted Pecans
Atop a Bouquet of Field Greens
Fresh Baked Melba Toast

"Superbowl Sportscaster"

Filet of Tenderloin
With Bernaise Sauce
Truffle Whipped Potatoes
Tomato Crown Filled with Creamed Spinach
Assorted Warm Dinner Rolls

"First Lady of Kentucky"

Flourless Chocolate Cake
Paired with Coffee Ice Cream and Frangelica Sauce

"Folk Artists' Spokesperson"

Freshly Brewed Colombian Coffee, Decaf and Teas
Beringer Chardonnay and Beringer Merlot Dinner Wines

"Learning makes a man fit company for himself."
- Anon

An event honoring Phyllis George featured an appropriate menu.

Sample Menu

*A salad of mixed greens with sliced pears and a
sprinkling of blueberries, slivers of toasted pecans, and a
wedge of Brie, complimented by a
light balsamic vinaigrette and
homemade Melba toast*

❧

*A petit filet of tenderloin with truffle whipped potatoes,
your choice of a mushroom or béarnaise sauce,
accompanied with a tomato crown filled
with creamed spinach*

❧

Warm dinner rolls and sweet butter

❧

Chocolate decadence cake with raspberry sauce

PLANNING THE DECORATIONS

When planning the décor for a special event, always consider your guests. Do everything you can to provide comfort and prevent slips, stumbles, and falls. If your gala has a theme and guests are asked to wear a mask, plan well so that ladies wearing long evening gowns won't have to negotiate steps up or down or maneuver a cluttered path.

When people are walking, most of the time they look straight ahead rather than down. Keeping pathways level and clear will help prevent an accident or potential injury. Keep the venue space from becoming overcrowded to allow comfortable passage for the guests as well as the waiters. Imagine a basket of rolls landing on a guest's head.

Take a Comfortable Chair, Please

Keep in mind the comfort level of guests when selecting rental chairs or choosing between chairs the venue has to offer. This is especially important when guests are seated for three to four hours. Guests come in all different sizes and heights, and you want them to be comfortable while they are seated. Ask one or two committee members to sit in several chairs before making the final selection. You don't want the only memory of your event to be uncomfortable chairs and aching backs.

Table Décor

Flowers require attention. Make sure you can keep the room where they are stored at the proper temperature—on the cool side. This is

Select table décor that reflects your theme.

especially important when you are making floral arrangements the day or night before an event. If you are hosting a series of related events in the same day, the floral centerpieces can be freshened and moved from a luncheon meeting to the evening occasion. This will save fundraising dollars and works well if both events are held at the same venue.

Consider the centerpieces part of your décor. On occasion, their design may dictate their placement and the direction they need to face on the table. For instance, Jeff Krause of the Roundtop Collection created a sphere with an Excalibur-like sword going through it for the Quest for Excellence Gala theme. All of the swords needed to be angled in the same direction. It made a powerful impact when guests entered the room. All of these details are part of the look and mood you are creating. In fact, it is a good idea to do a mock-up of your table and photograph it with everything in its proper place—place cards, programs, favors, chocolates, table tent cards, centerpiece, candles, napkin, crystal, china, and flatware. Recently, there was an

The centerpieces for the Quest for Excellence
Gala captured the essence of the event.

event at which the person in charge of the floral arrangements became ill. His assistants were able to take over because we had documented the way the centerpieces were to look.

If you are planning to offer your centerpieces for sale at the end of the evening, be sure to promote them in the invitation and event program. The master of ceremonies can give a reminder to guests that the centerpieces are available for purchase during the course of the evening. Invited guests of table sponsors may choose to support the cause—as well as to take home a remembrance from the event—by purchasing a centerpiece. The concept of recycling is yet another way to defray event expenses. When there are floral centerpieces leftover, and guests don't take them home, they can be delivered to a seniors' facility or a hospital.

Avoid white cotton table napkins since the lint has a tendency to stick to dark colors and adhere to certain fabrics. The decorations chairperson should take this under consideration when selecting the color of the napkin. Avoid slippery fabrics when selecting chair covers. You don't want to see your guests on the floor.

In the event there is an unforeseeable emergency, such as a contract decorator becoming ill, a contingency person should have the timeline and be totally familiar with the set up for the special event. Concerns that might arise could be the location of different props in the ballroom, the positioning of the dance floor, placement of the podium on the stage (to the right or to the left), and whether there is a color plan for the floral centerpieces.

Other Forms of Decoration

Lilly Pulitzer and Jay Mulvaney's book signing was a benefit where the guests became the décor dressed in their Lilly Signature prints. Models lounged around the pool and in the water, and guests danced to Calypso music. Everything was "very Lilly" in her fabulous print fabric from the tabletops to the potted pink hydrangeas that lined the swimming pool. Even the margaritas were mango flavored.

The design for this event honoring Lilly Pulitzer
reflected her signature style.

For "A Night at the Alhambra," the table coverings in the
"Perfumed Garden" ballroom evoked a Spanish Arabian-inspired
elegance and exoticism. In creating the look, Francesca Nilsen of
Distinctive Details and I went through her inventory of table coverings in search of the old world look we wanted. We also decided to
go to the Indian marketplace in our city, where we found one fabric
more beautiful than the other. We put our heads together and decided to use the cloths from her store as the table coverings, and then
buy saris and make them into the overlays to dress the tables. We
had to measure the saris to see how many overlays we could get
from each one.

From the remaining fabric, we created pashminas that adorned
the backs of the chair covers in the ballroom, and the myriad of jew-
eled colors looked stunningly beautiful. We anticipated a thousand
guests, and this meant there would be one hundred tables, more or

less. We had to work out the details of how many saris we needed with the color pattern of the underskirts. It was like creating a painting. The pashminas were red, green, and gold, and available for guests to purchase at $150 each. The palm-like metal tree candelabras with hand-blown glass votives were unique works of art complementing the table décor and were offered at $275 each.

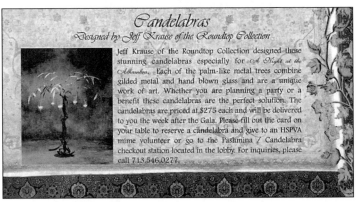

Candelabras
Designed by Jeff Krause of the Roundtop Collection

Jeff Krause of the Roundtop Collection designed these stunning candelabras especially for *A Night at the Alhambra*. Each of the palm-like metal trees combine gilded metal and hand blown glass and are a unique work of art. Whether you are planning a party or a benefit these candelabras are the perfect solution. The candelabras are priced at $275 each and will be delivered to you the week after the Gala. Please fill out the card on your table to reserve a candelabra and give to an HSPVA mime volunteer or go to the Pashmina / Candelabra checkout station located in the lobby. For inquiries, please call 713.546.0277.

When your centerpieces are for sale, be sure to feature them in the program.

For the Thyroid Society Gala with Joe Piscopo as our honoree, we decided to play up his Saturday Night Live role. We presented a comedy theater skit, complete with Church Lady, and adorned each table with metal sculptures representing New York icons—the Empire State and Chrysler Buildings and the Brooklyn Bridge. These sculptured centerpieces were available for purchase, once again adhering to the zero budget philosophy. A local grocer donated lots of red apples to add to the New York theme.

For the College of Architecture at the University of Houston, I used the reverse side of the table linens; the cloth was a black pinstripe, and using the reverse side of the fabric gave the tables a more architectural look. Black wooden chairs with white seat cushions continued the minimal design to complement the Philip Johnson building where the event was held. Each year an architect on the committee, George Atallah, creates a centerpiece as homage to the honored architect. Students at the college worked with him to complete the centerpieces in time for the event. Decorations on a budget can produce great results. The space at the college was well lit, and a few red roses as part of the centerpieces gave a dash of color.

The venue for this College of Architecture benefit was outfitted in elegant black décor for the occasion.

For the Challenger Gala, I enlisted a group of roller skaters known as the "Urban Animals." They donned futuristic space costumes and literally skated guests into the reception. Tribute banners commemorating the shuttle's heroic crew touched the guests as they ascended the escalators.

It was appropriate to bring in the Texas A&M Honor Guard for the Archives of American Art event. This added dignity to the occasion and created a special moment as guests entered the ballroom walking under the saber arch. Pomp and circumstance brings excitement to an event.

Decorating and Entertaining Ideas

- Go to a grocery store or florist and purchase bags of rose petals. They can be stored in a refrigerator until ready to use. Spread them around the tabletops at your event to create a pretty look.
- Votive candles add sparkle. Try covering the votive cups in acanthus leaves and tying your creation with a cording. Or for a different effect, place your candles in a hollowed out piece of fruit.
- Change all the light bulbs to pink in the chandeliers of a ballroom. People will love the glow. A wholesale lighting company may buy into the idea and supply the bulbs.
- Add panels of sheer silk organza draped strategically or wrapped around columns for a nice effect. Lighting to enhance this can add to the atmosphere.
- At an outdoor event at someone's home or a smaller venue, go to a market like Fiesta or Sam's and purchase tall religious candles in clear glass to create a special effect lining the pool or walkways.
- People love watching fish. How about a goldfish or two swimming in a bowl with a flower-shaped candle floating on the surface?
- For your next event, ask volunteers to make keepsake beaded or ceramic napkin rings.
- Let Carmen Miranda and her exotic turbans adorn the heads of your chair and committee members and serve as centerpieces for a benefit with a theme, "A Night in the Caribbean." Your guests will be fighting over which one takes the turban home.
- Offer walking sticks as favors for the gentlemen at an event with a Southern theme. The name of the event and year can be inscribed

continued

Decorating and Entertaining Ideas (continued)

on the top of the stick.

- Enlist the support of a nursery or floral shop to loan and transport palm trees and tropical plants to accentuate your theme.
- Marching bands outside a venue like a concert hall or theater can add hoopla and excitement and create the mood before guests enter.
- Mimes or a troop of actors can create a playful atmosphere.
- Add face painters, tarot readers, jugglers, a fire-eater, a sword swallower, a bagpiper, belly dancers, or strolling gypsies to the mix. They become the décor. You can see if there is a festival that takes place in your area and recruit performers, or you could call a talent agency.

The Best Things Are Unexpected

A chocolate vendor may want to introduce a new line of chocolates and decide to select your event to debut the candy. (For a Habitat for Humanity event, a chocolate house was created to represent the houses built by the volunteers.) Favors could be provided by a co-sponsoring retailer such as Saks Fifth Avenue, Bergdorf Goodman, or the Warner Brothers store. The item could be a new fragrance, a his/her gift, a funny T-shirt, or any other charming, eye-catching, and heartwarming memorabilia. These items can be sponsored by an organization's in-kind supporters.

When your organization is gifted with two hundred and fifty bottles of a new fragrance, add the extra touch that will make the favor even more special. The decorations committee members can enhance these perfumes by wrapping them in a lovely paper, tying a ribbon around them, and attaching a card acknowledging the donor's generosity.

You need to make certain that gift favors go to those who were intended to receive them. They should be kept in a safe, secure place until they are ready to be distributed. If there are leftover favors, give them to key volunteers and staff members as a thank-you.

The volunteer committee is responsible for placing the table favors on the tables as directed. More than half of those attending any function will be women, so a favor intended for the women would be placed at every other seat. Some gifts work for both genders, such as a gift bag of spa products, and should be placed at each seat. Try to think of unusual, commemorative, and meaningful favors for guests: magic wands, fans, engraved compacts, candles, bookmarks, picture frames, books, drawings, or something handmade by children to help the organization.

For example, for the "Quest for Excellence Award Gala" benefiting the College of Mathematics and Natural Science at the University of Houston, I used a molecule design as the graphic background on our special MCI calling card favor. The card was valid for thirty minutes of free long distance calling. There was a photograph of the honoree on the calling card and a message from the chair thanking the benefactors.

For the highest-level benefactors and the honoree of the 2001 Opera Ball, I commissioned a young sculptor, J. D. Peppers, who had been named "A Sculptor for the New Century," to create special pieces to show appreciation for their support. Mr. Peppers saw this as an opportunity to give back to the community and to put his work before leaders and philanthropists. The sculptures were on exhibit at the benefactors' dinner, and at the gala Mr. Peppers was brought on stage to present the award to the honoree.

THE PROGRAM

Choosing a Master of Ceremonies

The presence of a master of ceremonies always adds structure to the program and will get your guests out in a timely fashion. Busy people like to know that there is a beginning and an ending. A news anchor or media personality's presentation skills brings the event to order, guides the program along, and keeps everyone on schedule.

Try to keep the program to a maximum of forty-five minutes (thirty minutes is better). Guests should not be overwhelmed with a wordy emcee who looks upon this opportunity as a personal audition. Try to discourage a master of ceremonies who thinks he is a singer from spoiling the evening. Keep individual speeches and acceptance remarks in the two- to five-minute range. Your benefactors have stepped up to the plate and don't need repetitive reinforcement.

In the absence of an emcee, and if it is appropriate, you might consider inviting a member of the church community to deliver the invocation to bring the room to order. This helps signal the guests that lunch or dinner is about to be served.

At the beginning of the program, the emcee will recognize dignitaries and distinguished guests who are present in the audience. If a unique favor has been provided, the emcee will make guests aware of this special gift and recognize the donor.

Scripting the Event

Provide the master of ceremonies and any other participants in the program with a script in advance so they will be familiar with as many details as possible. As there is generally not time for a rehearsal, this is very helpful to the participants and will make your program flow smoothly. Also, don't forget to hand the emcee a revised script if changes are made at the last minute.

During the course of the evening program, the master of ceremonies can remind your guests of additional ways they can support your fundraising event. If your centerpieces or other items are for sale, the emcee can advise guests as to their availability and how to purchase them. If your event includes a silent auction, the emcee will give the guests several notices throughout the evening about what time the bidding will be closing.

Ask the Master of Ceremonies to remind people to turn off their cell phones or put them on vibrate. Nothing is more annoying than the ringing sound of a cell phone breaking the silence during a poignant moment in a ballroom. People feel very embarrassed when their cell phones go off during a stirring speech, an award presentation, or a touching movie clip.

Working Script

RAINFOREST GALA
November 2 Gala

8:15 p.m.
Once guests are seated for dinner, Master of Ceremonies Bob Boudreaux welcomes everyone, recognizes distinguished guests in the audience: actor Steven Seagal and possibly Cher, and any other Star Power in the audience.

8:45 p.m.
Once the dessert course has been placed on the table, Bob Boudreaux introduces Leon Hall, who then introduces the judges for Ms. Rainforest 2002 (former chairs of past Rainforest Galas: Jerry Allen, Susana Brener de Stern, Bill & Liz Decker, Gigi Huang, Olga & Jim Jeffries, John W Mecom, Jr., Jessica & Philipp Meyer, Ingrid K Moody, Renee & Fernando Somoza) to stand and be recognized.

Leon Hall presents the International Beauty Ambassadors of Goodwill in their official evening gowns, crowns, sashes.

Bob Boudreaux introduces Co-Chair Carolyn Farb, who makes remarks.

Co-Chair Carolyn Farb introduces Founder and Co-Chair Lucho, who makes remarks in Spanish.

continued

Carolyn and Lucho introduce the Sting Video.

Bob Boudreaux introduces Dr. Franca Sciuto, Chair of the Rainforest Foundation Fund. (Talk to Bright Star Productions about having poignant slides on screen.)

Bob Boudreaux introduces Rainforest Foundation Chairman USA (insert name).

Bob introduces Christie's Auctioneer and asks for the lights to be brought up and asks the spotters to take their places throughout the room.

Bob makes announcements about the Silent Auction closing at 10:45 to spur last-minute bidders; he lets guests know that the centerpieces will be available for sale.

Leon Hall brings out the Ambassadors of Beauty in their native costumes and presents Regina Duke Scholarship to Ms. Rainforest 2002. Leon Hall recognizes Regina Duke in the audience.

Carolyn & Lucho present the First Annual Foundation Guardian Award to Jaime Camille Garza and recognize art/sculptor Patricia Baez, who designed award.

Bob Boudreaux introduces Jaime Camil In Concert.

After the concert, Bob closes the evening out and introduces Commercial Art, who will provide the dance music.

Working the Crowd

If you're standing in a group and someone walks up and you don't know her name, you can say, "Have you met so-and-so?" Then, hopefully, that individual will respond with her name when you introduce the others. Have the volunteers who are working the event move about the crowd, offering assistance. Give everyone the opportunity to participate and support your cause. Let your guests leave with something commemorative that represents the organization, like an opera CD, coffee mug with the group's logo, or a T-shirt sporting your slogan. And always remind your guests of additional ways they can support your fundraising cause.

Ways to Maximize Your Event

- Several staff members should meet and greet guests.
- Staff members should be identified by special nametags or boutonnières.
- Volunteers should be positioned at entry elevators and escalators.
- Exchange business cards for future follow-up.
- Arrange introductions with other guests.
- Introduce guests to honorees and dignitaries.
- Make sure photographs are taken of key attendees.

 *Chapter Sixteen*

Down to the Details

*"Our main business is not to see what lies dimly in
the distance but to do what lies clearly at hand."*
—Thomas Carlyle

You can never be too meticulous when it comes to planning all the
details of a main event, from preparing a schedule for the evening to
organizing table seating and valet parking.

Make a Final Schedule for the Event

A reasonable time for the reception period of an evening event is
between 7:00 p.m. and 8:15 p.m. The dinner chimes should be
sounded from 8:00 p.m. to 8:05 p.m., and this will give your guests,
depending on the size of the crowd, ample time to be seated in the
ballroom. On a rare occasion, your reception may run longer than
anticipated, which may alter your event timeline. Any decision to
change the timetable should be left to the discretion of the event
chairman.

Taking into consideration the menu that the chef has prepared
and the number of courses planned, dinner would begin at 8:30
p.m., with the first course possibly being preset.

Generally, the program will begin at 9:15 or 9:30, after dessert
has been placed on the table. At this time the event chairs, major

benefactors, and honorees are recognized. Keep the program on the short side of thirty to forty-five minutes or the audience's attention will begin to wane. If you are holding a live auction, schedule it into the program before dancing or entertainment begins. The entertainment should begin at 10:00 p.m. or 10:15 p.m. and conclude by midnight. If your event is held during the week, you'll notice guests will begin leaving by 10:30 p.m.

PLACING THE TABLES

There is art and diplomacy in the seating of guests, and it comes with knowing your guests and being aware of sensitive situations. Once you know the number of full tables and individual seats that have been purchased, the banquet manager at the hotel can prepare a floor plan. The plan gives the scale of the dance floor and the required size of the bandstand. Ask the banquet manager to color code the most desirable tables on the floor plan and assign them according to different levels of sponsorship. The banquet manager will be more familiar with various aspects of the space—for example, which tables are located near a service door which might disturb guests, where the best handicap access would be, and the easiest access to the stage for participants in the program.

Combine individual reservations into tables of ten. You should always have open seats available to place guests who have purchased individual tickets at the last minute or who might drop in without having made a reservation. If you're anticipating a sell-out crowd, you want to make certain that there are no blank spaces in your room. Volunteers can fill in if necessary. People do not always use good manners and respond to an RSVP, but from a practical standpoint, a charity cannot afford to pay for an extra meal or have a seat vacant that they could have filled.

It is good planning to have a couple of extra tables at the back of the room in anticipation of unexpected guests or those who did not

RSVP. It's possible that their names did not appear on the reservation list due to the fault of a computer, a failed answering machine message, delays in the postal service, or a staff oversight. Always remember that the guest who appears unexpectedly must have assumed the RSVP had been handled and, upon arriving, discovers that there is no reservation. The best way to handle the situation is to accommodate the guest in an unflustered, welcoming manner.

A friend chaired a fashion show luncheon and an unexpected major table sponsor arrived wanting to be seated at her runway table. The room was at capacity, and there were no more tables available except a small nook near the front of the stage. Quickly a table appeared. The gracious benefactor took the error in stride and seated her group without incident. Mistakes do happen, and it is best when it can be resolved to the donor's satisfaction.

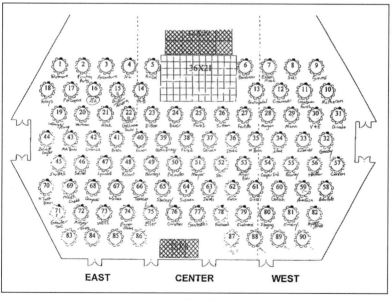

A seating chart provides event staff the big picture when seating guests.

Top-Level Seating

A benefactor host will want the evening to reflect his sense of gracious hospitality as if the event were being held in his home or at a private club. For top-level benefactors, the nonprofit organization may offer to prepare place cards for them and their guests. This can be done in a beautiful calligraphy by hand or on the computer. The nonprofit staff can place the cards in accordance with a seating diagram. Top-level benefactors will appreciate this special touch. In this way, when their guests enter the ballroom, they do not have to stand and wait to be seated by their hosts.

After the banquet manager has created the floor plan and numbered the tables accordingly, carefully work on your seating. The chair offers her input, along with others in the organization who may be familiar with guests who merit special consideration for past levels of giving. Make certain the person in charge of the seating arrangements is given as much information as possible about the guests (company, title, sponsorship level, or some other type of identifying information) in order to seat them well—especially if guests are unknown to one another. This helps make the task of deciding who sits with whom much easier. The goal is to seat everyone happily.

Your first priority is to seat the major table benefactors. Then combine high-level individual ticket holders at tables and, finally, place other levels of individual ticket holders. Sometimes individuals do not wish to go through the hassle of filling an entire table and will purchase two tickets at a higher level to demonstrate their support. Hopefully, there will be others choosing that same level of support on an individual basis, and you can seat them together, creating a table.

In another situation, if guests don't fill the entire table, you might ask them if you can seat another couple at their table. Most of the time, this does not create a problem, but there are exceptions. If this is the case, in order for the room not to have empty spaces, ask the banquet manager to set their tables for a specific number. On the occasion when someone has donated a table or purchased tickets but does not plan to attend, consider extending an invitation to in-kind donors who would like to attend.

Not everyone can have the best seat in the house. Guests will be content if they are in the company of people they know or other guests they would like to know. There is definitely a fine art to seating guests.

Making a Media Plan

When you have most of your information confirmed, set up your media plan for covering the gala event at least one to two weeks prior to the event. Schedule an on-site meeting so that everyone is familiar with the venue and the program. At the meeting, include the chairman, the media committee chair, any pro bono public relations representatives, and the photographer who will be covering the event.

When press or media are asked to cover an event, you should always arrange for them to be seated at the event. It is a courtesy to ask if they will be coming with a guest. A press kit can be held for them at the registration desk upon arrival. A representative from the nonprofit organization or a member of the media committee should meet them upon arrival and offer to be of assistance locating and identifying the individuals responsible for the success of the event such as the honoree, chairpersons, major benefactors, and generous in-kind donors.

Media Seating

Always provide good seating for the media because a happy reporter can give your cause much more exposure than one hundred events can. If the media does not like where they have been seated or feel that they have been slighted in any way, they may leave before the program begins. Don't group all the media representatives at the same table. Intersperse them throughout the audience, seated with the event chair, board members, celebrity guests, performing artists, visiting dignitaries, or volunteers. This is another way to make them more familiar with your organization.

PLANNING FOR TRANSPORTATION AND PARKING

Getting to the Venue

If the venue is located in an area where you might anticipate traffic congestion or new construction, tell your guests to allow an extra twenty to thirty minutes for driving and parking time. Offer alternative routes and a map. This will keep your event on schedule and help to soothe any unpleasant driving angst in getting to and from the venue. If the area where the event is scheduled has increased activity with limited parking space available, suggest old-fashioned carpooling.

Valet Parking

Valet parking can make or break an event. You want your guests' entrance and departure at an event to be equally pleasurable. Having purchased an expensive ticket or table for an event, donors resent being asked to pay for valet parking at the venue. See if you can negotiate with the hotel banquet manager to incorporate valet parking expenses into the cost per person for the meal. It is even more irritating if the parking service seems disorganized and it takes a long time to retrieve your car. Make certain the hotel has the correct number of valets in relation to the number of guests attending. Don't keep guests waiting.

Make sure that the parking attendants know in advance about the pre-arranged validated parking and do not hassle your guests as they are leaving. At registration, the guests should be given a sticker or stamp that validates their parking ticket. A tip to the valet is always appreciated, but the amount is up to your guests' personal discretion. At a recent fundraiser held at a museum on the West Coast, guests were advised upon departing the event that it was not necessary to tip the valet parkers. Their gratuity had been taken care of in advance. Not having to pull out the wallet was a nice touch for those in attendance.

Always try to do a dry run when a valet parking situation offers a challenge (a department store opening at a mall, a convention center, a rock concert), especially at larger events where a high volume of cars is involved. Estimate how long your guests will have to wait for their cars and evaluate what steps need to be taken to facilitate the situation.

Valet parking attendants need to know how many cars will be arriving so they can staff the event accordingly. Speak to the venue manager to make certain they have enough parking garage spaces and enough parking attendants based on the number of cars that will be parked. All of your hard work on the event can dissipate in a matter of moments if your guests' topic of conversation turns to their bad parking experience. For an Inside.com event in Beverly Hills, some partygoers waited forty-five minutes to retrieve their cars. You can have Wolfgang Puck, Spago, and all, but the evening is ruined if there is not a fast turn around in the valet parking.

If you choose to hold the event at a place other than a hotel, secure a bonded valet parking service. Be sure the valet company has handled numerous events in the same size range and with logistical challenges similar to yours. Schedule a site visit to determine the drop-off location, where the cars will be parked, how long it will take to retrieve guests' cars and how many attendants will be available. Also, if the parking is complimentary, this fact should be made known to the parking service.

For an independent valet service, a good formula to use in determining the number of valet parkers required is one valet parker per ten to fifteen cars. The number of valets depends on where the cars will be parked. If parking is easily accessible, you could use fewer valets. If you have four hundred guests, and they are mostly couples, you would have two hundred cars needing to be parked. You can figure thirteen to fifteen parkers to get the job done.

Give your valets specific instructions not to spend anymore time in your guests' cars than necessary. Valets should leave lights and other adjustments (the position of the driver's seat, the radio station, the climate control, and the viewing mirrors) as they were when they take the car to the parking garage. A valet is only in a guest's car for a matter of seconds, maybe minutes, so he doesn't need to check out all the features.

Accommodating Out-of-Town Guests

When fashion designer Zandra Rhodes hosted a benefit at actor Larry Hagman's home in Ojai, California, for the Fashion and Textile Museum in London, guests had the option of choosing their departure location. If they left from Los Angeles, the driving distance was an hour and a half, and from San Diego, three and a half hours, making the day trip from either location within reasonable driving distance. Arrangements were made for a group of benefactors to travel together by shuttle bus. Should one your two buses break down, be prepared to have backup transportation available. You want this excursion to be a pleasant memory. Sometimes the climate will vary, so provide your guests with the necessary details that will enable them to dress accordingly.

For the dedication of the George Bush Library in College Station, Texas, a special restored railroad car from Houston, Texas, transported guests. Try to enlist the partnership of a transportation company like Union Pacific Railroad to participate in your event.

It is common courtesy to offer certain amenities to visiting dignitaries, celebrities, or authors who are coming to participate in your special event. Their schedules are generally hectic and busy, and by providing a limousine to pick them up at the airport, you are assured that they will get to the event on time. Partner with a limousine company to be the official representative for your gala or concert. You can recognize the company in any advance publicity and in the event program. Encouraging your friends to use their services is another way to say thank you.

When making arrangements for out-of-town guests, negotiate with the host hotel for a discounted rate on rooms and parking, provide maps to pre-events, and list car services and available hair and make-up professionals.

Sometimes it's appropriate to go above and beyond these common courtesies when courting out-of-town benefactors. There were guests who traveled from abroad to attend the Quest for Excellence Award Gala honoring Eckhard Pfeiffer. We thought it would be nice to provide gift baskets to these special supporters when they checked into their hotel. I wrote a personal thank-you note and included any last-minute instructions or changes in plans.

For out-of-town guests who will be driving to events, it is helpful for them to know valet parking rates and different locations where they might park nearest to the event. To park at the Fairmont Hotel in Dallas might cost ten dollars, whereas parking in a nearby church parking garage may cost three dollars. For out-of-town guests, a listing of hotels in the district where the event is taking place, along with room rates, is also helpful.

EVENT LOGISTICS

Putting yourself through the paces a guest would experience at an event will help you work out the logistics. Having escorts and ushers take guests to their specific table locations in large venues can ease a challenging situation. Some people are claustrophobic and being in a large crowd is uncomfortable for them. Most people come to events hoping to enjoy themselves, relax, and support a worthwhile cause.

Also keep in mind that people prefer not to be shuttled from place to place during the course of an evening, unless each move is absolutely necessary. If you can keep the reception in one space, and the dinner and entertainment in another, your guests won't object to making that one transition. If they are transported from a pre-reception, to a reception, to a dinner, and then to a concert location, you might have some disenchanted guests.

Also, it may be difficult to reverse the flow of traffic, but it is worth a try when you are trying to summon hundreds of people to dinner on another floor up a single escalator. Check with the hotel manager to see if you might be able to have both of the escalators going up for a brief period to move the crowd more quickly, unless it proves hazardous or is against hotel fire regulations. When guests depart, they will be leaving at different times, so it does not present the same problem.

PLANNING THE LIGHTING AND SOUND SYSTEMS

Make certain you check out the technical equipment in advance. Schedule a rehearsal the afternoon of the event to review special lighting effects, slides, fireworks displays, video presentations, or even flaming desserts that are included in the program to ensure that all elements are working.

Perfect Lighting

This is a good time for your volunteers who will be setting up the ballroom to view a table complete with cloth, overlay, chair covers, napkin fold, china, centerpiece, candles, flowers, flatware, crystal, favors, and programs. You will be able to see how everything looks with the lighting in place. The lighting is a part of your overall theme for the event, and there may be additional lasers, pin lights, fog, or other special effects required for the entertainers, orchestra, backdrop, or program.

If the program is being filmed, be sure to give your lighting extra consideration. Working in advance with the sound and lighting crews will assure the success of any videos that are being produced. With the lights, excitement, and energy running high, have a makeup artist or volunteer off stage to powder or blot the faces of distinguished guests or speakers before they go on. Remember to check the ties on the gentlemen. When you go to the effort and expense of creating a video, be sure it is as representative of your event—and your organization—as it can be.

Sensitive Sound

Do sound checks from different locations in the venue. Have you ever begun to speak only to find that the audience cannot hear you? Or that the sound system has started to take on a life of its own? Especially at an outdoor function, the sound system needs to be tested in advance at the time of day or night the function will be held. Ask someone to spot the sound from several different locations to make certain it can be heard by all of your audience and that there are no dead spots. A good sound system also maximizes the performance of any musicians.

With outdoor events, remember to incorporate factors like wind, weather, and street noises into your sound check. The noise factor may be significantly different than when the sound was initially tested. Have a sound technician on hand to make any necessary adjustments to the sound system as soon as the first speaker is heard.

Provide a Podium

Many times, people will be speaking from a script or their own notes. Make arrangements for a podium with a light, or provide adequate lighting from above. It is up to the chairman or head of the decorations committee to choose the type of podium. A Plexiglas podium, if available, has a clean look. It's also helpful if a podium has a shelf for scripts and awards that may need to be presented. If there is not a shelf beneath the lectern, ask a volunteer to stand by at the side of the stage during the program to hand the awards to whoever will be presenting them. They can also assist people on and off the stage. Women in long ball gowns appreciate the helping hand

and thoughtfulness. Several glasses of water discreetly placed on a table onstage are a nice touch for participants in the program.

SCHEDULING THE EVENT VOLUNTEERS

Set up an event orientation at the venue beforehand so volunteers can become familiar with the space in which they will be performing various tasks. This helps to avoid confusion later on. Describe the flow of the event and distribute a timeline for the evening. Discuss parking, food and beverage arrangements, and attire. Set up a schedule of volunteer assignments, such as registration, logistics, seating assistance, auction set-up and tear-down, auction check-in and check-out, bid runners, spotters, etc.

Have a changing room for volunteers who work more than one shift (some need to switch from their work clothes to the appropriate attire for the event). Remember to thank volunteers often. They take care of numerous tasks that go unheralded. They are compassionate, unselfish, caring, patient, and loving. Never take volunteers for granted. Nurture them and appreciate their value.

Opera Ball 2001

Opera Staff - Volunteers

6:30 – 9:00 p.m. Registration – Development Staff

We need 10 volunteers from Development - Sonya, Rudy, Mindy, Tammy, Ila, Celia, Amy, Joy, LaShabriel, Mark, Kitty.

Their assignment is to meet and greet guests upon their arrival, at the registration desk as they come in from valet parking. Volunteers will also inform guests that if they haven't registered their credit cards for the auction that they can go to the computer banks and sign up during the one hour reception.

continued

Special Events will send out a mailing with Opera Ball Express Checkout on the outside so people will register in advance. This will avoid any delay for them at the Ball. They can fax or mail this back to Laura or Zack.

6:30 p.m. – 1:00 a.m. Auction Registration – Finance Department

We need 10 volunteers from this department - Judy, Ken, Jennifer M., Jennifer L, Rene, Kathy, Kisha, Joel, Maria, Bertha, Jocelyn.

They will sign in guests and register their credit cards. Some guests may have not been listed in the system at all and some guests may be substituting for another guest. We will need their name, address, and phone number.

Four volunteers are needed to man the computer terminal stations during the evening at all times. When the auction closes at 11 p.m., all 10 volunteers need to be manning this area.

8:00 p.m. – 11:00 p.m.

The Development Staff volunteers will have an alphabetical guest list and a table list. We will have two floor plans that Laura will get from Gary Marrero and have Kinko's enlarge and dry-mount them.

This station located directly outside the Ballroom also serves as an ad hoc registration and table locating station for those who arrive late or have forgotten where they are seated.

Six volunteers will man the Express Pashmina and Candelabra Station. Rody Kuchar's department (1-3 volunteers) plus 2 Development staff volunteers will move from the downstairs registration after guests go up to dinner at 8:15 p.m.

We are going to take reservations for the candelabras, which can be picked up the next day (Sunday) between 10 a.m. – 2 p.m. Gary Marrero is determining a room that can serve as a pickup station.

continued

9:30 – 10:30 p.m.

After guests have gone up to dinner by 8:30 p.m., Ken Vaughn and Joel Middents will move the auction registration desk to the checkout station between 9:30-10:00 p.m.

9:30 – 10:00 p.m. Live Auction Needs (Per the Auctioneer from Christie's)

The two artworks – the painting and sculpture plus the storyboard on the Chateau need to be presented when they are announced to auction. We will have slides on the car and these items as well displayed on the Screens.

We will need Marketing, Finance, Development, and Education Departments to serve as the 20 spotters during the Live Auction. Presently we have 825 plus guests attending and the opportunity to raise $200,000 or more with the help of our Christie's Auctioneer! He wants everyone to wave red napkins to indicate a bid and no shouting.

I would like Shane Gasbarra to stand by the Auctioneer's side to record the bids.

11:00 p.m.

When the Silent Auction closes, (Opera Guild and Houston Proud) volunteers will bring the bid sheets to auction checkout, which has been moved from the original valet to the departing valet exiting area.

All 10 Finance Dept. volunteers will input winning bids into HGO database.

11:30 p.m. Silent and Live Auction Checkout Begins

Mark Lear, Allen Naplan and Naomi with Guild or Houston Proud volunteers.

The Guild and Houston Proud volunteers who have been working the silent auction both in the lobby and outside the Ballroom will now bring the bid sheets to the checkout station and then pack the items and bring them to the Auction Warehouse, located

continued

next to auction checkout.

Guests go first to the auction checkout and get an invoice (a three part form); they will sign the top copy and leave it with the Finance Dept. and take the other two copies to the warehouse to pick up the item. They leave one copy of the invoice that has been initialed and the last copy is for their records.

Giving volunteers a detailed timeline with assignments at orientation will avoid confusion during the event.

Tips for Assisting Event Volunteers

- Never assume your volunteers can read your mind and that they will know how to handle things. Show them what tasks need to be done and how you would like them done.
- Provide volunteers with a timetable that gives them all the information they need about the special event, including where and when orientation takes place, when they are expected to arrive the day of the event, and where to park (is parking validation provided by the nonprofit in the form of a sticker?). Include specific duties (assisting the florist, loading and unloading props, placing signage, moderating the silent auction, handling reservations, or assisting with checkout or teardown), break schedules, the location of the break room, who will relieve them for breaks, where snacks and drinks are provided, and the changing-room location (especially if they work throughout the day into the evening).
- Provide a telephone contact sheet that includes cell phone numbers and responsibilities of key people and emergency contact numbers.
- Suggest a dress code so that the event will have a coordinated look (all black or black-and-white). You may want to give each volunteer

continued

Tips for Assisting Event Volunteers (continued)

a logo T-shirt as a nice thank-you that spreads the word about the organization. A T-shirt makes it easier for guests to locate someone associated with the event.

- Keep volunteers informed with an updated schedule of events for the evening.
- For an all day set-up schedule, organize volunteers into three shifts. You might consider 8:00 a.m. - 1:00 p.m., 12:00 p.m. - 5:00 p.m., and 5:00 p.m. - 1:00 a.m.
- If you are providing meals for volunteers, keep your budget in check. You can bring in sandwiches, snacks, and cold drinks, or ask the venue to provide them. Have food available throughout the day for the volunteers who work more than one shift.

PUTTING OUT FIRES

In spite of planning, no event is immune to major emergencies and minor mishaps. Be prepared to cope with the unexpected. The various committee chairs or members should work closely with venue personnel to make sure that their needs are being handled properly. For a large, multifaceted event that takes place on two levels, headsets attached to walkie-talkies can facilitate communication between key people involved in the event—venue staff, lighting and sound technicians, organization staff, and the overall coordinator.

Awards for honorees, favors, event programs, or other props essential to the program can be misplaced. There can also be problems with cooling and heating systems, microphones that don't work, and electrical failures. Should a mishap occur, the chairperson needs to use her best people skills to soothe the audience and keep them abreast of the situation. Have a back-up plan in place to correct the problem as quickly as possible. Most guests attending a benefit for a worthwhile cause are good-natured and will be good sports about such occurrences.

Keep Things Quiet

It is important to have a volunteer, staff person, or venue representative whose job it is to be aware of any background noises or disturbances during a concert, performance, or program and to rectify the problem. For example, when all the guests are seated, a designated volunteer should close the doors to the ballroom as quickly and quietly as possible to keep outside noises from interfering with the mood and program inside the ballroom.

It takes skill and tact to hush a noisy table. Always have someone who is part of the nonprofit staff or a diplomatic volunteer available to spot unexpected distractions, such as a noisy crowd or an unruly guest. Ask the emcee to address the matter from the podium so that the evening is not spoiled for everyone.

In Case of Emergency

If a serious emergency occurs, don't panic. Try to cope with the situation in a calm manner. In case of an accident or the sudden death of a guest, check to see if a physician is in the house, promptly call 9-1-1, and ask the venue manager to assist in handling the situation. If it turns out that someone becomes ill, but not seriously enough to be taken to a hospital, try and find a place where he can rest until feeling better. The venue can provide a place for the person to lie down, and volunteers can be of assistance without disrupting the entire ballroom.

If hecklers or demonstrators infiltrate the venue of a special event or if a security threat is posed, never try to establish order by yourself. Immediately call the police instead. If an event is being held at a hotel, in-house security can assist your group and will handle the emergency situation.

The Show Must Go On

If the guest of honor or chairman becomes suddenly unavailable due to a family emergency, it is best to go ahead with the benefit. When you postpone an event, the momentum is lost. If your guest of honor has passed on after she made the commitment, the event can be held in her memory. If your chairperson is unavailable, the chairman of the board of directors of the organization, a board member, or the executive director can take over. Should any of the above be the case, you will need to offer a delicate explanation for those who may not have been informed of the unforeseen unavailability.

You must have the courage to do whatever is necessary when an awkward situation arises. I recall once during the planning stage of a fundraising campaign for the Stehlin Foundation for Cancer Research, there had been a misunderstanding with the master of ceremonies, a famous comedian who had graciously donated his talent, energy, and time to help us reach our $1 million goal. He became very upset and was going to cancel his appearance, so I placed a call to him to discuss the problem. I tried to find a common ground from which to negotiate in good faith so that he would listen and let me work out the difficulty. I told him that what had happened had occurred in error, and unforeseeable things do happen. Following our discussion, the matter was resolved, and the show went on.

Weather or Not

Rain or shine, you must plan for both. If your event is outdoors, it is important to pay attention to the local extended weather forecast. This will help you decide whether or not you need to make other arrangements, such as providing a tent or, if possible, moving the event inside. Sometimes the weather is tricky. If the weather is extremely warm, offer old-fashioned handheld fans or small battery-operated table fans, and rent large standing fans to provide cross ventilation. On the other hand, if you have planned an outside event and a "Blue Norther" comes through, offer guests shawls, jackets, or even extra table cloths that could serve as a wrap. And don't forget to arrange for portable heaters. Valets also need to be prepared for inclement weather with large umbrellas and an arm to help guests to the door.

Should you have to bring in air conditioning for a venue, make certain an engineer or someone from the equipment rental company is on hand in case a problem should arise. Be sure that off-site maintenance service is provided for in the contract. This is especially important when the item from the rental equipment company is a generator that a volunteer can't manage.

Who's Responsible?

When you are planning an event in a private home, the owner may insist upon using a treasured family heirloom to hold ice, food, or a liquid item. If your better judgment says this won't work, speak out no matter what. You do not want your organization to end up making good on that item.

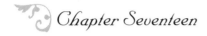 *Chapter Seventeen*

AT THE END OF THE DAY

*"There's no labor a man can do that's
undignified—if he does it right."*

— BILL COSBY

Once the event is over, nonprofit staff members and the volunteer crew responsible for this phase of the event need to supervise the teardown process. Have enough volunteers scheduled to pick up all the remaining programs, gift bags, favors, centerpieces, unsold auction items, auction items requiring special handling for delivery, borrowed items, and podiums. Make sure there is temporary storage space available at the venue for these items, or make advance arrangements for them to be picked up by the moving company and taken to a secured storage location.

Nonprofit staff members need to remain with the lighting, sound, and decorating crews to ensure they remove all their equipment according to the timeline. This may be the longest night of your life if the teardown is not properly orchestrated. Items sometimes disappear and can be damaged, so staff supervision is essential to avoid unexpected expenses due to unreturned or misplaced items.

If an event was held in a private home, it is possible for one of the host's dining room chairs or the carpet to be accidentally damaged by a guest or catering staff member. Other damage might occur (like the valet parking attendant backing into a guest's car.) The nonprofit organization's special events or development staff should take care of getting its insurance company representative to handle the matter. Even if there is no apparent damage, the event chairperson should call to thank the host the morning after the event to make certain that everything went smoothly and ask, "Is everything as we found it?"

KIND WORDS

The day following a major fundraising event, the nonprofit executive, managing director, or chairman of the board of directors should acknowledge the dedication and commitment of the event committee chair and the key volunteers. After all, this type of volunteering may take up a year of their personal lives and should be appropriately recognized. Sending flowers and a personal thank-you telephone call will make your chairperson feel appreciated. Bravos and bouquets are always welcome.

All donors, volunteers, and staff have this in common: They like to be thanked and acknowledged for their gifts, time, and hard work. Volunteers appreciate knowing that they have made a difference to your organization. Send a letter of appreciation to supervisors commending outstanding service by a group of corporate volunteers or staff at the venue.

The chairperson needs to remember throughout any campaign to thank the key staff members of the nonprofit group and recognize their supporting role with praise and kind words. After the event, it would be a nice gesture to treat the key volunteers to a night out at their favorite restaurant. When a printer or advertising company has done an exceptional job in the production of the printed matter, acknowledge their generosity, as well.

Send a program and a video of the evening as a thank-you to major benefactors. Make a copy of the video to be included in your organization's archives. Try to enlist a video company to underwrite producing the video. Ask the videographer to incorporate footage from the pre-events into the final main event video. A well-produced video will keep the momentum going long after the event is over and can be used as a presentation tool to cultivate new benefactors and prospective corporate donors. The journey for the next chair and team of volunteers can benefit from the video as well.

POST-EVENT ASSESSMENT

A good review can help alleviate any concerns and disappointments, as well as help eliminate potential problems for the next upcoming event. Was inadequate buffet line service causing a bottleneck of disgruntled patrons? Was there poor signage at the silent auction reception? Were volunteers guilty of oversocializing, rather than paying attention to their responsibilities? Were there enough volunteers throughout the day to set up the event? Did they need additional orientation? How did they handle the silent auction reception?

Go over the highs and lows of the menu with the catering service and let the venue manager know which format would work best for the future. How many people enjoyed the eggplant and scallop mousse, corn soufflé and unadorned fish? Did the spa meal have appeal?

Evaluate what you may have learned from the event about the organization, its dynamics, and its shortcomings. One important realization that came out of a performing arts event was the need to make the public more aware of the educational and community outreach programs of the arts group. This new focus proved to be a key ingredient in improving individual, corporate, and foundation support. The information was there, but it needed to be well presented to the community at large.

The past chairperson can help the board, executive director, and new chairperson evaluate the assistance and support they did or did not receive from the nonprofit development staff. If there were problems in working with the organization's staff, a volunteer will do service to the organization if he brings the situation to the attention to the board chairman or a group of board members.

At the end of each year, the board, executive director, development manager, marketing coordinator, and past chair should evaluate all the special events that took place. In this way, you can determine which one of the fundraising formats—symposium, distinguished lecture series, retailer partnership, sporting tournament, or auction—works to the best advantage for your organization. You may decide to eliminate one or two events because they are too time consuming, labor intensive, or nonproductive.

TACTFUL DEPARTURES

If this is an annual event, plans for next year's event should begin immediately. It's not too soon to reflect on the menu and entertainment and to begin thinking about a theme for the next event.

When your organization begins working with the next year's chairman, invite the past chair to give her input as to what changes she might offer. Remember that the past chair has valuable information to share.

The new chairperson should be given a list of work and cell phone numbers for the subcontractors such as caterers, florists, and wine purveyors. Also, include the storage location of any materials that can be used again. The outgoing chair should pass on his archives, such as samples of all documents and suggestions of potential donors.

There may have been a situation where a benefactor made a one-time gift to the organization. It is important that the following year's event chair or auction chair respect that "one-time ask" and not violate the special relationship that existed between the former chair and a one-time donor. When in doubt about soliciting a donor, always ask the original contact (former chair, auction chair, or development director) for guidance to avoid hard feelings.

FINAL WRAP-UP

Following an event, the event chair, media committee member, or staff from the nonprofit should be responsible for getting a press release with labeled photographs to local publications. If the publications have space available, they will do their best to accommodate the organization. The press release should be confined to one page, giving pertinent details—who benefits from the event, where it was held, the honoree, the number of guests, and the net amount raised.

 **NEWS RELEASE**

American Film Institute

FOR IMMEDIATE RELEASE

HOUSTON COMMUNITY WELCOMES AFI AT BRUNCH
HONORING JACK VALENTI, FOUNDING TRUSTEE

LOS ANGELES, CALIFORNIA, May 13, 2003—The American Film Institute (AFI) was warmly welcomed by author and philanthropist Carolyn Farb and members of the Houston, Texas community at a brunch event on May 4th honoring AFI Founding Trustee and President of the Motion Picture Association of America, Jack Valenti.

The event at Ms. Farb's home introduced AFI in greater detail as the nation's preeminent arts organization dedicated to the moving image. Mr. Valenti, a former Texan, serves as one of AFI's founding members of its prestigious Board of Trustees. As part of the midday event, John Campbell, AFI's Chief Development Officer, spoke about one of AFI's most prominent events—the upcoming 31st AFI Life Achievement Award honoring Robert De Niro to be held in Hollywood, California, on June 12, 2003.

Among the guests attending the May 4th brunch were Molly and Jim Crownover, Astrid and Gene Van Dyke, Eckhard Pfeiffer and La Nese Marshall, Angus Wynne III, Erin and Nic Florescu, Frances and Don Baxter, Rudy and Karen Wildenstein, Kathi Walsh, Linda Able, and Lorraine Dinerstein (Mr. Valenti's sister) with her son Jack Caltagirone.

AFI is the preeminent organization dedicated to advancing and preserving the art of film, television and other forms of the moving image. AFI trains the next generation of filmmakers, coordinates nationwide film preservation efforts and explores new technologies in moviemaking. AFI also presents the best of film through the AFI Los Angeles International Film Festival (AFI FEST); the AFI National Film Theater at the John F. Kennedy Center for the Performing Arts in Washington, D.C.; the AFI Silver Theatre and Cultural Center in Silver Spring, Maryland; and the AFI Life Achievement Award, the highest honor given for a career in film. AFI's annual almanac for the 21st century, **AFI AWARDS**, honors the most outstanding motion pictures and television programs of the year. In addition, **AFI's 100 Years . . . 100 Movies, 100 Stars, 100 Laughs, 100 Thrills, 100 Passions** and **100 Heroes & Villains** (airing June 2003) have ignited extraordinary public interest in classic American movies. More information about AFI can be found by visiting its Web site, located at www.AFI.com.

PHOTOS AVAILABLE

CONTACT:
Liza deVilla
American Film Institute
323-856-7896 or ldevilla@AFI.com

A post-event press release is essential to wrapping up a major event.

After an event has been held and funds have not been received in a timely manner, send an invoice and follow up with a call. Make certain the invoice is being sent to the responsible party. There will always be some individuals or companies that pay slowly, and some who don't honor their commitments. You have a degree of leverage in that situation because those individuals, corporations, or foundations have been recognized publicly in pre-event coverage and printed materials. This recognition will encourage them to honor their commitments.

PLANNING FOR NEXT YEAR

Fundraising doesn't stop at the end of the special event; it's just the beginning. Stay in touch with those who participated in the event. Look for and nurture potential leadership and volunteers for next year's event. Evaluate the results, assess the degree of success, and discuss future directions your fundraising might take. Your guests leave the venue with a better understanding of why their commitment is so invaluable. They now have knowledge about a cause that has touched them, and they know they have made a difference. Donors take pride in having shared a memorable evening with friends and associates in support of a worthwhile cause. They leave the event with a sense of where their gifts will go. The energy they created lives on to regenerate continuing support for your organization.

The staff, board members, and volunteers also leave with a feeling of accomplishment. They shared their hopes and dreams about the mission of their favorite charitable cause. They were able to network, make new acquaintances, and reconnect with friends they hadn't seen in years past.

The true art of volunteer fundraising is in determining the next steps. It's now appropriate to sit down face-to-face with the organization's other key players in a nonparty atmosphere to talk about the progress you've made, your mission, the next step, and the future. It's time to discuss the financial goals of the needed projects, and the many ways the event's benefactors can be part of attaining those goals. At the same time, begin to plan the next series of events, where you can continue building relationships among donors to raise funds and awareness.

"Success is a journey, not a destination. The doing is often more important than the outcome."

—ARTHUR ASHE

 *Appendix*

Use this case study of one large-scale fundraising event to model your own.

Timeline

"A Night at the Alhambra"
March 31, 2001

March 2000
>I was selected by the Houston Opera to Chair the 2001 Opera Ball. I immediately began creating a timeline, which evolved during the planning process.

April 2000 (One year before the event)
1. Mail honorary committee letter request and select other committee chairs
2. Set goals
3. Decide on the format
4. Identify theme for the event
5. Select the venue and determine event capacity
6. Finalize the date
7. Formulate media plan; announce chair
8. Schedule all committee member meetings
9. Begin working on the mailing list
10. Select an honoree
11. Find an auctioneer

May 2000 (Eleven months before the event)
1. Find a graphic designer
2. Look for a printer
3. Create a timeline for all printed materials
4. Work with public relations professionals
5. Meet with the banquet manager, linen company, florist, video, and sound

August 2000 (Eight months before the event)

1. Establish benefactor incentives
2. Draft benefactor letter and event fact sheet
4. Create response form
5. Draft the auction solicitation letter and donor response form
6. Mail first pre-event invitations

September 2000 (Seven months before the event)

1. Mail benefactor letter and response form
2. Mail auction solicitation letter
3. Secure a moving service and storage facility
4. Meet with auction Web site designer
5. Find an operatic performer for the event
6. Book the dance orchestra
7. Secure local talent for pre-events
8. Secure a photographer
9. Meet with Saks Fifth Avenue for Sultan's Treasure
10. Find media person for master of ceremonies
11. Arrange for sculptor to create gifts for benefactors
12. Secure donated wines
13. Plan November pre-event and mail invitations
14. Send press release announcing honoree
15. Host first pre-event

October 2000 (Six months before the event)

1. Print save-the-date cards
2. Meet with centerpiece designer
3. Send mailing to previous attendees about auction Web site
4. Follow-up calls to benefactors and auction donors
5. Plan activities for pre-event and mail invitations
6. Press release for auction—highlighting auction items
7. Arrange for pickup and storage of auction Items
8. Send out updated fact sheets

November 2000 (Five months before the event)
1. Recommend theme attire for the wait staff
2. Review plans for Sunday brunch for out-of-town donors
3. Create mock agenda for benefactor dinner and gala
4. Determine content and format for online registration
5. Host pre-event: a preview of auction items
6. Make follow-up calls to benefactors and auction donors
7. Pick up and store auction Items
8. Approve sample of candelabra
9. Discuss band member attire (fezzes)

December 2000 (Four months before the event)
1. Prompt online bidders to begin registration
2. Make follow-up calls to benefactors and auction donors
3. Deadline for auction catalog entries
4. Proof invitation and auction catalog

January 2001 (Three months before the event)
1. Print invitations and auction catalog
2. Organize security for auction and gala
3. Online bidding begins
4. Make follow-up calls to benefactors
5. Proof event program
6. Mail invitations to benefactor dinner
7. Plan benefactor dinner menu and entertainment
8. Create timeline for benefactor dinner
9. Meet with sculptor regarding benefactor gifts and award
10. Tasting for event

February 2001 (Two months before the event)
1. Mail invitations and auction catalogs
2. Print event program
3. Set up schedule of volunteer assignments
4. Host benefactor dinner

March 2001 (One month before the event)

1. RSVPs due
2. Plan seating for event
3. Organize volunteer teams for online bidding
4. Volunteer orientation at venue
5. Schedule setup and tear-down for the event
6. Schedule piano tuner for tenor
7. Script the program
8. Finalize transportation and other needs for band and tenor
9. Touch base and confirm silent auction reception entertainers

March 30, 2001 (Day before the event)

1. Update script
2. Prepare press release with blanks to fill in
3. Check in with photographer and send shot list

- **1:30 p.m.** – Audio-visual company due at the loading dock
- **2:00 p.m.** – Begin installing and focusing the light system (three hours)
  - Set up continuous loop recorded operatic music system
  - Install plasma screens and monitors
  - Install stage floor in ballroom
- **2:30 p.m.** – Decorating team due at loading dock
- **3:00 p.m.** – Decorator to install decorations and signage for auction
  - Piano company to deliver baby grand
- **10:00 p.m.** – Centerpieces to be delivered and placed in cool storage area
  - Hyatt to begin lobby setup for silent auction tables
  - Saks to set up Sultan's Tent and auction props
  - Movers to load auction items into truck for early morning delivery.

March 31, 2001 (Day of the event)

- **6:00 a.m.** – Setup Continues
  - Uniformed Security on-site through remainder of evening in silent auction area and to direct traffic at both entrances for gala
- **6:00 a.m. – 8:00 a.m.** – Mover to unload auction items and meet with auction coordinator
  - Portrait lights to be set up by audio-visual company

- Volunteers to set up auction items; artist and art crew volunteers set up gallery for paintings
- Duplicate set of display tables to be set up outside the main ballroom with clipboards and display photos representing silent auction items
- Additional registration tables to be set up outside the main ballroom
- Round tables to be set up in the ballrooms by Hyatt staff (without chairs to avoid interfering with lighting crew)
- **8:00 a.m.** – Lighting company to focus pin beam lighting on each table
- **9:00 a.m.** – Linens placed on tables in ballrooms
- **10:00 a.m.** – Chair covers to be placed
  - Registration tables to setup with ten computers for opera finance staff
- **11:30 a.m.** – Event volunteer orientation
- **12:00 p.m. – 4:00 p.m.** – Volunteers to place silver boxes at every other place, programs at every place, alternate his and hers Gucci fragrances, place tent cards with information about sale of pashminas and centerpieces
- **12:00 p.m.** – Mercedes Benz to deliver car to lobby entrance
- **1:00 p.m.** – Carolyn to check slides that will be viewed during the event
- **2:00 p.m.** – Plasma screens and monitors to be set up in lobby area
- **3:30 p.m.** – Guest tenor Rodrick Dixon to rehearse
- **4:00 p.m.** – Mike Carney orchestra to rehearse
- **5:30 p.m.** – Lobby music and lighting to be checked
- **6:00 p.m.** – Volunteers to be in place at registration
- **7:00 p.m. – 8:30 p.m.** – Silent auction and reception
  - Camel to be in place in hotel lobby
  - Banquet staff to begin passing hors d'ouevres at reception
- **8:15 p.m.** – Master of ceremonies to invite guests to "The Perfumed Garden" for dinner
  - Bagpiper to lead the group up the escalator to the dinner
  - Pianist to begin playing dinner music
  - Registration volunteers to move upstairs registration area
- **8:25 p.m.** – Emcee to announce second call for dinner
- **8:30 p.m.** – Guests will sit down to pre-set first course

- **8:40 p.m. – 9:00 p.m.** – Team of volunteers to move the bid sheet clipboards and descriptions of the auction items upstairs and place them in the duplicate auction stations after the guests move into the ballroom for dinner
    - The upstairs reservation/check-in table to be converted to the Express Pashmina/Candlebra checkout station
- **9:30 p.m.** – Dessert served
    - Program begins
- **10:00 p.m.** – Lights up—live auction to begin
- **10:30 p.m.** – Bars reopen; dancing begins
- **11:00 p.m.** – Silent auction bidding closed
- **11:30 p.m.** – Auction checkout to begin in the lobby
- **1:00 a.m.** – Teardown begins

April 1-6, 2001 (Week after the event)

1. Return borrowed fezzes worn by band members
2. Send thank-you notes to all donors, in-kind donors, volunteers, committee members, and vendors
3. Schedule formal debriefing with all committee members
4. Return any loaned props
5. Make arrangements to deliver large auction items
6. Get ID photos back from photographer
7. Finalize press release and send photos to press
8. Pay bills and prepare invoices

About the Author

Carolyn Farb is a fundraising visionary who has raised more than thirty
million dollars for a wide variety of
causes, including the March of Dimes,
the Rainforest Foundation, the
University of Houston, and a number
of organizations dedicated to fighting
cancer. She has received countless
awards honoring her service, and has
been featured widely in magazines and
on television. She is the author of
*How to Raise Millions: Helping
Others and Having a Ball!*
She lives in Houston, Texas.

Jean-Daniel Lorieux